ISBN 978-1-331-85393-0
PIBN 10242401

1 MONTH OF
FREE
READING

at

www.ForgottenBooks.com

By purchasing this book you are eligible for one month membership to ForgottenBooks.com, giving you unlimited access to our entire collection of over 700,000 titles via our web site and mobile apps.

To claim your free month visit:
www.forgottenbooks.com/free242401

English
Français
Deutsche
Italiano
Español
Português

www.forgottenbooks.com

Mythology Photography **Fiction**
Fishing Christianity **Art** Cooking
Essays Buddhism Freemasonry
Medicine **Biology** Music **Ancient
Egypt** Evolution Carpentry Physics
Dance Geology **Mathematics** Fitness
Shakespeare **Folklore** Yoga Marketing
Confidence Immortality Biographies
Poetry **Psychology** Witchcraft
Electronics Chemistry History **Law**
Accounting **Philosophy** Anthropology
Alchemy Drama Quantum Mechanics
Atheism Sexual Health **Ancient History**
Entrepreneurship Languages Sport
Paleontology Needlework Islam
Metaphysics Investment Archaeology
Parenting Statistics Criminology
Motivational

HISTORY

OF THE

ENNONITES

STORICALLY AND BIOGRAPHICALLY ARRANGED FROM THE TIME
OF THE REFORMATION; MORE PARTICULARLY FROM THE
TIME OF THEIR EMIGRATION TO AMERICA. CON-
TAINING SKETCHES OF THE OLDEST MEET-
ING HOUSES AND PROMINENT
MINISTERS.
ALSO, THEIR CONFESSION OF FAITH, ADOPTED AT
DORTRECHT, IN 1632.

BY

DANIEL K. CASSEL.

WITH ILLUSTRATIONS.

PHILADELPHIA:
DANIEL K. CASSEL.
1888.

Press of
Globe Printing House,
Philadelphia.

DEDICATED TO THE MEMORY

OF

WILLEM RUDDINGHUYSEN [RITTENHOUSE],

FIRST MENNONITE BISHOP

IN AMERICA.

Introduction.

THIS volume, containing brief sketches of the Mennonites in America, beginning with the first settlement
and organization at Germantown, Pa., is the result of researches originally intended as sketches for the public
press, but at the earnest solicitation of many friends it is
now offered in its present form, as a memorial of the two
hundredth anniversary of their first organization in
America.

A history of the Mennonites, and more especially of
those in America, is a task surrounded with many difficulties. But few collections of their books exist in
America; in many of their churches no records have been
kept, or have been lost; and many old and valuable papers
and records that did exist, which would have been the
ordinary source of information, have been destroyed or
lost, not being regarded at the time of any value.

Material facts have been diligently sought after and
patient labor cheerfully bestowed upon the work; events
and facts have been gathered, both from American and
European sources, in order to make it a valuable work
for the present and future generations. It is submitted

to a generous and intelligent people in the belief that it will meet their approval.

BANCROFT says of the Germans in America: "Neither they nor their descendants have laid claim to all that is their due." This is attributable partly to language, partly to race instincts and hereditary tendencies. Quiet in their tastes, deeply absorbed in the peaceful avocations of life, undemonstrative to the verge of diffidence, without clannish propensities, they have permitted their more aggressive neighbors to deny them a proper place even on the historic page.

At the close of the Thirty Years' War there ran through Protestant Germany a broad line; upon the one side of that line stood the followers of Luther and Zwingli, of Melancthon and Calvin—these were called the church people; upon the other side stood Menno Simons, Dietrich Philips, Casper Schwenkfeld, the Silesian Knight, and "The Separatists"—these were called the sect people. It was a line which divided persecution by new bound aries, and left the fagot and the stake in new hands, for the Peace of Westphalia had thrown the guarantees of its powerful protection only over one side of this Protestant division. It was a line which in the New World, though less discernible than in the Old, is only becoming obliterated in the widening philanthropy of our own times.

"While the German Church people have some written

history in America, the sect people have yet very little of their history written."—*E. K. Martin.*

DANIEL WEBSTER, in one of his speeches said, as if to commend our kind of notices : " There is still *wanting* a history which shall trace the Progress of Social Life. We still need to learn how our ancestors, in *their* houses, were fed, lodged and clothed, and what were their employments. We wish to see and know more of the *changes* which took place from age to age in the homes of the first settlers," etc.

We want a History of Firesides.

I have endeavored to some extent to cover *this* ground —as the reader will find in the settlements of Germantown, Lancaster, Ohio and Canada.

I believe the work to be as reliable as the nature of things will permit.

Should the reader discover differences in dates or ages of persons, he will remember that where the month is designated by a number, that March counts as the first month, April the second, etc.

The days also differ from our reckoning. The improved *Gregorian* Calendar was not adopted in Pennsylvania till 1752, which accounts for the great discrepancy in ancient dates.

I have also endeavored to retain the old or ancient phraseology in my quotations, as well as the old mode of spelling, especially names of places and persons, in order not to destroy the original.

It is, therefore, in the hope of stimulating investigation into the past life of this most interesting of all those sects, who, during the last century or two, have landed upon our shores, that these brief sketches of the Mennonites have been given to the public.

Hoping that my efforts may be of some benefit to the Mennonite Church and people in America.

THE AUTHOR.

Preface.

A LARGE portion of the material composing this volume, which more immediately concerns the Mennonite Church in America, has to a considerable extent been derived from original documents, some of which have never been on historic pages before, and from the records of churches wherever such existed, such as the records of the Mennonite Church at Germantown, also that of Skippack and others, as well as the writings of Dr. Ludwig Keller, Royal Librarian at Münster; J. T. V. Braght's *Martyrs' Mirror*, and *Biographical Sketches*, by S. W. Pennypacker; *The Mennonites*, by E. K. Martin; B. Carl Roosen, Dr. A. Eby and a number of others.

Special thanks for assistance and valuable information furnished during my labors in compiling this work, rendered in various ways, are due to Abraham Blosser, of Virginia; John F. Funk, of Elkhart, Ind.; Sam'l Stauffer, Berks Co., Pa.; John B. Bechtel, Boyertown, Pa.; Jacob S. Moyer, Bucks Co., Pa.; A. B. Shelly, Milford Square, Bucks Co., Pa.; Sam'l K. Cassel, Blooming Glen, Pa.; A. H. Cassel, Harleysville, Pa.; Abel Horning, Telford, Pa.; William S. Godshall, Schwenksville, Pa.;

Jacob C. Loux, Lansdale, Pa.; John C. Boorse, Esq.,
Kulpsville, Pa.; Herman Godshall, Souderton, Pa.; M.
S. Moyer, of Missouri; George S. Nyce, of Frederick,
Pa.; N. B. Grubb, Philadelphia; John B. Tyson, Skip-
pack, Pa.; Christian Schowalter, Primrose, Iowa; Hon.
Horatio Gates Jones, Roxborough, Phila.; Welty and
Sprunger, Berne, Ind.; and S. S. Haury, Cantonment,
Indian Territory. The author is also under many obligations to Prof. J. G. De Hoop Scheffer, of Amsterdam,
Holland, and many others. The collection of the material
for this volume has been a tedious and difficult work;
and though conscious that this work is in many respects
incomplete and deficient, the author is encouraged in its
publication by the fact that his researches in certain
periods of the American history of the Mennonite Church
have not proved unsuccessful. The book is now sent
forth with all its imperfections, hoping that it may help
to awaken the members of the Mennonite Church to a
consciousness of their precious historical inheritance.

There are, no doubt, many inaccuracies and omissions
and the author will be grateful for such information as
may hereafter enable him to give a more complete record.

Contents.

(3)

APPENDIX

Menno Simons' Renunciation of the Church of Rome.

THE names of Œcolampadius, Luther, Zwinglius, Melanchton, Bucer, Bullinger, Calvin and others, whom God in His providence raised up as humble instruments to reform to no small extent abuses which had crept into the Church, are familiar to almost every ordinary reader; while that of Menno Simons is little known, although he was contemporary with Luther, Zwinglius and others, and with some of whom he had personal interviews—with Luther and Melanchton in Wittemberg; with Bullinger at Zurich; and at Strasburg with Bucer.

It has been a mooted question for many years whether or not the Mennonites were descendants from the Wal denses, but the testimony of Dr. Ypeij, a professor of theology at Groningen and a member of the Dutch Reformed Church, in a book published by him in 1813, ought to set the question forever at rest. The eminent Doctor says in his excellent work that the Baptists, who were formerly called Anabaptists and in latter times Mennonites, were the original Waldenses. Testimony of this character from such high authority in the Dutch Reformed Church must carry conviction with it.

There is apparently no reason to question the antecedents of the Mennonites, but as misrepresentation has always been more or less their bane, we suppose it will so continue to be until the end of time, when, if not before, justice will assuredly be done them.

The name Mennonite came from Menno Simons,* a native of Witmarsum, a small town about half-way between Bolsward and Harlingen, and the year of his birth 1492; he was reared as a Catholic. We find in his writings that he was appointed chaplain in Pingium, a small town which he called his father's town, where he was stationed as a priest and preached for two years, without ever having read the Scripture, or touched it, for fear he might be mislead.

In the third year (1527) he concluded to read the Scripture and soon found that he was in error. He continned reading the Scripture daily, and was soon called an evangelical preacher, but still, as he says, he loved the world and the world loved him.

It occurred in the year 1531 that a very devout Christian named Sicke Schneider, a native of Switzerland, was beheaded, being condemned by the Catholics as a heretic, because he renewed his baptism. Menno Simons had never heard of a second baptism, therefore it seemed to him very strange. He then commenced to examine the Scripture closely in regard to infant baptism, but, as he says, he soon found that infant baptism had no foundation in the Scripture.

Shortly after 1531 Menno Simons left Pingium and was stationed in Witmarsum, his birthplace, as a Catholic priest.

---

* Or Symons, read Seemons.

After remaining at the latter place about one year, the first evangelical people teaching the doctrine of adult baptism settled also in the neighborhood, and soon after, the Münsterites also made their appearance among them and elected John Bockhold their king. A riot took place and the Münsterites were driven out, in 1534, by Count Waldeck, its expelled bishop, and in February, 1535, about 300 men, with their wives and children, entrenched themselves in the so-called old cloister, near Witmarsum, where on the 7th of April, 1535, they were overpowered; many were taken prisoners, many were killed, women were drowned. Menno Simons' own brother, Peter Simons, also lost his life in this riot, and many of the quiet and peaceable evangelical people who lived among them suffered much.

All this took place while Menno Simons was yet in the Catholic Church, but his teaching and his life became quite changed. During this time he wrote a book against the Münsterites, shortly before he left the Catholic Church. In that book he speaks of John Bockhold, of Leyden, as yet living, and who was executed January 22d, 1536.

Menno Simons left the Catholic Church January 12th, 1536 (see *Berend Karl Roosen, p. 24*). According to the foregoing statement it is clearly shown that Menno Simons never had any connection or anything common with the Münsterites, because he was yet in the Catholic Church.

Menno renounced the Catholic faith January 12th, 1536, and shortly afterwards he was baptized at Leeuwarden (see *B. Karl Roosen, p. 25*) by Johann Matthys (see *Gemeindeblatt für Mennoniten, Bände 4 und 5, Jahrg. 1836*).

After his severance from the Catholic Church he lived retired, spent his time in reading and writing, until the year 1537.

Ubbo Philipps, a brother of Dirk Philipps, was ordained to the ministry by Johann Matthys, says *Berend Karl Roosen, of Hamburg, Altona,* and Menno Simons was ordained a minister by Ubbo Philipps in 1537, in the Old Evangelical (*Taufgesinnten,* or *Waldenser*) Church, afterwards called Mennonites.

Menno Simons' departure from the teachings of his childhood naturally caused the greatest indignation in Catholic circles, and from that time on he and his followers were subjected to the basest persecution—a persecution which has been transmitted through successive generations and exists to-day, although not to such an extent.

After Menno's ordination to the ministry in 1537, he exercised an influence upon the remaining Münsterites, strong enough to cause them to renounce their warlike attitude and become peaceable Christians. He tried to persuade them to hold peace, even when he was yet a Catholic priest.

The quiet Old Evangelical Baptists, who strongly renounced every kind of warfare, called upon Menno in 1537, after he had renounced his office as Catholic priest, and only after much deliberation and prayer he consented to accept the call and become their bishop (see *B. K. Roosen, p. 33*), and, being a learned and eloquent man, he accomplished a vast amount of good, the effect of which is felt in Mennonite circles to-day. His unquestioned piety and sincerity, together with his eloquence, swayed the multitudes and many thousands en-

Nach dem der Mennoniten Kirche in Hamburg und Altona gehörendem Bildnisse.

MENNO SIMONS.

BORN 1492.   DIED 1559.

listed in the good cause. In the year 1537 Menno Simons commenced traveling throughout Northern Germany as a teacher of the Scriptural truth. Everywhere he went his life was endangered by indignant followers of the faith he had renounced, but he was not dismayed, and went on in his laudable effort to convert men to be believers in and followers of the teachings of Christ. He founded many congregations in Europe, and labored assiduously in his undertaking until death put an end to his earthly career.

The exact date of Menno Simons' birth and death is somewhat shrouded in mystery. Nearly all writers in the home of Menno Simons have fixed 1496 as the year of his birth, and 1561 as the year of his death. We find in his foundation book, in late German editions, "that it [the dawning of the new spiritual light] occurred in 1524, in his twenty-eighth year," which would make the year of his birth 1496; but the first Dutch collected edition to which we have access does not contain any such date. It appears, then, he never wrote this sentence; it has evidently been added by some writer or printer in later years.

E. K. Martin, Esq., of the Lancaster Bar, in his pamphlet called the "Mennonites," fixes the year of Menno's birth in 1492.

Professor J. G. De Hoop Scheffer, who has charge of the Mennonite archives at Amsterdam, in Holland, whom we must acknowledge as good authority, and have no reason to doubt has better facilities of ascertaining than many others, also fixes the year of Menno's birth, A.D. 1492, and that of his death 1559, on the 13th of January.

Much could be written on this subject and explanations given, but this must suffice. The good that Menno

Simons had done in life did not end at his death; it lived
after him. The seed he had sown took deep root in the
hearts of those he had taught, and although some writers
accuse his followers of degenerating after Menno's death,
they continued to labor on in the good cause. There is
no evidence to prove the theory that his followers became
lukewarm after his death. There has been a disposition
in some quarters to depreciate the work accomplished by
Menno Simons, and much of the credit that rightfully
belongs to him was given to Luther and Calvin and others
of his contemporaries. The time will come, however,
when the concession will be made that he did as much
towards the enlightenment of mankind as did those illustrious personages who shed such lustre on the history of
the Reformation.

The persecution of the Mennonites continued long after
the death of Menno Simons. They were compelled to
flee from one country to another. The band of followers
of the Mennonite doctrine was compelled to disperse.
Some of them went to Russia, others to Prussia, Poland,
Holland and Denmark, and others to America.

The alleged peculiarity of the faith of the Mennonites,
even after they came to America, was still the subject of unfavorable comment and much ridicule. The Mennonites
do not parade their doctrine like other denominations,
and their form of religious worship is free from every
semblance of ostentation. They prefer not to let their
good works be seen of men. Nevertheless, having en
dured the ridicule of those antagonistic to their manner
of worship as long as they could, they prepared a work
called *Articles of Faith*, which was executed and finished
in the United Churches in the city of Dortrecht, April

21st, 1632, subscribed by delegates from all the churches (see *Articles of Faith*, page 25). One feature of their faith, and one to which they cling with most praiseworthy tenacity, is this: They believe that the doctrine of Christ forbids the resentment of wrongs and the showing of any spirit of revenge. They believe their mission to be one which will redound to the benefit of all men, and they are assiduous in their efforts to that end. They never turn a stranger from their door, but they do not give aims to be seen of men. They are very careful in this respect. If an enemy comes to them in distress, they help him. What an example they set for many professing Christians! One portion of their faith may possibly be termed peeuliar; yet when one looks at it in the right light, there is nothing so objectionable in it. In forming marital relations, the Mennonites adhere to the doctrine that two believers in the same faith should marry. This is a custom of the Church which is still strictly adhered to by many. They base this portion of their belief upon the ordainment of God in the garden of Eden, when he instituted an honorable union between Adam and Eve. In their code they cite many more Scriptural teachings which carry them out in their belief that there should be no marriage consummated except between two members of the same Church.

The Mennonites do not believe in any great flourish of trumpets; so they seldom make known the number of their communicants. In short, they believe in doing all the good they can, but in a quiet way. In this they observe a simplicity worthy of emulation. Too many of our churches make a great flourish, and ministers and members speak glowingly of what ought to be done; but they seldom find time to do it. On the other hand, the Mennonites indulge in no braggadocia, and go around quietly doing the work which they believe has been made imperative on them by the command of the Master.

Descriptive of the trials and tribulations that the ear lier Mennonites underwent, nothing can be more beauti ful than the following, which is taken from an ably written pamphlet on the "Mennonites," composed by E. K. Mar- tin, Esq., a member of the Lancaster Bar: "A recent his- torian says: 'The philologist who seeks to know some thing of the language of the primeval man of Europe, finds amid the mountains of the Pyrenees the Basques, who have preserved down to the present time the tongue of their remote forefathers.'

"Whether we regard their personal history or the result of their teaching, the Mennonites were the most interest ing people who came to America. There is scarcely a family among them which cannot be traced to some an- cestor burned to death because of his faith. Their whole literature smacks of the fire. Beside a record like theirs the sufferings of Pilgrim and Quaker seem trivial. A hundred years before the time of Roger Williams, George Fox and William Penn, the Dutch reformer, Menno Simons, contended for the complete severance of Church and State, and the struggles for religious and political liberty which convulsed England and led to the English colonization of America in the seventeenth century, were logical results of docrines advanced by the Dutch and German Anabaptists in the one which preceded. This is a bold and sweeping claim for a place in history for the Mennonites; but *let him who challenges it look well to the ground on which he stands.*

"The sixteenth century was a period of unrest in the Old World. Europe was at length standing at the foot of the long ascent which was to lead out of Middle Age superstition and servitude to false and degrading religious pretensions. Of all the dreadful visitations to Europe in which this sixteenth century spirit sought expression, the Peasants' war of Germany was the worst. A hundred thousand of them fell in battle or were driven into exile, and their cause was stamped out in blood; not so, however, their ideas. The Middle Age spirit the brave peasants had challenged, and it must henceforth fight for its existence alongside of Popery and whatever else men saw fit to condemn, when the smoke of the pillaged castles and ruined vineyards had ascended to heaven, and the earth had drunk up the blood from the hundred battle-fields, and the last remnant of the warlike Anabaptists had fallen under the mercenary's heel or the headsman's axe, when the detonations of the fierce popular explosion had ceased longer to terrify, and the empire, surfeited with bloodshed, had begun to stay the hand of destruction, out of the vast chaos, the confusion of beliefs, the contempt for creed, arose a new apostle with a new doctrine. And yet it was not new; the same fundamental belief had been promulgated by Waldus in the twelfth century and by Wickliffe in the fourteenth. It was Christianism in humility, and the apostle was Menno Simons. In 1536 Menno renounced Popery altogether, and shortly after a number of persons came to him, whom he describes as of one heart and soul with himself, and these earnestly besought him to take upon himself the ministry of the Word. In this little handful of believers we have the first Mennonite congregation, and the first

Mennonite pastor, and the continuation of the Apostolic Church. They were undoubtedly Waldenses who had survived the fire of persecution and the fury of the Peasant war. There are many things besides creed and religious practices, the implications of contemporary writers and the direct testimony of the historians, Van Braght, Roosen, Mehrning and others, that lead to this conclusion. The Waldenses had been the valley people of the Alpine fastnesses, almost the only places in Europe where the corroding influences of the Church had failed to destroy the simplicity of primitive Christianity. Neander says : 'They not only disapproved of oaths, but held it unchristian to shed blood,' which are among the fundamental teachings of Menno. Frank, a very ancient writer, speaking of the Waldenses says: 'They reject infant baptism, they live a blameless, Christian life, invoke no saints or any creature; they call upon God alone, they swear not at all, and maintain that no Christian is allowed to swear. They have no mendicants among them, but they help each other as brethren. These are the true Waldenses.' Since they likewise opposed war and taking part in civil government, the stricter of them could not become Lutherans, Zwinglians or Calvinists, and the inference is irresistible that they lost their identity in that sect which has preserved to our own day their practices and belief, and which in the nineteenth century exacts the rigid simplicity and stout self-denial which succesfully resisted Roman absolutism in Europe during the fifteenth century. Of course, the Mennonites inherited at the same time the terms of opprobrium with which the Papists had for centuries been pleased to stigmatize all those who differed with themselves. The followers of Menno have frequently been confounded with the Münsterites, or warlike section of the Anabaptists, among whom the enthusiasm of the Reformation led to frightful excesses. There is nothing in ecclesiastical history better authenticated than not only his lack of sympathy with, but his utter abhorrence and detestation of, their practice, one of the first acts of Menno's ministry being the preparation of a work stigmatizing the Münster king and his "ungodly doctrine." With reference to the unjust confounding of these sects, because they agreed in the visible act of repeating baptism, history is rapidly changing front, and the furious and fanatical are being separated from the gentle and pious, as it is being discovered and brought to light that these terms of opprobrium have been for centuries fastened upon great numbers of people whom history has dealt with unjustly and harshly, because historians were enemies or the tools of enemies, and because the learning of the period was sifted through bigotry and intolerance. A sect must be judged by its principles, not by its slanderers.

"*Herzog's German Encyclopædia*, a high authority, thus treats of the great apostle: 'The ground thought from which Menno proceeded was not, as with Luther, justification by faith, or, as with the Swiss reformers, the absolute dependence of the sinner upon God in the work of salvation. The holy Christian life in opposition to worldliness was the point whence Menno proceeded, and to which he always returned. In the Romish Church we see the ruling spirit of Peter; in the Reformed Evangelical, of Paul; in Menno we see arise again James the Just, the brother of the Lord.'

"Luther's conception undoubtedly was that of a State Church. It was in accordance with the spirit of his

times, the religious temper of his age, and grandly did
the problem work itself out from the impulse he gave it.
Menno Simons had a scheme equally grand, more devout
and of more exalted piety.   He saw the north of Europe
the home of haunted sects ; he saw in these, or thought
he saw, the outlines of the ancient religion, obscured and
distorted, it is true, by the traditions in which it had been
preserved, but consonant still with the teachings of Christ
the Redeemer as He interpreted them to the multitude
by the Sea of Galilee, and to the eleven on the Mount of
the Ascension.   To gather these sects, which under various names were becoming entangled in the dangerous
heresies of the Reformation period, and unite them under
one fold, free alike from the plagues of Rome and the delusions of the world, was the work he set before himself.
In order to accomplish this, Menno insisted on the most
careful attention to moral duties and exercised the
severest discipline towards offenders, employing even
the ban of excommunication from fellowship of the
Church.   About Menno there grew up a large and flourishing sect.   On questions of discipline after a time they
became divided into the Flemings or Flandrians, and the
Waterlanders, from districts of Holland in which each
resided.   These divisions led to intestine discords, which
were finally settled at a Synod held in Amsterdam in
1630.   Their early history is a story of frightful persecutions endured with rare and heroic fortitude.   Three
thousand of them suffered martyrdom in Suabia, Bavaria,
Austria and the Tyrol; six thousand under the rule of
Philip II of Spain.

"Pennypacker says : 'There were nearly as many martyrs among the Mennonites in the City of Antwerp alone

as there were Protestants burned to death in England during the whole reign of Bloody Mary.' Menno himself, during the greater part of his ministry, went about with a price on his head; malefactors were promised pardon and murderers absolution if they would deliver him up. Sometimes clad like a peasant, with an axe on his shoulder, to disarm suspicion, he would go into the depths of the forest to minister to his scanty flock assembled there; again in the caves of the earth he gathered his faithful ones, and when persecution was sorest they ofttimes held these Christian communions in the dead of the night, purposely avoiding the knowledge of each other's names, that, if apprehended and put to the rack or instrument of torture, no unguarded word in the awful extremity of the hour might escape their lips to betray one another. Of course their meetings and their practices were thus shrouded with an almost impenetrable obscurity, which was constantly taken advantage of by their enemies to proclaim them as plotters of sedition as well as practicers of heresy. They were persecuted by Catholics and Protestants alike. In Switzerland, the land of William Tell and Ulrich Zwingli, when the Reformed Church was yet but five years old and its members were themselves still the subjects of persecution, the Protestant State Church inaugurated a frightful persecution of the Old Evangelical Baptists, to be followed during the next century and a quarter by every appliance of vengeance, until the persecution of 1659, exceeding all its predecessors in severity, almost totally annihilated the sect.

"These Swiss persecutions of the Mennonites must ever stand as a blot on the pages of the Protestant Reforma

tion, and more especially as they were perpetrated chiefly
by that Church which they most closely resembled of all
Protestant communions. We know there are excuses
offered, but they are the excuses of cowardice. It is
attempted to palliate the naked ugliness of these under
takings by saying that to have permitted their religious
irregularities longer would have invoked the wrath of the
powerful emperor, and perhaps subjected all the cantons
to Papal persecution and the destruction of their ancient
liberties.

"The Mennonite persecutions were then a bid for political favor and protection. The extreme severity of the
Swiss Protestants against the Mennonites sent a chill of
horror through all Holland, and drew a memorable protest from the burgomasters and lords of Rotterdam. An
ambassador went out from the Hague loaded with remon-
strances, but they seem all to have been of no avail, for
Swiss Mennonites, branded with the arms of the Canton
of Berne and chained to their seats, continued to pull
galleys in the Mediterranean, to work on the fortifications
of Malta, and to be sold to Barbary pirates, principally
because they differed from their Protestant brethren as to
whether a child should be held at the baptismal font as
soon as it could be carried there by its nurse, or whether
the age of discretion was the appropriate period to receive
the holy ordinance.

"But while the iron hold of persecution was tightening
its grip at one end of the Rhine Valley, it was relaxing
its hold at the other. Towards the close of the sixteenth
century a grand and historic personage advanced upon
the scene and became sponsor for the persecuted Mennonites. Mosheim says : 'The Mennonites, after having

been long in an uncertain and precarious situation, obtained a fixed and unmolested settlement in the United Provinces, under the shade of a legal toleration procured for them by William, Prince of Orange, the glorious founder of the liberty of the Netherlands. This illustrious chief, who acted from principle in allowing liberty of conscience and worship to Christians of different denominations, was moreover engaged by gratitude to favor the Mennonites, who had assisted him in the year 1572 with a comfortable sum of money, when his coffers were nearly exhausted.

"' He was frequently urged to persecute the Mennonites, and violently assaulted for his refusal to do so. His trusted friend, Saint Aldegonde, the distinguished patriot of the Netherlands, complained because he would not do it; and Peter Dathenus denounced him as an atheist for the same reason. Both civil magistrates and clergy made a long and obstinate opposition to his proclaimed toleration towards this people, an opposition not entirely conquered by him at the time of his death, but which on every occasion he resolutely discountenanced through his whole life.'

"In 1710, finding themselves studiously and persistently misrepresented and misunderstood, the Swiss Mennonites at length broke their long silence by publishing to the world their Confession of Faith,* at Amsterdam, which

---

* First, Of the Magistracy; Second, Of Defence or Revenge; Third, Of Oath or Swearing. The above-named Articles are the same as the 13th, 14th and 15th Articles of the Dortrecht Confession of Faith adopted in 1632.

The above exiled petitioners requested us, the regents or burgomasters of the City of Amsterdam, that we should have the above Statement or Con-

secured them absolute tranquillity in Holland ever after. (See *Mennonite History, by Ben. Eby, Berlin, Canada, 1841.*) They, in common with all Holland, shared the advantages which the revocation of the Edict of Nantes brought to the Dutch nation, and grew rich and numerous. Many now became well educated, and occupied high social and commercial relations. The deft Flemish weavers, the rare lacemakers, the skillful artisans who made the Low Countries the home of superior trades found among their sect unrivaled craftsmen. The famous linens and silks of Crefeld were woven on Huguenot and Mennonite looms, and there was an entire class of fabric known at that time in the Dutch trade as Mennonite goods. Mosheim said of them at a little later period: ' It is certain that the Mennonites in Holland, at this day, are in their tables, their equipages and their country seats the most luxurious of the Dutch nation. This is more especially true of the Mennonites of Amsterdam, who are numerous and exceedingly opulent.' "

As the question is frequently asked, What is the belief of the Mennonites, or in what respect do they differ from other denominations, I will give the leading Articles of the Christian Faith of the Churches of the United Flemish, Friesland and other Mennonites, adopted in 1632, at a conference held in the city of Dortrecht.

---

fession in writing, that it might be preserved in our archives for future reference, but being they could not speak the Dutch language, and their language (the Swiss) was hard to be understood, they had it translated by a notary-public under a solemn promise.

And for the purpose of having a reliable record, we caused the town seal to be appended to the Articles, and subscribed to by one of our secretaries, dated May the 22d, A.D. 1710.

By order of the authorities, burgomasters or regents as above.

J. HEES, Secretary.

Articles of Faith.

---

1. OF GOD, OF THE CREATION OF ALL THINGS, AND OF MAN.—Since it is testified that without faith it is impossible to please God, and that whosoever would come to God must believe that God is, and that He is a rewarder of all those who seek Him, we therefore confess and believe, according to the Scriptures, with all the pious, in one eternal, omnipotent and incomprehensible God: The Father, Son and Holy Ghost; and in no more and none other; before whom there was no God, nor shall there be any after Him; for from Him, by Him and in Him are all things; to whom be praise, honor and glory for ever and ever. Amen.

We believe in this one God, who works all in all; and confess that He is the Creator of all things, visible and invisible, who in six days created heaven and earth, the sea and all that is therein; and that He governs and upholds all His works by His wisdom, and by the word of His power. Now, as He had finished His work, and had ordained and prepared every thing good and perfect in its nature and properties, according to His good pleasure, so at last He created the first man, Adam, the father of us all; gave him a body, formed of the dust of the earth and breathed into his nostrils the breath of life, so that he became a living soul, created by God after His own image and likeness, in righteousness and true holiness, unto eternal life. He esteemed him above all

(25)

creatures, and endowed him with many and great gifts; placed him in a delightful garden or paradise, and gave him a command and a prohibition; afterwards He took a rib from Adam, made a woman, and brought her to Adam for a helpmate, consort and wife. The consequence is, that from this first and only man, Adam, all men that dwell upon the earth have descended.

II. Of the Fall of Man.—We believe and confess, according to the tenure of the Scriptures, that our first parents, Adam and Eve, did not remain long in the glorious state in which they were created; but being deceived by the subtlety of the serpent and the envy of the devil, they transgressed the high commandment of God and disobeyed their Creator, by which disobedience sin entered the world, and death by sin, which has thus passed upon all men, in that all have sinned, and hence incurred the wrath of God and condemnation. They were, therefore, driven of God out of paradise, to till the earth, to toil for sustenance, and to eat their bread in the sweat of their face, till they should return to the earth whence they had been taken. And that they, by this one sin, fell so far as to be separated and estranged from God, that neither they themselves, nor any of their posterity, nor angel, nor man, nor any other creature in heaven or on earth, could help them, redeem them or reconcile them to God; but they must have been eternally lost, had not God, in compassion for His creatures, made provision for them, interposing with love and mercy.

III. Of the Restoration of Man by the Promise of Christ's Coming.—Concerning the restoration of the first man and his posterity, we believe and confess that God, notwithstanding their fall, transgression, sin and perfect inability, was not willing to cast them off entirely, nor suffer them to be eternally lost; but that He called them again to Him, comforted them, and testified that there was yet means of reconciliation; namely, the Lamb without spot, the Son of God, who was appointed for this purpose before the foundation of the world, and was promised while they were yet in paradise, for consolation, redemption and salvation unto them and all their posterity; nay, from that time forth was bestowed upon them by faith; afterwards all the pious forefathers, to whom this promise was frequently renewed, longed for, desired, saw by faith, and waited for the fulfillment, that at his coming He would redeem, liberate and release fallen man from sin, guilt and unrighteousness.

IV. OF THE COMING OF CHRIST AND THE CAUSE OF HIS COMING.—We further believe and confess that when the time of His promise, which all the forefathers anxiously expected, was fulfilled, promised Messiah, Redeemer and Saviour, proceeded from God, was sent, and according to the predictions of the prophets and the testimony of the Evangelist, came into the world; nay, was made manifest in the flesh, and thus the Word was made flesh and man; He was conceived by the Virgin Mary, who was espoused to Joseph, of the house of David; and that she brought forth her first-born son at Bethlehem, wrapped Him in swaddling clothes and laid Him in a manger.

We confess and believe that this is He whose going forth is from everlasting to everlasting, without begin-

ning of days or end of life; of whom it is testified that
He is Alpha and Omega, the beginning and the end, the
first and the last; that He is the same and no other who
was provided, promised, sent and came into the world,
and who is God's first and only Son, and who was before
John the Baptist, Abraham, and prior to the formation of
the world; nay, who was the Lord of David, and the
God of the universe; the first-born of all creatures, who
was sent into the world and yielded up the body which
was prepared for Him, a sacrifice and offering, for a
sweet savor to God; nay, for the consolation, redemption and salvation of the world; we believe also in the
Apostles' Creed, as given by the Evangelists.

But as to how and in what manner this worthy body
was prepared, and how the Word became flesh, we are
satisfied with the statement given by the Evangelists;
agreeably to which, we confess with all the saints, that
He is the Son of the living God, in whom alone consists
all our hope, consolation, redemption and salvation.

We further believe and confess with the Scriptures, that
when He had fulfilled His course and finished the work
for which He had been sent into the world, He was,
according to the providence of God, delivered into
the hands of wicked men; that He suffered under
Pontius Pilate; was crucified, dead and buried; rose
again from the dead on the third day; ascended to
heaven, and sits on the right hand of the majesty of God
on high; whence He will come again to judge the living
and the dead.   And also that the Son of God died, tasted
death and shed His precious blood for all men, and that
thereby He bruised the serpent's head, destroyed the
works of the devil, abolished the handwriting, and

obtained the remission of sins for the whole human family; that He became the means (*author*) of eternal salvation to all those who, from Adam to the end of the world, believe in and obey Him.

V. OF THE LAW OF CHRIST, THE GOSPEL OF THE NEW TESTAMENT.—We believe and confess that previous to His ascension He made, instituted and left His New Testament, and gave it to His disciples, that it should remain an everlasting testament, which He confirmed and sealed with His blood, and commended it so highly to them that it is not to be altered, neither by angels nor men, neither to be added thereto, nor taken therefrom. And that inasmuch as it contains the whole will and counsel of His Heavenly Father, as far as is necessary for salvation, he has caused it to be promulgated by His Apostles, missionaries and ministers, whom He called and chose for that purpose, and sent into all the world, to preach in His name among all people, and nations, and tôngues, testifying repentance and the forgiveness of sins; and that consequently He has therein declared all men, without exception, as His children and lawful heirs, so far as they follow and live up to the contents of the same by faith, as obedient children; and thus He has not excluded any from the glorious inheritance of everlasting life, except the unbelieving, the disobedient, the obstinate and the perverse, who despise it, and by their continual sinning, render themselves unworthy of eternal life.

VI. OF REPENTANCE AND REFORMATION.—We believe and confess, since the thoughts of the heart are evil from youth, and prone to unrighteousness, sin and wickedness,

that the first lesson of the New Testament of the Son of
God is repentance and reformation. Men, therefore, who
have ears to hear and hearts to understand, must bring
forth fruits meet for repentance, reform their lives, believe
the Gospel, eschew evil and do good, desist from sin and
forsake unrighteousness, put off the old man with all his
works, and put on the new man, created after God in
righteousness and true holiness ; for neither baptism, supper, church, nor any other outward ceremony can, without faith, regeneration, change or reformation of life,
enable us to please God, or obtain from Him any consolation or promise of salvation. But we must go to God,
with sincere hearts and true and perfect faith, and believe
on Jesus Christ, according to the testimony of the Scriptures ; by this living faith we obtain remission or forgiveness of sins, are justified, sanctified, nay, made children of
God, partakers of His image, nature and mind; being
born again of God from above, through the incorruptible
seed.

VII. OF BAPTISM.—As regards Baptism, we confess
that all penitent believers, who by faith, regeneration and
renewing of the Holy Ghost are made one with God and
written in heaven, must, upon their Scriptural confession
of faith and reformation of life, be baptized with water,* in
the name of the Father, and of the Son, and of the Holy
Ghost, agreeably to the doctrine and command of Christ
and the usage of His Apostles to the burying of their
sins, and thus be received into fellowship with the saints,
whereupon they must learn to observe all things which

* The Mennonites baptize by pouring water upon the head of the person
baptized when in a kneeling position.

the Son of God taught, left to and commanded His disciples.

VIII. OF THE CHURCH OF CHRIST.—We believe and confess there is a visible Church of God, namely, those who, as aforementioned, do works meet for repentance, have true faith and receive a true baptism, are made one with God in heaven, and received into fellowship of the saints here upon earth: those we profess are the chosen generation, the royal priesthood, the holy nation, who have the witness that they are the spouse and bride of Christ, nay, the children and heirs of everlasting life; a habitation, a tabernacle, a dwelling-place of God in the Spirit, built upon the foundation of the Apostles and the Prophets, Christ being the chief corner-stone (upon which his Church is built)—*this Church of the living God*, which He bought, purchased and redeemed with His own precious blood, with which *Church*, according to His promise, He will always remain to the end of the world as protector and comforter of *believers;* nay, will dwell with them, walk among them, and so protect them, that neither floods nor tempests, nor the gates of hell shall prevail against or overthrow them. This Church is to be distinguished by Scriptural faith, doctrine, love, godly walk or deportment, as also by a profitable or fruitful conversation, use and observance of the true ordinances of Christ, which He strictly enjoined upon His followers.

IX. OF THE ELECTION AND OFFICE OF TEACHERS, DEACONS AND DEACONESSES IN THE CHURCH.—As regards offices and elections in the Church, we believe and confess, since the Church cannot subsist in her growth, nor remain an edifice without officers and discipline, that, therefore, the Lord Jesus Christ Himself instituted and ordained officers and ordinances, and gave commands and directions how every one ought to walk therein, take heed to his work and vocation and do that which is right and necessary; for He, as the true, great and Chief Shepherd and Bishop of our souls, was sent and came into the world, not to wound or destroy the souls of men, but to heal and restore them; to seek the lost; to break down the middle wall of partition; of two to make one; to gather together out of Jews, Gentiles and all nations a fold to have fellowship in His name, for which, in order that none might err or go astray, He laid down His own life, and thus made a way for their salvation, redeeming and releasing them when there was no one to help or assist.

And further, that He provided His Church before His departure with faithful ministers, evangelists, pastors and teachers, whom He had chosen by the Holy Ghost, with prayers and supplications, in order that they might govern the Church, feed His flock, watch over them, defend and provide for them; nay, do in all things as He did, going before them, as He taught, acted and commanded, teaching them to do all things whatsoever He commanded them.

That the Apostles, likewise, as true followers of Christ and leaders of the Church, were diligent with prayers and supplication to God in electing brethren, providing every city, place or church with bishops, pastors and leaders, and ordaining such persons as took heed to themselves and to the doctrine and flock who were sound in the faith, virtuous in life and conversation, and were of good report, that they might be an example, light and pattern in all godliness, with good works, worthily administering the Lord's ordinances, baptism and supper, and that they might appoint in all places faithful men as elders, capable of teaching others, ordaining them by the imposition of hands in the name of the Lord; further, to have the care, according to their ability, for all things necessary in the Church; so that, as faithful servants, they might husband well their Lord's talent, gain by it, and consequently save themselves and those who hear them.

That they should also have a care for every one of whom they have the oversight; to provide in all places deacons who may receive contributions and alms, in order faithfully to dispense them to the necessitous saints with all becoming honesty and decorum.

That honorable and aged widows should be chosen deaconesses, who, with the deacons, may visit, comfort and provide for poor, weak, infirm, distressed and indigent persons, as also to visit widows and orphans, and further assist in taking care of the concerns of the Church according to their ability.

And further, respecting deacons, that they particularly, when they are capable, being elected and ordained thereto by the Church, for the relief and assistance of the elders, may admonish the members of the Church being appointed thereto, and labor in the Word and doctrine, assisting one another out of love with the gift received of the Lord; by which means, through the mutual service and assistance of every member, according to his measure, the body of Christ may be edified, and the vine and Church of the Lord may grow up, increase and be preserved.

X. OF THE HOLY SUPPER.—We likewise confess and observe a breaking of bread, or supper, which the Lord Jesus Christ instituted with bread and wine before His passion, did eat it with His Apostles, and commanded it to be kept in remembrance of Himself; which they con sequently taught and observed in the Church, and commanded to be kept by believers in remembrance of the sufferings and death of the Lord, and that His body was broken and His precious blood was shed for us and for the whole human family; as also the fruits thereof, namely, redemption and everlasting salvation, which He procured thereby, exhibiting so great love towards sinners by which they are greatly admonished to love one another, to love our neighbor, forgiving him as He has done unto us, and we are to strive to preserve the unity and fellowship which we have with God and with one another, which is also represented to us in the breaking of bread.

XI. OF WASHING THE SAINTS' FEET.—We also confess the washing of the saints' feet, which the Lord not only instituted and commanded, but He actually washed His Apostles' feet, although He was their Lord and Master, and gave them an example that they should wash one another's feet, and do as He had done unto them; they, as a matter of course, taught the believers to observe this as a sign of true humility, and particularly as directing the mind by *feet-washing* to that right washing, by which we are washed in His blood and have our souls made pure.

XII. OF MATRIMONY, OR STATE OF MARRIAGE.—We confess that there is in the Church an honorable marriage between two believers, as God ordained it in the beginning in paradise, and instituted it between Adam and Eve; as also the Lord Jesus Christ opposed and did away the abuses of marriage which had crept in, and restored it to its primitive institution.

In this manner the Apostle Paul also taught *marriage* in the Church, and left it free for every one, according to its primitive institution, to be married in the Lord to any one who may consent; by the phrase, *in the Lord*, we think it ought to be understood, that as the patriarchs had to marry among their own kindred or relatives, so likewise the believers of the New Testament are not at liberty to marry except among the chosen generation and the spiritual kindred or relatives of Christ; namely, such and no others as have been united to the Church as one heart and soul, having received baptism and stand in the same communion, faith, doctrine and conversation before they became united in marriage. Such are then joined together according to the original ordinance of God in His Church, and this is called *marrying in the Lord.*

XIII. OF THE MAGISTRACY.—We believe and confess that God instituted and appointed authority and a magistracy for the punishing of the evildoers and to protect the good; as also to govern the world, and preserve the good order of cities and countries; hence, we dare not despise, gainsay or resist the same, but we must acknowlededge the magistracy as the minister of God, be subject and obedient thereunto in all good works, especially in all things not repugnant to God's law, will and commandment; also faithfully pay tribute and tax, and render that which is due, even as the Son of God taught and practiced and commanded His disciples to do; that it is our duty constantly and earnestly to pray to the Lord for the government, its prosperity and the welfare of the country, that we may live under its protection, gain a livelihood, and lead a quiet, peaceable life in all godliness and sobriety. And further, that the Lord may reward them in time and eternity for all the favors, benefits and the liberty we here enjoy under their praiseworthy administration.

XIV. OF DEFENSE OR REVENGE.—As regards revenge or defense, in which men resist their enemies with the sword, we believe and confess that the Lord Jesus Christ forbade His disciples, His followers, all revenge and defense, and commanded them, besides, not to render evil for evil, nor railing for railing, but to sheath their swords, or, in the words of the prophet, "to beat them into ploughshares."

Hence it is evident, according to His example and doctrine, that we should not provoke or do violence to any man, but we are to promote the welfare and happiness of all men; even, when necessary, to flee for the Lord's sake from one country to another and take patiently the spoiling of our goods, but to do violence to no man; when we are smitten on one cheek to turn the other, rather than take revenge or resent evil. And, moreover, that we must pray for our enemies, feed and refresh them when they are hungry or thirsty, and thus convince them by kindness and overcome all ignorance. Finally, that we should do good and approve ourselves to the consciences of all men; and, according to the law of Christ, do unto others as we would wish them to do unto us.

XV. OF OATHS OR SWEARING.—Respecting judicial oaths, we believe and confess that Christ our Lord did forbid His disciples the use of them and commanded them that they should not swear at all, but that yea should be yea, and nay, nay. Hence we infer that all oaths, greater and minor, are prohibited; and that we must, instead of oaths, confirm all our promises and assertions, nay, all our declarations or testimonies in every case, with the word yea in that which is yea, and with nay in that which is nay; hence we should always and in all cases perform, keep, follow and live up to our word or engagement, as fully as if we had confirmed and established it by an oath. And we do this, we have the confidence that no man, not even the magistrate, will have just reason to lay a more grievous burden on our mind and conscience.

XVI. OF ECCLESIASTICAL EXCOMMUNICATION OR SEPARATION FROM THE CHURCH.—We also believe and profess a ban, excommunication, or separation and Christian correction in the Church, for amendment and not for destruction, whereby the clean or pure may be separated from the unclean or defiled. Namely, if anyone, after having been enlightened and has attained to the knowl edge of the truth and has been received into the fellow ship of the saints, sins either voluntarily or presump tuously against God, or unto death, and falls into the unfruitful works of darkness, by which he separates himself from God and is debarred His kingdom; such a person, we believe, when the deed is manifest and the Church has sufficient evidence, ought not to remain in the congregation of the righteous, but shall and must be sep-

arated as an offending member and an open sinner, be
excommunicated and reproved in the presence of all and
purged out as leaven ; and this is to be done for his own
amendment and as an example and terror to others,
that the Church be kept pure from such foul spots ; lest,
in default of this, the name of the Lord be blasphemed,
the Church dishonored and a stumbling-block and cause
of offense be given to them that are without ; in fine, that
the sinner may not be dammed with the world, but become convicted, repent and reform.

Further, regarding brotherly reproof or admonition, as
also the instruction of those who err, it is necessary to
use all care and diligence to observe them, instructing
them with all meekness to their own amendment, and
reproving the obstinate, according as the case may require. In short, that the Church must excommunicate
him that sins either in doctrine or life, and no other.

XVII. OF SHUNNING OR AVOIDING THE SEPARATED
OR EXCOMMUNICATED —Touching the avoiding of the
separated, we believe and confess that if any one has so
far fallen off, either by a wicked life or perverted doctrine,
that he is separated from God, and, consequently, is justly
separated from and corrected or punished by the Church,
such a person must be shunned, according to the doctrine
of Christ and His Apostles, and avoided without partiality
by all the members of the Church, especially by those to
whom it is known, whether in eating or drinking, or
other similar temporal matters, and they shall have no
dealings with him ; to the end that they may not be con-
taminated by intercourse with him, nor made partakers
of his sins ; but that the sinner may be made ashamed,
be convicted, and again led to repentance.

That there be used, as well in the avoidance as in the separation, such moderation and Christian charity as may have a tendency not to promote his destruction, but to insure his reformation; for if he is poor, hungry, thirsty, naked, sick or in distress, we are in duty bound, according to necessity and agreeably to love and to the doctrine of Christ and His Apostles, to render him aid and assistance; otherwise, in such cases, the avoidance might tend more to his ruin than to his reformation.

Hence we must not consider excommunicated members as enemies, but admonish them as brethren, in order to bring them to knowledge, repentance and sorrow for their sins, that they may be reconciled with God and His Church, and, of course, be received again into the Church, and so may continue in love toward him as his case demands.

XVIII. Of the Resurrection of the Dead and the Last Judgment.—Relative to the resurrection of the dead, we believe and confess, agreeably to the Scriptures, that all men who have died and fallen asleep shall be awakened, quickened and raised on the last day by the incomprehensible power of God; and that these, together with those that are then alive and who shall be changed in the twinkling of an eye, at the sound of the last trumpet, shall be placed before the judgment seat of Christ, and the good be separated from the wicked; that then every one shall receive in his own body according to his works, whether they be good or evil, and that the good and pious shall be taken up with Christ as the blessed, enter into everlasting life, and obtain that joy which no eye hath seen, nor ear heard, nor mind conceived, to reign and triumph with Christ from everlasting to everlasting. And that, on the contrary, the wicked or impious shall be driven away as accursed, and thrust down into utter darkness nay, into everlasting pains of hell, where the worm dieth not and the fire is not quenched; and that they shall never have any prospect of hope, comfort or redemption.

May the Lord grant that none of us may meet the fate of the wicked, but that we may take heed and be dili gent, so that we may be found before Him in peace, without spot and blameless. Amen.

Done and finished in our United Churches, in the city of Dortrecht, April 21st, A.D. 1632. Subscribed:

Dortrecht.

Isaac de Koning,
John Jacobs,
Hans Corbryssen,
Jaques Terwen,
Nicholas Dirkson,
Mels Gylberts,
Adriaan Cornelisson.

Zeeland.

Cornelius de Moir,
Isaac Claasz.

Flissingen.

Dillaert Willeborts,
Jacob Pennen,
Lieven Marynehr.

Harlem.

Jan Doom,
Peter Gryspeer,
Dirk W. Kolenkamp,
Peter Joosten.

Bommel.

Wilhelm J. von Exselt,
Gispert Spiering.

Rotterdam.

Balten C. Schumacher,
Michael Michiels,
Israel von Halmael,
Heinrich D. Apeldoren,
Andreas Lucken.

Germany.

Peter von Borsel,
Anton Hans.

Arnheim.

Cornelius Jans,
Dirk Rendersen.

Amsterdam.

Tobias Gewerts,
Peter Jansen Mayer,
Abraham Dirks,
David ter Haer,
Peter Jan von Zingel.

Middleburg.

Bastian Willemsen,
Jan Winkelmans.

Schiedam.

Cornelis Bom,
Lambrecht Paeldink.

Leyden.

Christian Koenig,
Jan Weyns.

Utrecht.

Herman Segers,
Jan Heinrich Hochfeld,
Daniel Horens,
Abraham Spronk,
W. von Brockhuysen.

Krevelt.

Herman op den Graff,
Wilhelm Kreynen.

Blockziel.

Claes Claessen,
Peter Petersen.

Zurich Zee.

Anton Cornelius,
Peter E. Zimmermann.

Gorcum.

Jacob von Sebrecht,
Jan J. von Kruysen.

General Adoption of the Articles of Faith.

THE foregoing articles are received, accepted and maintained by all the Mennonites throughout the United States, Territories, and in Canada, wherever they have been dispersed; for since the first immigration of the Mennonites to this country, they have been spread over a great portion of Pennsylvania.

Bishops, elders or ministers and deacons are usually chosen by casting lots. In general, their pastors neither receive nor accept stipulated salaries, nor any kind of remuneration for preaching the Gospel, or in attending to the functions of their office. They are distinguished above all others for their plainness in dress, economy in their domestic arrangements, being frugal, thrifty, and withal very hospitable. They take in strangers; treat them kindly without charge. They suffer none of their members to become a public charge. Nothing can be purer and gentler than the inner motives of Mennoniteism. What thought so near the practice of the blessed Master and so far from the acrimony and bitterness of men, as their scruple which makes all strife and warfare unchristian, and the iron purpose they have exhibited now for four centuries in maintaining their doctrine that the only genuine baptism could be that in which the matured consciousness of the individual took part? Who dares to assail it as an inexorable prejudice? Then there is their brotherly charity, which counts it so unworthy to leave their poor to be cared for even by the public institutions which their toil most largely contributes to maintain.

Hannibal is said to have complained that he made his tory, but the Romans wrote it. So the history of the subjects of this sketch has hitherto been written almost exclusively by their enemies (see *E. K. Martin's Sketches*, p. 17). The Roman Catholics and the large Protestant denominations, the Lutherans, the Reformed, and even Episcopalians have been characterized by jealousy towards new sects. To this day the State Churches of Europe look down with disdain upon " the Separatists." In the noisy clamor for worldly recognition the Mennonites have fared ill indeed. The story of the suffering Puritans, which at most extended over a few generations and a small area of territory, has been told and re-told with almost distressing particularity. There is not an event or object, from the departure at Delfthaven to the chair of Carver and the pot and platter of Miles Standish, that has not been held up to veneration, by poet, painter and orator. Even the German school boy is taught to regard these Pilgrim sacrifices of a handful of Englishmen as the noblest ever laid upon the altar of conscience and humanity. Yet if he but turned to the history of his own ancestors and read there the story of sufferings, persecutions, stout abnegation through eight centuries, in which cruel selfishness and heartless bigotry assumed the wardship of conscience, he would find the trials of these Puritans, great as they were, compared with the trials of his own people but the waters of Marah beside the plagues of Egypt; and while New England to-day laments the loss of its sons, swept into the vortex of national life setting westward, in danger of losing her distinctive characteristics by the Teutonic and Celtic influences that are clambering into their places, complaining that her stony acres must soon be tilled by an alien race or left barren and valueless, the Mennonite lands of Eastern Pennsylvania still remain in the descendants of the first hardy stock, who hold them by ancient indentures, supplemented by grant from father to son, reaching backward in one ever strengthening chain of titles to the original patents of Penn, implanting in a glorious Commonwealth a true conservatism, and adorning it continually with renewed evidences of prosperity and thrift.

The Lutherans have a well-defined literature which preserves their achievements in Church and State. The Reformed Church of Germany and Switzerland points with pardonable pride to the triumphs of Calvin, Zwingli and Ursinus, and a literature which has preserved the almost sacred teachings of their scholars and martyrs to our own time. The Presbyterian will show you in Edinburgh the monument of Margaret Wilson, who, fastened to a stake driven in the sands where the Galway overflowed by the tide, was sustained by her lofty enthusiasm until the waves drowned her prayers and the waters choked her songs, and who tasted this death unflinchingly for the faith that was in her. The Moravians will tell you how the ashes of Huss were borne on the bosom of the Rhine to the Scheldt, and on the bosom of the Scheldt to the sea, fit type of the great missionary work they were to record in the annals of every tongue and people and clime.

But the poor Mennonites, in journeyings oftener, in perils of robbers, in perils by their own countrymen, in perils by the heathen, in perils in the city, in perils in the wilderness, in perils in the sea, in perils among false brethren, in weariness and painfulness, in watchings, in hunger and thirst, in fastings, in cold and nakedness, the thousandth part of which can never be known, who have gone through the centuries their silent and uncomplaining way, believing that the glory of this world was but the mammon of unrighteousness, that it was enough for Him to know their deeds by whom the hairs of the head are numbered, and without whose knowledge the sparrow falls not to the earth—their story is yet untold.*

---

* For the above I feel greatly indebted to E. H. Martin, of the Lancaster Bar.

King Charles II and William Penn.

WE now come to where the widening influences of this people touch the rim of our own age and history.

On the 4th of March, 1681, Charles II, of England, granted William Penn a great tract of land in the New World. Penn was a Quaker. The Quakers may be called the Mennonites of England, or English Menno nites. Professor Oswald Seidensticker, an eminent Ger man-American authority, thus treats of their relationship: "The affinity between the religious principles of the Friends and the Mennonites is so obvious, and in many respects so striking, that an actual descent of the former from the latter has been hinted at as highly probable." "So clearly," says Barkley, "do their views (*i. e.*, those of the Mennonites) correspond with those of George Fox, that we are compelled to view him as the unconscious exponent of the doctrine, practice and discipline of the ancient and stricter parties of the Dutch Mennonites." Arguments are cumulative on this point, but cannot be indulged in here.

It is certain that the two visits of William Penn to Holland and Germany in the years 1671 and 1677, and his contact with the Mennonites there, had much to do with preparing his philanthropic mind for erecting an asylum for the persecuted of all classes in the New World.

The following poem is from the Latin of Daniel Francis Pastorius in the *Germantown Records*, 1688, first published by Professor Oswald Seidensticker:

(46)

Hail to posterity!
Hail, future men of Germanopolis!
Let the young generations yet to be
Look kindly upon this.
Think how your fathers left their native land,
Dear German land, O! sacred hearts and homes!
And where the wild beasts roam
In patience planned
New forest homes beyond the mighty sea,
There undisturbed and free
To live as brothers of one family.
What pains and cares befell,
What trials and what fears,
Remember, and wherein we have done well
Follow our footsteps, men of coming years;
Where we have failed to do \
Aright, or wisely live,
Be warned by us, the better way pursue.
And knowing we were human, even as you,
Pity us and forgive.
Farewell, Posterity;
Farewell, dear Germany,
Forever more farewell!   —WHITTIER.

When the history of Pennsylvania comes to be thoroughly understood, it will be found that the Dutchman, as he is generally called, occupies a position by no means so inconspicuous as that which the most of us are apt to assign to him. Every one is willing to admit that to him is due much of the material prosperity for which this State is so noted, that his hogs are fat, his butter is sweet, his lands are well-tilled, and his barns are capacious. But the claims that there is anything distinguished in his origin or brilliant in his career is seldom made, and that he has approached his English associates in knowledge of politics, literature or science, those of us who get our Saxon blood by way of the Mersey and the Thames would quickly deny. The facts which tell in his favor, however, are many and striking. Pastorius possessed probably more literary attainments and produced more literary work than any other of the early emigrants to this province, and he alone of them all, through the appreciative delineation of a New England poet, has a permanent place in the literature of our own time. Willem Rittinghuysen, the first Mennonite minister known in America, came to Germantown in 1688,* and in 1690 built on a branch of the Wissahickon Creek the first paper mill in the Colonies. The Bible was printed in German in America thirty-nine years before it appeared in English.. The first edition of Christopher Saur's quarto Bible was completed on the 16th of August, 1743, consisting of one thousand copies; a second edition in 1763 of two thousand copies, and a third edition in 1776 of three thousand copies. The first English Bible printed in America was the Aitkins' Bible, printed in 1782, the New Testament of which was printed in 1781. The Douay or Catholic Bible was printed in 1790. The first Protestant or King James Bible in quarto was printed by Isaac Collins at Trenton, and was completed in June, 1791. Isaiah Thomas, of Worcester, Massachusetts, also undertook to publish FOLIO and ROYAL QUARTO editions of the English Bible, and both editions were finished in December, 1791 (*from original documents in possession of* A. H. CASSEL). No other known literary work undertaken in the Colonies equals in magnitude the Mennonite "Martyr's Mirror" by Van Braght, printed at Ephrata in 1748, whose publication required the labors of fifteen men for three years.

---

* From New Amsterdam; probably he lived there a few years.

Settlement of Germantown.

An examination of the earliest settlement of the Germans in Pennsylvania, and a study of the causes which produced it, may, therefore, well be of interest to all who appreciate the value of our State history. The first impulse followed by the first wave of immigration came from Crefeld, a city of the lower Rhine, within a few miles of the borders of Holland. On the 10th of March, 1682, William Penn conveyed to Jacob Telner, of Crefeld, doing business as a merchant in Amsterdam, Jan Streypers, a merchant of Kaldkirchen, a village in the vicinity, still nearer to Holland, and Dirk Sipman, of Crefeld, each five thousand acres of land to be laid out in Pennsylvania. As the deeds were executed upon that day, the design must have been in contemplation and the arrangements made some time before. Telner had been in America between the years 1678 and 1681, and we may safely say that his acquaintance with the country had much influence in bringing about the purchase. In November, 1682, we find the earliest reference to the enterprise which subsequently resulted in the formation of the Frankfort Company. At that date Pastorius heard of it for the first time, and he, as agent, bought the lands when in London between the 8th of May and 6th of June, 1683 (*Pastorius MS. in the Historical Society of Pa.*). The eight original purchasers were Jacob Van de Walle, Dr. Johann Jacob Schutz,

4   (49)

Johann Wilhelm Uberfeldt, Daniel Behagel, Casper Merian, George Strauss, Abraham Hasevoet and Jan Laurens, an intimate friend of Telner, apparently living at Rotterdam. Before November 12th, 1683, on which day, in the language of the Manatawny patent, they "formed themselves into a company", the last named four had withdrawn and their interest had been taken by Francis Daniel Pastorius, the celebrated Johanna Eleanora von Merlau, wife of Dr. Johann Wilhelm Peterson, Dr. Gerhard von Mastricht, Dr. Thomas von Wylich, Johannes Lebrun, Balthaser Jawert and Dr. Johannes Kemler.

That this was the date of the organization of the company is also recited in the power of attorney which they executed in 1700.* Up to the 8th of June, 1683, they seem to have bought 15,000 acres of land, which were afterwards increased to 25,000 acres. Of the eleven members nearly all were followers of the pietist Spener, and five of them lived at Frankfort, two in Wesel, two in Lubeck and one in Duisberg. Though to this company has generally been ascribed the settlement of Germantown, and with it the credit of being the originators of German emigration, no one of its members, except Pastorius, ever came to Pennsylvania, and of still more significance is the fact that, so far as known, no one of the early emigrants to Pennsylvania came from Frankfort. On the 11th of June, 1683, Penn conveyed to Govert Remke, Lenart Arets and Jacob Isaacs Van Bebber, a paker, all of Crefeld, one thousand acres of land each, and they, together with Telner, Streypers and Sipman, constituted the original Crefeld purchasers. It is evident

---

* Both the original agreement and the letter of attorney, with their autographs and seals, are in the possession of Samuel W. Pennypacker.

that their purpose was colonization and not speculation.
The arrangement between Penn and Sipman provided
that a certain number of families should go to Pennsylvania within a specified time, and probably the other
purchasers entered into similar stipulations (see Dutch
deed from Sipman to Peter Schumacher in the Germantown Book in the Recorder's Office). However that may
be, ere long thirteen men with their families, comprising
thirty-three persons, nearly all of whom were relatives,
were ready to embark to seek new homes across the
ocean. They were Lenart Arets, Abraham Op den Graeff,
Dirk Op den Graeff, Herman Op den Graeff, Willem
Streypers, Thones Kunders, Reynier Tyson, Jan Seimans,
Jan Lensen, Peter Keurlis, Johannes Bleikers, Jan Lucken
and Abraham Tunes. The three Op den Graeff's were
brothers. Herman was a son in-law of Van Bebber, accompanied by their sister Margaretha, and they were
cousins of Jan and Willem Streypers, who were also
brothers. The wives of Thones Kunders and Lenart
Arets were sisters of the Streypers, and the wife of Jan
was the sister of Reynier Tyson. Peter Keurlis was also
a near relative, and the location of the signature of Jan
Lucken and Abraham Tunes on the certificate of the
marriage of a son of Thones Kunders with a daughter of
Willem Streypers in 1710, indicates that they too were
connected with the group by family ties (Streeper MSS. in
the Historical Society). On the 7th of June, 1683, Jan
Streypers and Jan Lensen entered into an agreement at
Crefeld, by the terms of which Streypers was to let Lensen
have fifty acres of land at a rent of a rix dollar and half a
stuyver, and to lend him fifty rix dollars for eight years
at the interest of six rix dollars annually. Lensen was

to transport himself and wife to Pennsylvania, to clear eight acres of Streyper's land and to work for him twelve days in each year for eight years.

The agreement proceeds: " I further promise to lend him a linen-weaving stool with three combs and he shall have said weaving stool for two years . . and for this Jan Lensen shall teach my son Leonard in one year the art of weaving, and Leonard shall be bound to weave faithfully during said year." On the 18th of June the little colony were in Rotterdam, whither they were accompanied by Jacob Telner, Dirk Sipman and Jan Streypers, and there many of their business arrangements were completed. Telner conveyed two thousand acres of land to the brothers Op den Graeff, and Sipman made Herman Op den Graeff his attorney. Jan Streypers conveyed one hundred acres to his brother Willem, and to Seimens and Keurlis each two hundred acres. Bleikers and Lucken each bought two hundred acres from Benjamin Furly, agent for the purchasers at Frankfort. At this time James Claypoole, a Quaker merchant in London, who had previously had business relations of some kind with Telner, was about to remove with his family to Pennsylvania, intending to sail in the Concord, William Jeffries, master, a vessel of five hundred tons burthen. Through him a passage from London was engaged for them in the same vessel, which was expected to leave Gravesend on the 6th of July, and the money was paid in advance.* It is now ascertained definitely that eleven of these thirteen emigrants were from Crefeld, and the presumption that their two companions, Jan Lucken and Abraham Tunes, came from the same city

---

* Letter Book of James Claypoole in the Historical Society.

is consequently strong (*S. W. Pennypacker*). This presumption is increased by the indications of relationship, and the fact that the wife of Jan Seimens was Merken Williamsen Lucken. Unfortunately, however, we are wanting in evidence of a general character. Pastorius, after having an interview with Telner at Rotterdam, a few weeks earlier, accompanied by four servants, who seem to have been Jacob Schumacher, Isaac Dilbeeck, George Wertmüller and Koenradt Rutters, had gone to America, representing both the purchasers at Frankfort and Crefeld. In his references to the places at which he stopped on his journey down the Rhine he nowhere mentions emigrants, except at Crefeld, where he says: "I talked with Tunes Kunders and his wife, Dirk, Herman and Abraham Op den Graeff, and many others, who six weeks later followed me" (*Pastorius MS.*). For some reason the emigrants were delayed between Rotterdam and London, and Claypoole was in great uneasiness for fear the vessel should be compelled to sail without them, and they should lose their passage money. He wrote several letters about them to Benjamin Furly at Rotterdam. June 19th he says: "I am glad to hear the Crevill ffriends are coming." July 3d he says: "Before I goe away wch now is like to be longer than we expected by reason of the Crevill friends not coming we are fain to loyter and keep the ship still at Blackwell upon one pretence or another," and July 10th he says: "It troubles me much that the friends from Crevillt are not yet come." As he had the names of the thirty-three persons, this contemporary evidence is very strong, and it would seem safe to conclude that all of this pioneer band, which, with Pastorius, founded Germantown, came from Crefeld.

Henry Melchior Muhlenberg says the first comers were
Plattdeutsch from the neighborhood of Cleeves (*Hallische
Nachrichten*).   Despite the forebodings of Claypoole, the
emigrants reached London in time for the Concord, and
they set sail westward on the 24th of July, 1683.   While
they were for the first time experiencing the dangers and
trials of a voyage across the ocean, doubtless sometimes
looking back with regret, but oftener wistfully and won-
deringly forward, let us return to inquire who these
people were who were willing to abandon forever the
old homes and old friends along the Rhine, and commence new lives with the wolf and the savage in the
forests upon the shores of the Delaware.

Origin of the Sect of Mennonites.

As the origin of the sect of Mennonites is somewhat involved in obscurity, their opponents, following Sleidanus and other writers of the sixteenth century, have reproached them with being an outgrowth of the Anabaptists of Münster. On the contrary, their own historians, Mehrning, Van Braght, Schynn, Maatschoen and Roosen, trace their theological and lineal descent from the Waldenses, some of whose congregations are said to have existed from the earliest Christian times, and who were able to maintain themselves in obscure parts of Europe against the power of Rome, in large numbers, from the twelfth century downward. The subject has of recent years received thorough and philosophical treatment at the hands of S. Blaupot Ten Cate, a Dutch historian.* The theory of the Waldensian origin is based mainly on a certain similarity in creed and Church observances; the fact that the Waldeness are known to have been numerous in those portions of Holland and Flanders, where the Mennonites arose and throve, and to have afterward disappeared, the ascertained descent of some Mennonite families from Waldenses, and a marked similarity in habits and occupations. This last fact is

---

* *Geschiedkundig Onderzock naar den Waldenzischen oorsprung van de Nederlandsche Doopsgezinden*, Amsterdam, 1844.

especially interesting in our investigation, as will be hereafter seen.

The Waldenses carried the art of weaving from Flan
ders* into Holland, and so generally followed that trade
as in many localities to have gone by the name of *Tisserands, or weavers* (see *Ten Cate's Onderzock*, p. 42). It
is not improbable that the truth lies between the two
theories of friend and foe, and that the Baptist movement,
which swept through Germany and the Netherlands in
the early part of the sixteenth century, gathered into its
embrace many of these communities of Waldenses. At
the one extreme of this movement were Thomas Münzer,
Bernhard Rothman, Jean Matthys and John, of Leyden ;
at the other were Menno Simons, Dirk Philips and
Casper Schwenkfeld. Between them stood Battenburg
and David Joris, of Delft. The common ground of them
all, and about the only ground which they had in common, was opposition to the baptism of infants.

Menno Simons was educated for the priesthood, and
entered upon its duties early in life. The beheading of
Sicke Snyder for re-baptism in the year 1531 in his near
neighborhood, called his attention to the subject of infant
baptism, and after a careful examination of the Bible and
the writings of Luther and Zwinglius, he came to the conclusion there was no foundation for it in the Scriptures.
He left the Catholic Church in 1536. Ere long he began
to be recognized as the leader of the Taufgesinnte, and
gradually the sect assumed from him the name of Mennonites. His first book was a dissertation against the
errors and delusions in the teachings of John of Leyden,
and after a convention held at Buckhold in Westphalia,
in 1538, at which Battenburg and David Joris were

present, and Menno and Dirk Philips were represented, the influence of the fanatical Anabaptists seems to have waned. (See *Nippold's Life of David Joris; Roosen's Menno Simons*, p. 32). His entire works, published at Amsterdam in 1861, make a folio volume of 642 pages. Luther and Calvin stayed their hands at a point where power and influence would have been lost, but the Dutch reformer, Menno, far in advance of his time, taught the complete severance of Church and State, and the principles of religious liberty, which have been embodied in our own federal constitution, were first worked out in Hol land.* The Mennonites believed that no baptism was efficacious unless accompanied by repentance, and that the ceremony administered to infants was vain. Their meetings were held in secret places, often in the middle of the night, and in order to prevent possible exposure under the pressure of pain, they purposely avoided knowing the names of the brethren whom they met, and of the preachers who baptized them. (See *Van Braght's Martyrer Spiegel.*) A reward of one hundred gold guilders was offered for Menno; malefactors were promised pardon if they should capture him. Tjaert Ryndertz was put on the wheel in 1539 for having given him shelter, and a house in which his wife and children had rested, unknown to its owner, was confiscated. He was, as his followers fondly thought, miraculously protected however, died peacefully in 1559, and was buried in his own garden. The natural result of this persecution was much dispersion. The prosperous communities of Hamburg

---

* *Barclay's Religious Societies of the Commonwelth*, pp. 78, 676; *Menno's " Exhortation to all in Authority,"* Funk's edition, Vol. 1, p. 75; Vol. 2, p. 303.

and Altona were founded by refugees. The first Mennonites in Prussia fled there from the Netherlands, and others found their way up the Rhine. (See *Life of Gerhard Roosen*, p. 5.) Crefeld is chiefly noted for its manufactures of silk, linen and other woven goods, and these manufactures were first established by persons fleeing from religious intolerance.

From the Mennonites sprang the general Baptist churches of England, the first of them having an ecclesiastical connection with the parent societies in Holland, and their organizers being Englishmen, who, as has been discovered, were actual members of the Mennonite Church at Amsterdam. (See *Barclay's Religious Societies*, pp. 72, 73, 95.) It was for the benefit of these Englishmen that the well-known Confession of Faith* of Hans de Ries and Lubbert Gerritz was written, and according to the late Robert Barclay, whose valuable work bears every evidence of the most thorough and careful research, it was from association with these early Baptist teachers that George Fox, the founder of the Quakers, imbibed his views. Says Barclay: "We are compelled to view him as the unconscious exponent of the doctrine, practice and discipline of the ancient and stricter party of the Dutch Mennonites." (*Barclay*, p. 77.) If this be correct, to the spread of Mennonite teachings we owe the origin

---

* The preface to that Confession, Amsterdam, 1686, says : " Ter cause, also daer eenige Englishe uyt Engeland gevlucht ware, om de vryheyd der Religie alhier te genieten, en alsoo sy een schriftelijcke confessie (*van de voornoemde*) hebben begeert, want veele van hare gheselschap inde Duytsche Tale onervaren zijnde, het selfde niet en konde verstaen, ende als dan konde de ghene die de Tale beyde verstonde de andere onderrechten, het welche oock niet onvruchtbaer en is ghebleven, want na overlegh der saecke zijn sy met de voernoemde Gemeente vereenight."

of the Quakers and the settlement of Pennsylvania. The doctrine of the inner light was by no means a new one in Holland and Germany, and the dead letter of the Scriptures is a thought common to David Joris, Casper Schwenkfeldt and the modern Quaker. The similarity between the two sects has been manifest to all observers, and recognized by themselves. William Penn, writing to James Logan, of some emigrants in 1709, says : " Herewith comes the Palatines, whom use with tenderness and love, and fix them so that they may send over an agreeable character ; for they are a sober people, divers Mennonists, and will neither swear nor fight. See that Guy has used them well." Thomas Chalkley, writing from Holland the same year, says : "There is a great people which they call Mennonists, who are very near to truth, and the fields are white unto harvest among that people, spiritually speaking." When Ames, Caton, Stubbs, Penn and others of the early Friends went to Holland and Germany, they were received with the utmost kindness by the Mennonites, which is in strong contrast with their treatment at the hands of the established Churches.

The strongest testimony of this character, however, is given by Thomas Story, the recorder of deeds in Pennsylvania, who made a trip to Holland and Germany in 1715. There he preached in the Mennonite meetinghouses at Hoorn, Holfert, Drachten, Goredyke, Herveen, Jever, Oudeboone, Grow, Leeuwarden, Dokkum and Henleven, while at Malkwara no meeting was held because "a person of note among the Menists being departed this life," and none at Saardem because of "the chief of the Menists being over at Amsterdam." These meetings were attended almost exclusively by Mennonites and they entertained him at their homes. One of their preachers he describes as "convinced of truth," and of another he says that after a discourse of several hours about religion they "had no difference." Jacob Nordyke, of Harlingen, "a Menist and friendly man," accompanied the party on their journey, and when the wagon broke down near Oudeboone he went ahead on foot to prepare a meeting. The climax of this staid, good fellowship was capped, however, at Grow. Says Story in his journal: "Hemine Gosses, their preacher, came to us, and taking me by the hand he embraced me and saluted me with several kisses, which I readily answered, for he expressed much satisfaction before the people, and received us gladly, inviting us to take a dish of tea with him. He showed us his garden and gave us of his grapes to eat, but first of all a dram lest we should take cold after the exercise of the meeting, and treated us as if he had been a Friend, from which he is not far, having been as tender as any at the meeting."

William Sewel, the historian, was a Mennonite (says Pennypacker), and it certainly was no accident that the first two Quaker histories were written in Holland (*Sewel and Gerhard Creese*). It was among the Mennonites they made their converts (*Sewel, Barclay and Seidensticker*). In fact, transition between the two sects both ways was easy. Quakers became members of the Mennonite Church at Crefeld (*Life of Gerhard Roosen*, p. 66), and at Harlem (*Story's Journal*, pp. 490), and in the reply which Peter Henrichs and Jacob Claus, of Amsterdam, made in 1679 to a pamphlet by Heinrich Kassel, a Mennonite preacher at Krisheim they quote him as saying "that the so-called Quakers, especially here in the

Palatinate, have fallen off and gone out from the Mennonites."*

These were the people who, some as Mennonites and
others, perhaps, as recently converted Quakers, after
being unresistingly driven up and down the Rhine for a
century and a half, were ready to come to the wilds of
America. Of the six original purchasers, Jacob Telner
and Jacob Isaacs Van Bebber are known to have been
members of the Mennonite Church ; Govert Remke
(*Johann Remke was the Mennonite preacher at Crefeld in
1752*), January 14th, 1686, sold his land to Dirk Sipman,
and had little to do with the emigration; Sipman selected
as his attorneys here, at various times, Hermann Op den
Graeff, Hendrick Sellen and Van Bebber, all of whom
were Mennonites ; and Jan Streypers was represented
also by Sellen, was a cousin of the Op den Graeffs and
was the uncle of Hermannus and Arnold Kuster, two of
the most active of the early Pennsylvania members of
that sect. Of the emigrants Dirk, Herman and Abraham
Op den Graeff were Mennonites, and were grandsons of
Hermann Op den Graeff, the delegate from Crefeld to the
Council which met at Dortrecht in 1632 and adopted a
Confession of Faith.† Many of the others, as we have
seen, were connected with the Op den Graeffs by family
ties. Jan Lensen was a member of the Mennonite
Church here. Jan Lucken bears the same name as the
engraver who illustrated the edition of Van Braght, pub-

---

* This rare and valuable pamphlet is in the library of A. H. Cassel, at
Harleysville.

† Scheuten Genealogy in the possession of Miss Elizabeth Müller, of
Crefeld, Extracts from MS. which begins with the year 1562 to Frederick
Müller, the celebrated antiquary and bibliophile of Amsterdam.

lished in 1685, and others of the books of the Mennonite
Church, and the Dutch Bible which he brought with him
is a copy of the third edition of Nicolaes Biestkens, the
first Bible published by the Mennonites.*   Lenart Arets,
a follower of David Joris, was beheaded at Poeldyk
in 1535.   The name Tunes occurs frequently on the
name lists of the Mennonite preachers about the time of
this emigration, and Hermann Tunes was a member of
the first church in Pennsylvania.   This evidence, good
as far as it goes, but not complete, is strengthened by the
statement of Mennonite writers and others upon both
sides of the Atlantic.   Roosen tells us " William Penn
had, in the year 1683, invited the Mennonites to settle in
Pennsylvania.   Soon many from the Netherlands went
over and settled in and about Germantown."   Funk, in
his account of the first church, says : " Upon the invitation of William Penn to our distressed forefathers in the
faith, it is said a number of them emigrated either from
Holland or the Palatinate and settled in Germantown in
1683, and there established the first church in America."
Rupp asserts that " in Europe they had been sorely persecuted, and, on the invitation of the liberal-minded
William Penn, they transported themselves and families
into the Province of Pennsylvania as early as 1683."
Those who came that year and in 1698 settled in and
about Germantown.   Says Haldeman : " Whether the
first Taufgesinneten, or Mennonites, came from Holland
or Switzerland I have no certain information, but they
came in the year 1683."   Richard Townsend, an eminent

* The Bible now belongs to Abel Lukens, of North Wales, Montgomery
County, Pennsylvania.

Quaker preacher, who came over in the "Welcome" and settled a mile from Germantown, calls them a "religious, good people," but he does not say they were Friends, as he probably would have done had the facts justified it. (*Hazard's Register*, Vol. 6, p. 198.) Abraham, Dirk and Hermann Op den Graeff, Lenart Arets, Abraham Tunes and Jan Lensen were linen weavers, and in 1686 Jan Streypers wrote to his brother Willem inquiring "who has wove my yarns, how many ells long and how broad the cloth made from it, and through what fineness of comb it has been through." (*Deeds, Stryper's MSS.*)

Arrival of Mennonites at Germantown.

THE pioneers had a pleasant voyage and reached Philadelphia on the 6th of October, 1683. In the language
of Claypoole: "The blessing of the Lord did attend us
so that we had a very comfortable passage and had our
health all the way (*Claypoole's Letter Book*). Unto Johannes Bleikers a son Peter was born while at sea. Cold
weather was approaching and they had little time to waste
in idleness or curiosity. On the 12th of the same month
a warrant was issued to Pastorius for six thousand acres
"on behalf of the German and Dutch purchasers." On
the 24th Thomas Fairman measured off fourteen divisions of land, and the next day meeting together in the
cave of Pastorius they drew lots for the choice of location. Under the warrant 5,350 acres were laid out May
2d, 1684, having been allotted and shared out by the said
Francis Daniel Pastorius, as trustee for them and by their
own consent to the German and Dutch purchasers, after
named as their respective several and distinct dividends,
whose names and quantities of the said land they and the
said Pastorius did desire might be herein inserted and
set down, viz.: The first purchaser of Frankfort, Germany, Jacobus Van de Walle 535, Johan Jacob Schutz
428, Johan Wilhelm Uberfeld 107, Daniel Behagel 356⅔,
George Strauss 178⅓, Jan Laurens 535, Abraham Hase

voet 535, in all 2,675 acres of land.   The first purchasers
of Crefeld in Germany, Jacob Telner 989, Jan Streypers
275, Dirk Sipman 588, Govert Remke 161, Lenert Arets
501, Jacob Isaacs 161, in all 2,675 acres." In addition 200
acres were laid out for Pastorius in his own right, and
150 to Jurian Hartsfelder, a stray Dutchman or German,
who had been a deputy sheriff under Andross in 1676,
and who now cast his lot in with the settlers at Germantown. (*Exemplification Records*, Vol. 1, p. 61. *It is also
said that Heinrich Frey* was here before the landing of
Penn.*)   Immediately after the division in the cave of
Pastorius they began to dig the cellars and build the huts
in which, not without much hardship, they spent the
following winter.   Thus commenced the settlement of
Germantown.   Pastorius tells us that some people were
making a pun upon the name and called it *Armentown,*
because of their lack of supplies, and adds, " it could not
be described, nor would it be believed by coming generations, in what want and need and with what Christian
contentment and persistent industry this Germantownship
started."   Willem Streypers wrote over to his brother
Jan on the 20th of second month, 1684, that he was
already on Jan's lot to clear and sow it and make a dwelling, but that there was nothing in hand and he must
have a year's provision, to which in due time Jan replied
by sending a " box with 3 combs and 5 shirts and a
small parcel with iron ware for a weaving stool," and
telling him " to let Jan Lensen weave a piece of cloth to
sell and apply it to your use."

---

* Heinrich Frey and Joseph Blattenbach were the two first German emigrants who came to Pennsylvania.   They emigrated in 1680 and settled
in Philadelphia. (*Hallische Nachrichten.*)

In better spirits Willem wrote October 22d, 1684: "I have been busy and made a brave dwelling house, and under it a cellar fit to live in, and have so much grain, such as Indian Corn and Buckwheat that this winter I shall be better off than what I was last year."*

. Other emigrants ere long began to appear in the little town. Cornelis Bom, a Dutch baker, whom Claypoole mentions in association with Telner, and who bears the same name as a delegate from Schiedam to the Menno- nite convention at Dortrecht, arrived in Philadelphia before Pastorius. David Scherkes, perhaps from Mühl- heim on the Ruhr, and Walter Seimens and Isaac Jacobs Van Bebber, both from Crefeld, were in Germantown, November 8th, 1684. Van Bebber was a son of Jacob Isaacs Van Bebber, and was followed by his father and brother Matthias in 1687. Jacob Telner, the second of the six original Crefeld purchasers to cross the Atlantic, reached New York after a tedious voyage of twelve weeks' duration, and from there he wrote December 12th, 1684, to Jan Laurens, of Rotterdam, that his wife and daughter were "in good health and fat," that he had made a trip to Pennsylvania, which "he found a beautiful land with a healthy atmosphere, excellent fountains and springs running through it, beautiful trees, from which can be ob- tained better firewood than the turf of Holland," and that he intended to take his family there the following spring.†
He seems to have been the central figure of the whole emigration. As a merchant in Amsterdam his business

---

* Streeper MSS.

† Two letters in Dutch from Bom and Telner to Jan Laurens were printed in Rotterdam in 1685. The only known copy is in the Moravian Archives at Bethlehem.

was extensive. He had transactions with the Quakers in London, and friendly relations with some of the people in New York. One of the earliest to buy lands here, we find him meeting Pastorius immediately prior to the latter's departure, doubtless to give instructions, and later personally superintending the emigration of the Colonists. During his thirteen years' residence in Germantown his relations, both in a business and social way with the principal men in Philadelphia, were apparently close and intimate. Penn wrote to Logan in 1703: "I have been much pressed by Jacob Telner concerning Rebecca Shippen's business in the town."* Both Robert Turner and Samuel Carpenter acted as his attorneys. He and his daughter Susanna were present at the marriage of Francis Rawle and Martha Turner in 1689, and witnessed their certificate. The harmonious blending of the Mennonite and the Quaker is nowhere better shown than in the fact of his accompanying John Delavall on a preaching and proselyting tour to New England in 1692. He was the author of a "Treatise" in quarto, mentioned by Pastorius, and extracts from his letters to Laurens were printed at Rotterdam in 1685 (*MS. Historical Society*). About 1692 he appears to have published a paper in the controversy with George Keith, charging him with "impious blasphemy and denying the Lord that bought him."† He was one of the first burgesses of Germantown, the most extensive landholder there, and promised to give ground enough for the erection of a market house, a promise,

---

* *Smith's History, Hazard's Register*, Vol. 6, p. 309. Smith adopts him as a Friend, but in his own letter of 1709, written while he was living among the Quakers in England, he calls himself a Mennonite.

† A True Account of the Sense and Advice of the People called Quakers.

which we will presume, he fulfilled. In 1698 he went to London, where he was living as a merchant as late as 1712, and from there, in 1709, he wrote to Rotterdam concerning the miseries of some emigrants, six of whom were Mennonites from the Palatinate who had gone that far on their journey and were unable to proceed. " The English friends who are called Quakers," he says, had given material assistance.*   Doubtless European research would throw much light on his career.   He was baptized at the Mennonite church in Amsterdam, March 29th, 1665. His only child, Susanna, married Albertus Brandt, a merchant of Germantown and Philadelphia, and after the death of her first husband, in 1701, she married David Williams (*Exemp. Records*, Vol. 7, p. 208). After deducting the land laid out in Germantown, and the two thousand acres sold to the Op den Graeffs, the bulk of his five thousand acres was taken up on the Skippack, in a tract for many years known as Telnor's Township.   In 1684 also came Jan Willemse Bockanogen, a Quaker cooper from Harlem.†   October 12th, 1685, in the " Francis and Dorothy," arrived Hans Peter Umstat from Crefeld, with his wife Barbara, his son John, and his daughters Anna Margaretta and Eve;‡ Peter Schumacher, with his son Peter, his daughters Mary, Frances and Gertrude, and his cousin Sarah ; Gerhard Hendricks, with his wife Mary, his daughter Sarah and his servant Heinrich Frey, the last

---

* Dr. Sheffer's Paper in the *Pennsylvania Magazine*, Vol. 2, p. 122.

† Among his descendants was Henry Armitt Brown, the orator. The old Bockenogens were Mennonite weavers, who fled to Harlem because of persecution about 1578.

‡ " He brought over with him the family Bible of his father, Nicholas Umstat, which I have inherited through his daughter Eve," says S. W. Pennypacker.

named from Altheim in Alsace; and Heinrich Buchholtz
and his wife Mary. Peter Schumacher, an early Quaker
convert from the Mennonites, is the first person definitely
ascertained to have come from Kriesheim, the little village
in the Palatinate, to which so much prominence has been
given. Fortunately we know under what auspices he
arrived. By an agreement with Dirk Sipman, of Crefeld,
dated August 16th, 1685, he was to proceed with the first
good wind to Pennsylvania, and there receive two hundred
acres from Herman Op den Graeff, on which he should
erect a dwelling, and for which he should pay a rent of two
rix dollars a year.* Gerhard Hendricks also had bought
two hundred acres from Sipman (*Deed Book*, Ed. IV, vol.
7, p. 180). "He came from Kriesheim, and I am inclined
to believe that his identity may be merged in that of Gerhard Hendricks Dewees," says Saml. W. Pennypacker.
If so, he was associated with the Op den Graeffs and
Van Bebbers, and was the grandson of Adrian Hendricks
Dewees, a Hollander, who seems to have lived in Amsterdam (see *Rath's Buch*). This identification, however,
needs further investigation. Dewees bought land of Sipman, which his widow, Zytien, sold in 1701. The wife
of Gerhard Hendricks in the court records is called Sytje.
On the tax list of 1693 there is a Gerhard Hendricks,
but no Dewees, though the latter at that time was the
owner of land (*S. W. Pennypacker*). Hendricks, after
the Dutch manner, called one son William Gerrits and
another Lambert Gerrits, and both men, if there were
two, died about the same time. Much confusion has resulted from a want of familiarity on the part of local his-

---

* See his Deed in Dutch in the Germantown Book.

torians with the Dutch habit of omitting the final or local
appellation.   Thus the Van Bebbers are frequently re-
ferred to in contemporaneous ,records as Jacob Isaacs,
Issac Jacobs and Matthias Jacobs, the Op den Graeffs as
Dirk Isaac, Abraham Isaacs and Herman Isaacs, and
Van Burklow as Reynier Hermanns.   In 1685 also came
Heivert Papen, afterwards married to Elizabeth Rittenhouse, daughter of Willem Rittenhouse, and on the 20th
of March, 1686, Johannes Kassel, a weaver, and another
Quaker convert from the Mennonites, from Kriesheim,
aged forty-seven years, with his children, Arnold, Peter,
Elizabeth, Mary and Sarah, both having purchased land
from individual members of the Frankfort Company.
About the same time Klas Tamsen arrived.   In the vessel
with Kassel was a widow, Sarah Schumacher, from the
Palatinate and doubtless from Kriesheim, with her children George, Abraham, Barbara, Isaac, Susanna, Elisabeth
and Benjamin.   Isaac Schumacher married Sarah, only
daughter of Gerhard Hendricks.   Their son Benjamin
and their grandson Samuel were successively Mayors of
Philadelphia, and a great granddaughter was the wife of
William Rawle (*W. Brooks Rawle, Esq.*).

Among the Mennonite martyrs mentioned by Van
Braght there are several bearing the name of Schoen-
maker, and that there was a Dutch settlement in the
neighborhood of Kriesheim is certain.   At Flomborn, a
few miles distant, is a spring which the people of the
vicinity still call the " Hollander Spring."*   The Panne-

* This and other information is from Herr Johannes Pfannebecker,
Geheimer Regierungs-Rath (of Germany), living in Worms, who at the
request of Dr. Seidensticker and S. W. Pennypacker, made an investigation
at Kriesheim.

bakkers went there at some remote date from North Brabant in Holland. S. W. Pennypacker says: "I have a
Dutch medical work, published in 1622, which belonged
to Johannes Kassel." Many Dutch books from the same
family are in the possession of that indefatigable anti
quary, Abraham H. Cassel, and the deed of Peter Schu
macher is in Dutch. The Kolbs, who came to Pennsyl
vania later, were grandsons of Peter Schumacher and
were all earnest Mennonites. The Kassels brought over
with them many of the manuscripts of one of their
family, Ylles Kassel, a Mennonite preacher at Kriesheim,
who was born before 1618 and died after 1681, and some
of these papers are still preserved. The most interesting
is a long poem in German rhyme which describes vividly
the condition of the country, and throws the strongest
light upon the character of the people and the causes of
the emigration. The writer says that it was copied off
with much pain and bodily suffering November 28th,
1665. It begins: "O Lord! to Thee the thoughts of
all hearts are known. Into Thy hands I commend my
body and soul. When Thou lookest upon me with Thy
mercy all things are well with me. Thou hast stricken
me with severe illness, which is a rod for my correction.
Give me patience and resignation. Forgive all my sins
and wickedness. Let not Thy mercy forsake me. Lay
not on me more than I can bear." And continues: "O
Lord God! Protect me in this time of war and danger,
that evil men may not do with me as they wish. Take
me to a place where I may be concealed from them, free
from such trials and cares. My wife and children, too,
that they may not come to shame at their hands. Let
all my dear friends find mercy from Thee." After noting

a successful flight to Worms, he goes on : " O dear God and Lord ! to Thee be all thanks, honor and praise for Thy mercy and pity, which Thou hast shown to me in this time. Thou hast protected me from evil men, as from my heart I prayed Thee. Thou hast led me in the right way, so that I came to a place where I was concealed from such sorrows and cares. Thou hast kept the way clear till I reached the city, while other people about were much robbed and plundered. I have found a place among people who show me much love and kindness.

Gather us into heaven of which I am unworthy, but still I have a faith that God will not drive me into the Devil's kingdom with such a host as that which now in this land with murder and robbery destroys many people in many places, and never once think how it may stand before God. Well is it known what misery, suffering and danger are about in this land, with robbing, plundering, murdering and burning. Many a man is brought into pain and need and abused even unto death. Many a beautiful home is destroyed. The clothes are torn from the backs of many people. Cattle and herds are taken away. Much sorrow and complaint have been heard. The beehives are broken down, the wine spilled." *

The first to die was Jan Seimens, whose widow was again about to marry in October, 1685. Bom died before 1689, and his daughter Agnes married Anthony Morris, the ancestor of the distinguished family of that name. In 1685 Wigard and Gerhard Levering came from Mühlheim on the Ruhr, a town also far down the Rhine, near Holland, which next to Crefeld seems to have sent the

---

* These papers also belong to A. H. Cassel, his descendant.

largest number of emigrants.   In 1687 Arents Klinken arrived from Dalem, in Holland, and Jan Streypers wrote: " I intend to come over myself," which intention he carried into effect before 1706, as at that date he signed a petition for naturalization.   All of the original Crefeld purchasers, therefore, came to Pennsylvania sooner or later, except Remke and Sipman.   He, however, returned to Europe, where he and Willem had an undivided inheritance at Kaldkirchen, and it was agreed between them that Jan should keep the whole of it and Willem take the lands here.   The latter were 275 acres at Germantown, 50 at Chestnut Hill, 275 at the Trappe, 4,448 in Bucks County, together with 50 acres of Liberty lands, and three city lots, the measurement thus considerably overrunning his purchase.

Another arrival of importance was that of Willem Rittinghuysen, in 1688, a Mennonite minister, who, with his two sons, Gerhard and Klaas, or Nicholas, and a daughter, who later married Heivert Papen, came from Broich, in Holland.   His forefathers had long carried on the business of manufacturing paper at Arnheim, and in 1690 he built the first paper mill in America, on a branch of the Wissahickon Creek.   There he made the paper used by William Bradford, the earliest printer in the middle colonies.   It appears from a letter in the Mennonite archives, at Amsterdam, that he endeavored to have the Confession of Faith translated into English and printed by Bradford, and that he died in 1708, aged sixty-four years.*   The Mennonites had their Confession of Faith

* *Jones' Notes to Thomas on Printing; Barton's Life of David Rittenhouse; Penna. Magazine,* Vol. 2, p. 120.

printed in English, in Amsterdam, in 1712; and a reprint by Andrew Bradford, in 1727, with an appendix, is the first book printed in Pennsylvania for the Germans. The erection of the paper mill is likely to keep his memory green for many generations to come, and its value was fully appreciated by his contemporaries. In a *Description of Pennsylvania*, in verse, by Richard Frame, in 1692, we are told, "A papermill near Germantown does stand," and says the quaint Gabriel Thomas, six years later, "all sorts of very good paper are made in the German town."

About 1687 came Jan Duplouvys, a Dutch baker, who married, by Friends' ceremony, Weyntie Van Sanen, in the presence of Telner and Bom, on the third of third month, of that year; and Dirk Keyser, a silk merchant, of Amsterdam, and a Mennonite, connected by family ties with the leading Mennonites of that city, arrived in Germantown, in 1688, by way of New York. If we can rely on tradition, the latter was a descendant of that Leonard Keyser who was burned to death at Scharding, in 1527, and who, according to Ten Cate, was one of the Waldenses (see *Pennypacker Reunion*, p. 13). There was a rustic murmur in the little burgh (Germantown) that year, which time has shown to have been the echo of the great wave that rolls around the world. The event, probably, at that time produced no commotion and attracted little attention. It may well be that the consciousness of having won immortality never dawned upon any of the participants, and yet a mighty nation will ever recognize it in time to come as one of the brightest pages in the early history of Pennsylvania. On the 18th of April, 1688, Gerhard Hendricks, Dirk Op den Graeff, Francis Daniel Pastorius and Abraham Op den Graeff sent to the Friends'

Meeting the first public protest ever made on this Continent against the holding of slaves. A little rill there started which further on became an immense torrent, and whenever thereafter men trace analytically the causes which led to Shiloh, Gettysburg and Appomattox, they will begin with the tender consciences of the linen weavers and husbandmen of Germantown.

The protest is as follows:

THIS IS TO Y^E MONTHLY MEETING HELD AT RIGERT WORRELLS.

These are the reasons why we are against the traffick of mens-body, as followeth. Is there any that would be done or handled at this manner? viz. to be sold or made a slave for all the time of his life? How fearful & faint-hearted are many on sea, when they see a strange vassel being afraid it should be a Turck, and they should be tacken and sold for Slaves in Turckey. Now what is this better done as Turcks doe? yea rather is it worse for them, wch say they are Christians; for we hear, that ye most part of such Negers are brought heither against their will & consent, and that many of them are stollen. Now tho' they are black, we cannot conceive there is more liberty to have them slaves, as it is to have other white ones. There is a saying, that we shall doe to all men, licke as we will be done our selves: macking no difference of what generation, descent or Colour they are. And those who steal or robb men, and those who buy or purchase them, are they not all alicke? Here is liberty of Conscience, wch is right & reasonable, here ought to be likewise liberty of ^{ye} body, except of evildoers, wch is an other case. But to bring men hither, or to robb and sell them against their will, we stand against. In Europe there are many oppressed for Conscience sacke; and here there are those oppressed wch are of a black Colour. And we who know that men must not comitt adultery, some doe comitt adultery, in others, separating wifes from their housbands, and giving them to others and some sell the children of those poor Creatures to other men. Oh! doe consider well this things, you who doe it, if you would be done at this manner? and if it is done according Christianity? you surpass Holland & Germany in this thing. This mackes an ill report in all those Countries of Europe, where they hear off, that ye Quackers doe here handel men, Licke they handel there ye Cattle; and for that reason some have no mind or inclination to come hither. And who shall maintaine this your cause, or plaid for it? Truely we can not do so except you shall inform us better hereoff, viz. that christians have liberty to practise this things. Pray! What thing in the world can be done worse towarts us then if men should robb or steal us away & sell us for slaves to strange Countries; separating housbands from their wife & children. Being now this is not done at that manner we will be done at, therefore we contradict & are against this traffick of men body. And we who profess that it is not lawfull to steal, must lickewise avoid to purchase such things as are stolen, but rather help to stop this robbing and stealing if possibel and such men ought to be delivred out of ye hands of ye Robbers and set free as well as in Europe. Then is Pensilvania to have a good report, in stead it hath now a bad one for this sacke in other Countries. Especially whereas ye Europeans are desirous to know in what manner ye Quackers doe rule in their Province & most of them doe loock upon us with an envious eye. But if this is done well, what shall we say, is don evil?

If once these slaves (wch they say are so wicked and stubbern men) should joint themselves, fight for their freedom, and handel their masters and mastrisses, as they did handel them before; will these masters & mastrisses tacke the sword at hand & warr against these poor slaves, licke we are able to belive, some will not refuse to doe? Or have these negers not as much right to fight for their freedom, as you have to keep them slaves?

Now consider well this thing, if it is good or bad? and in case you find it to be good to handel these blacks at that manner, we desire & require you hereby lovingly that you may informe us herein, which at this time never was done, viz. that Christians have Liberty to do so, to the end we shall be satisfied in this point, & satisfie lickewise our good friends & acquaintances in our natif Country, to whose it is a terrour, or fairfull thing that men should be handeld so in Pensilvania.

This was is from our meeting at Germantown hold ye 18 of the 2 month 1688 to be delivred to the monthly meeting at Richard Warrel's.

> gerret hendericks
> derick op de graeff
> Francis daniell Pastorius
> Abraham op den graef.

"At our monthly meeting at Dublin, ye 30 2 mo. 1688, we having inspected ^{ye} matter, above mentioned & considered of it, we finde it so weighty that we think it not Expedient for us to meddle with it here, but do Rather comitt it to ^{ye} consideration of ^{ye} Quarterly meeting, ye tennor of it being nearly Related to ye truth.

> on behalfe of ye monthly meeting.
> signed, pr. Jo. Hart."

"This above mentioned was Read in our Quarterly meeting at Philadelphia, the 4 of ye 4 mo. '88, and was from thence recommended to the Yearly Meeting, and the above-said Derick, and the other two mentioned therein, to present the same to ye above-said meeting, it being a thing of too great a weight for this meeting to determine.

> Signed by order of ^{ye} meeting,
> Anthony Morris.

YEARLY MEETING MINUTE ON THE ABOVE PROTEST.

At a Yearly Meeting held at Burlington the 5th day of the 7th month, 1688.

A Paper being here presented by some German Friends Concerning the Lawfulness and Unlawfulness of Buying and keeping Negroes, it was adjudged not to be so proper fot this Meeting to give a Positive Judgment in the Case, It having so General a Relation to many other Parts, and therefore at present they forbear It.

As to the origin of the above protest, there is a difference of opinion as to who is entitled to the credit. Mrs. Anna Brons, of Holland, writes in an historical sketch of the Mennonites, stating that a copy of the above protest was in possession of the chief burgomaster at Crefeld. She further says : " The feeling of personal liberty probably was the cause of several brethren meeting together on the 18th of April, 1688, and resolved to enter a protest against slavery." Whether Garret Hendricks was connected with the Mennonite Church is not positively known, but the Hendricks generally were Mennonites; their descendants now living in Bucks County are of that faith, and in an article published in the *Germantown Independent* of July 28th, 1883, it says : " It is held quite probable that Hendricks was of that faith, and Laurence Hendricks was a Mennonite minister in the Palatinate, as appears in his letter written April 9th, 1710.

Derick up de Graeff and Abraham up Den Graef were Mennonites, says S. W. Pennypacker, in his *Biographical Sketches*, p. 28, and were grandsons of Herman Op den

Graeff,* the delegate from Crefeld to the Council which
met at Dortrecht in 1632, and adopted a Confession of
Faith.

Further, it is said by some that Pastorius was a Quaker
and by others that he was a Dunkard, but it appears by
close investigation that he was neither. It is held that he
was a Pietist; on one occasion he called the Pietists his
friends; afterward he wrote two pamphlets in the controversy with George Keith, in 1697, printed at Amsterdam, by Jacob Claus, to the so-called Pietists in Germany.†
Neither is it known where he is buried. If he had been
a Quaker his grave would undoubtedly be known.

Dr. Ludwig Keller, Royal Librarian at Münster, Germany, in his history of the " Altevangelischen Gemeinden," printed at Berlin, says the following on p. 51 :

" It is by no means yet generally known what prominent merits these old congregations deserve, not only in
establishing freedom of conscience, but also in the attempt
to abolish slavery and witchcraft."

" The German Mennonites were the first who protested
against slavery, as they found it in America, by entering
an earnest protest against it ; and to the Quakers belong

---

* Foot-note, p. 206, *Historical and Biographical Sketches*, by S. W.
Pennypacker, reads thus :

" When this article was written I had no knowledge of the Scheuten genealogy. That valuable MS. says that Herman Op den Graeff was born November 26th, 1585, at Aldekerk, a village near the borders of Holland. He
moved to Crefeld, and there married a Mennonite girl, Grietjen Pletjes,
daughter of Driessen, August 16th, 1605. He died December 27th, 1642,
and she died January 7th, 1643. They had eighteen children, among whom
was Isaac, who was born February 28th, 1616, and died January 17th,
1679. He had four children, Herman, Abraham, Dirk and Margaret,
all of whom emigrated to Germantown.

† See *Pennypacker's Sketches*, pp. 17 and 49.

the credit of having successfully carried the work further, also the same with witchcraft."

Dr. W. J. Mann, of Zion's Church, Franklin Street, Philadelphia (*Lutheran*), in an address delivered on the bi-centennial of Germantown, and published in the *Philadelphia Press*, October 8th, 1883, says: "Two hundred years ago the first German emigrants .came to our beautiful Pennsylvania; they were small (few) in numbers, but they were an energetic, industrious and persevering people. They came as Christians, and not being provided with churches they united with the Quakers and worshiped with them, and indeed, in 1688, undertook to lay the first protest against slavery before the monthly meeting of the Quakers."

In the Catalogue of the Library of the "Vereenigde Doopsgezinde Gemeente" at Amsterdam, by Prof. J. G. De Hoop Scheffer, we find the following on p. 46:

"Germantown Friends' protest against slavery, 1688 fol. (fotogr. afdruk 1880)."

"Yearly meeting minutes on the above protest. Burlingt, 1788 fol. (fotogr. afdruck 1880.) (Van de vier onderteekenaars van het protest zijn er drie doopsgesinnten uit Crefeld afkomstig.)"*

It took almost one hundred and eighty years and a mighty war which shook our whole Union to the foundation, to bring about what those Germans in their simpleheartedness had considered as the right and Christian thing at too early a period. It is conceded generally

---

* Among the four signers of the above protest were three baptism-minded from Crefeld.

Von den vier Unterschreibern des obigen Protests waren drei Taufgesinnten aus Crefeld.

that the Quakers and Mennonites worshiped together before the Mennonites had a meeting-house, but that they
connected themselves with the Quakers Dr. Mann does
not say. By reading the above protest carefully it can
plainly be seen that it has not been written by Quakers,
because if written by them they would not have used the
word Quakers, but Friends. Again, it accuses the Quakers
in strong terms of holding slaves and dealing in them
themselves, where they say: " Oh, doe consider well this
thing, you who doe it," and " That ye Quakers do here
handel men," and " Who shall maintain this *your* cause
or plead for it ?" " Truly we can not do so except *you*
shall inform us better hereof," etc. Further the protest goes
on and says: " Now consider well this thing, if it is good
or bad ? and in case *you* find it to be good to handel these
blacks at that manner, *we* desire and require *you* hereby
lovingly that *you* may informe *us* herein, which at this
time never was done." (*I hereby follow the original as
to language and orthography.*)

The residents in 1689, not heretofore mentioned, were
Paul Wolff, a weaver from Fendern, in Holstein, near
Hamburg, Jacob Jansen Klumpges, Cornelis Siverts,
Hans Millan, Johan Silans, Dirk Van Kolk, Hermann
Bom, Hendrick Sellen, Isaac Schaffer, Ennecke Klosterman, from Mühlheim on the Ruhr, Jan Doeden and Andries Souplis. Of these, Siverts was a native of Friesland,
the home of Menno Simons (see *Rath's Buch*). Sellen,
with his brother Dirk, were Mennonites from Crefeld, and
Souplis was admitted as a burgher and denizen of the
city of New York, September 17th, 1685, with a right to
trade anywhere in his majesty's dominions. The origin
of the others I have not been able to ascertain, says

6

Pennypacker. Hendrick Sellen was very active in affairs
at Germantown. According to Funk he gave the ground
for the Mennonite church there, was a trustee of the
church on the Skippack, and in 1698 made a trip to Crefeld, carrying back to the old home many business communications, and we may well suppose many messages
of friendship.

On the 14th of January, 1690, two thousand nine hun-
red and fifty acres north of Germantown were divided
into three districts, and called Kriesheim, Sommerhausen,
from the birthplace of Pastorius, and Crefeld.

An effort at naturalization, made in 1691, adds to our
list of residents Reynier Hermanns Van Burklow, Peter
Klever, Anthony Loof, Paul Karstner, Andris Kramer,
Jan Williams, Hermann Op de Trap, Hendrick Kasselberg,
from Bakersdorf in the country of Brugge, and Klas
Jansen. The last two were Mennonites, Jansen being
one of the earliest preachers. Op de Trap, or Trapman, as
he is sometimes called, appears to have come from Mühlheim on the Ruhr, and was drowned at Philadelphia in
1693. Gisbert Wilhelms died the year before.

Pastorius served in the Assembly in the years 1687
and 1691, and Abraham Op den Graeff in the years 1689,
1690 and 1692, though they were both still aliens.

Francis Daniel Pastorius was a son of Melchior Adam
Pastorius, who was converted to the Protestant faith.
Francis Daniel was born at Sommerhausen, September
26th, 1651. When he was seven years old his father removed to Windsheim, and there he was sent to school.
Later he spent two years at the University of Strasburg,
in 1672 went to the high school at Basle, and afterwards
studied law at Jena. He was thoroughly familiar with

the Greek, Latin, German, French, Dutch, English and Italian tongues, and at the age of twenty-two publicly disputed in different languages upon law and philosophy. On the 24th of April, 1679, he went to Frankfort, and there began the practice of law; but on June, 1680, he started with Johan Bonaventura von Rodeck, "a noble young spark," on a tour through Holland, England, France, Switzerland and Germany, which occupied over two years. On his return to Frankfort, in November, 1682, he heard from his friends the Pietists of the contemplated emigration to Pennsylvania, and with a sudden enthusiasm he determined to join them, or in his own words, "a strong desire came upon me to cross the seas with them." He sailed from London June 10th, 1683, and arrived at Philadelphia, August 20th. His great learning and social position at home made him the most conspicuous person at Germantown. He married November, 1688, Ennecke Klosterman, and had two sons, John Samuel and Henry.

The village had now become populous enough to warrant a separate existence, and on May 31st, 1691, a charter of incorporation was issued to Francis Daniel Pastorius, bailiff; Jacob Telner, Dirk Op den Graeff, Hermann Op den Graeff and Thones Kunders, burgesses; Abraham Op-den Graeff, Jacob Isaacs Van Bebber, Johannes Kassel, Heivert Papen, Hermann Born and Dirk Van Kolk, committeemen (council), with power to hold a court and a market, to admit citizens, to impose fines and to make ordinances. The bailiff and first two burgesses were constituted justices of the peace—they did not want their laws to go unheeded. It was therefore ordered that "On the 19th 1st month in each year the people shall be called together and the laws and ordinances read aloud to them." Oh, ye modern legislators! think how few must have been the statutes and how plain the language in which they were written in that happy community. As we have seen, the greater number of the first Crefeld emigrants were weavers. This industry increased so that Frame describes Germantown as a place

> " Where lives High *German* people and Low *Dutch*,
> Whose trade in weaving linen cloth is much ;
> There grows the Flax as also you may know
> That from the same they do divide the tow ;"

and Thomas says they made "very fine German linen, such as no Person of quality need be ashamed to wear."

When, therefore, Pastorius was called upon to devise a town seal, he selected a clover on one of whose leaves was a vine, on another a stalk of flax, and on the third a weaver's spool, with the motto "Vinum, Linum et Textrinum." This seal happily suggests the relations of the town with the far past, and it is a curious instance of the permanence of causes that these simple people, after the lapse of six centuries, and after-being transplanted to a distance of thousands of miles, should still be pursuing the occupation of the Waldenses of Flanders. The corporation was maintained until January 11th, 1707, but always with considerable difficulty in getting the offices filled. Says Löher : " They would do nothing but work and pray, and their mild consciences made them opposed to the swearing of oaths and courts, and would not suffer them to use harsh weapons against thieves and trespassers." Through conscientious scruples Arent Klincken declined to be burgess in 1695, Heivert Papen in 1701, Cornelis Siverts in 1702, and Paul Engle in 1703, Jan Lensen to be a committeeman in 1701, Arnold Kuster and Daniel Geissler in 1702, Matteus Millan to be constable in 1703, and in 1695 Albertus Brandt was fined for a failure to act as juryman, "having no other escape but that in court in Philadelphia he was wronged upon the account of a jury." New comers were required to pay one pound for the right of citizenship, and the date of the conferment of this right doubtless approximates that of the arrival (*Rath's Buch and Court Records*). In 1692 culminated the dissensions among the Quakers caused by George Keith, and the commotion extended to the community of Germantown. At a public meeting Keith called Dirk Op den Graeff an " impudent rascal," and since, as we have seen, the latter was a justice of the peace, in the right of his position as a burgess it was looked upon as a flagrant attack upon the majesty of the law. Among those who signed the testimony of the yearly meeting at Burlington 7th of 7th month, 1692, against Keith were Paul Wolff, Paul Kastner, Francis Daniel Pastorius, Andries Kramer, Dirk Op den Graeff and Arnold Kassel. The certificate from the quarterly meeting at Philadelphia, which Samuel Jennings bore with him to London in 1693, when he went to present the matter before the yearly meeting there, was signed by Dirk Op den Graeff, Reynier Tyson, Peter Schumacher and Casper Hoedt. Pastorius wrote two pamphlets in the controversy. The titles of these hitherto unknown pamphlets are :

I. Ein Sendbrieff Offenhertziger Liebsbezeugung an die so genannte Pietisten in Hoch Teutschland. Amsterdam, 1697.

II. Henry Bernhard Kuster, William Davis, Thomas Rutter and Thomas Bowyer, four Boasting Disputers of this world, *Rebuked* and *Answered* according to their folly, which they themselves have manifested in a late pamphlet, entitled *"Advice for all Professors and writers."*—(*William Bradford, New York*, 1697.)

On the other hand, Abraham Op den Graeff was one of five persons who, with Keith, issued the *Appeal*, for publishing which William Bradford, the printer, was committed, and a testimony in favor of Keith was signed by Herman Op den Graeff, Thomas Rutter, Cornelis Siverts, David Scherkes and Jacob Isaacs Van Bebber (*Pott's Memorial*, p. 394). Op den Graeff and Van Bebber were Mennonites. This furnishes us with another instance of two known to have been Mennonites acting with the Friends, and Sewel, the Quaker historian, says concerning Keith, "and seeing several Mennonites of the county of Meurs lived also in Pennsylvania, it was not much to be wondered that they who count it unlawful for a Christian to bear the sword of the magistracy did stick to him."

Casper Hoedt, then a tailor in New York, married there 6th month 12th, 1686, Elizabeth, eldest daughter of Nicolaes De la Plaine and Susanna Cresson, who were French Hugenots. James De la Paine, a relative and probably a son of Nicolaes, came to Germantown from New York prior to August 28th, 1692, on which day he was married by Friends' ceremony to Hannah Cock.

Susanna, a daughter of Nicolaes, became the wife of Arnold Kassel 9th month 2d, 1693.*

* Notes of Walter Cresson.

A tax list, made by order of the Assembly in 1693, names the following additional residents, viz : Johanna Pettinger, John Van de Woestyne and Paulus Kuster. Kuster, a Mennonite, came from Crefeld with his sons Arnold, Johannes and Hermannus and his wife Gertrude. She was a sister of Jan and Willem Streypers.

In 1662, twenty years before the landing of Penn, the city of Amsterdam sent a little colony of twenty-five Mennonites to New Netherlands under the leadership of Pieter Cornelisz Plockhoy, of Zierik Zee. They were to have power to make rules and laws for their own government, and were to be free from taxes and tenths for twenty years. Each man was loaned a hundred guilders to pay for his transportation. They settled at Horekill, on the Delaware, and there lived on peaceful terms with the Indians. The hand of fate, however, which so kindly sheltered Telner and Pastorius, fell heavily upon their forerunner, Plockhoy. An evil day for this colony soon came. When Sir Robert Carr took possession of the Delaware on behalf of the English, he sent a boat, in 1664, to the Horekill, and his men utterly demolished the settlement and destroyed and carried off all the property, " even to a naile." What became of the people has always been a mystery. History throws no light on the subject, and of contemporary documents there are none. *

In the year 1694 there came an old blind man and his

---

* Col. W. W. H. Davis, in his " History of Bucks County, Pa.," states that they were taken South and sold as slaves, but I had two interviews with him on the subject, and he acknowledged that he could not give any authority for said statement.

I also examined Egley's History, containing Capt. Carr's Day Book, but found no mention of it there.—AUTHOR.

wife to Germantown. His miserable condition awakened the tender sympathies of the Mennonites there. They gave him the citizenship free of charge. They set apart for him on Ent Street, by Peter Kleever's corner, a lot twelve rods long and one rod broad, whereon to build a little house and make a garden which should be his as long as he and his wife should live. In front of it they planted a tree. Jan Doeden and Willem Ritting-huysen were appointed to take up "a free-will offering" and to have the little house built. This is all we know, but it is surely a satisfaction to see a ray of sunlight thrown upon the brow of the helpless old man as he neared his grave. After thirty years of untracked wanderings on these wild shores friends had come across the sea to give him a home at last. His name was Cornelis Plockhoy.*

On the 24th of June of the same year Johannes Kelpius, Henry Bernhard Koster, Daniel Falkner, Daniel Lutke, Johannes Seelig, Ludwig Biderman and about forty other Pietists and Chiliasts arrived in Germantown and soon after settled on the Wissahickon, where they founded the society of the "Woman in the Wilderness." The events in the strange life of Kelpius, the hermit of the Wissa-hickon, have been fully told by Seidensticker and Jones. Together with Johannes Jawert and Daniel Falkner he was appointed an attorney for the Frankfort Company in 1700, but he never acted. Falkner had more to do with the affairs at Germantown, being bailiff in 1701, and in Montgomery County *Falkner's Swamp* still preserves the remembrance of his name. In 1700 he went to Holland

---

* *Rath's Buch, Broadhead's History of New York*, Vol. I, p. 688.

where he published a small volume in German, giving information concerning the province, to which he soon
returned.*

George Gottschalk, from Lindau, Bodensee, Daniel
Geissler, Christian Warner and Martin Sell were in Ger-
manton in 1694, Levin Harberdinck in 1696, and in
1698 Jan Linderman came from Mühlheim on the Ruhr.
During the last year the right of citizenship was conferred
upon Jan Neuss, a Mennonite and silversmith; William
Hendricks, Frank Houfer, Paul Engle, whose name is on
the oldest marked stone in the Mennonite graveyard on
the Skippack under date of 1723, and Reynier Jansen.
Though Jansen has since become a man of note, absolutely nothing seems to have been known of his antecedents, and I will, says Pennepacker, " therefore give in
detail such facts as I have been able to ascertain concerning him."   On the 21st of May, 1698, Cornelis Siverts,
of Germantown, wishing to make some arrangements
about land he had inherited in Friesland, sent a power of
attorney to Reynier Jansen, lace-maker at Alkmaer in
Holland.   It is consequently manifest that Jansen had not
then reached this country.   On the 23d of April, 1700,
Benjamin Furly, of Rotterdam, the agent of Penn at that
city, gave a power of attorney to Daniel and Justus
Falkner to act for him here.   It was of no avail, however, because, as appears from a confirmatory letter of
July 28th, 1701, a previous power " to my loving friend,
Reynier Jansen," lace-maker, had not been revoked,
though no intimation had ever been received that use had

---

* *Curieuse Nachricht von Pennsylvania in Norden America von Daniel
Falknern, Professor etc.*   Frankfurt und Leipzig, 1702.

been made of it.   It seems, then, that between the dates
of the Siverts and Furly powers Jansen had gone to
America.   On the 29th of November, 1698, Reynier Jansen, who afterwards became the printer, bought of Thomas
Tresse twenty acres of Liberty lands here, and on the 7th
of February, 1698–9, the right of citizenship, as has been
said, was conferred by the Germantown Court upon Reynier Jansen, lace-maker.   These events fix with some
definiteness the date of his arrival.   He must soon afterwards have removed to Philadelphia, though retaining his
associations with Germantown, because ten months later,
December 23d, 1699, he bought of Peter Klever seventy-
five acres in the latter place by a deed in which he is described as a *merchant* of Philadelphia.   This land he, as
a *printer*, sold to Daniel Geissler October 20th, 1701.
Since the book called "God's Protecting Providence," etc.,
was printed in 1699, it must have been one of the earliest
productions of his press, and the probabilities are that he
began to print late in that year.   Its appearance indicates
an untrained printer and a meagre font of type.   He was
the second printer in the middle colonies, and his books
are so rare that a single specimen would probably bring
at auction now more than the price for which he then
sold his whole edition.   He left a son, Stephen, in business at Amsterdam whom he had apportioned there, and
brought with him to this country two sons, Tiberius and
Joseph, who, after the Dutch manner, assumed the name
Reyniers, and two daughters, Amity, who married
Matthias, son of Hans Millan, of Germantown, and Alice,
who married John Piggot.   His career as a printer was
very brief.   He died about March 1st, 1706, leaving personal property valued at £226 1s. 8d., among which was

included " a parcell of books from William Bradford £4 2s. od." We find among the residents in 1699 Heinrich Pennepacker, the first German surveyor in the province, and Evert In den Hoffen, from Mühlheim on the Ruhr, with Herman, Gerhard, Peter and Annecke, who were doubtless his children, some of whom are buried in the Mennonite graveyard on the Skippack.

Four families, members of the Mennonite Church at Hamburg, Harman Karsdorp and family, Claes Berends and family, including his father-in-law, Cornelius Claessen, Isaac Van Sintern and family, and Paul Roosen and wife, and two single persons, Heinrich Van Sintern and the widow Trientje Harmens, started for Pennsylvania, March 5th, 1700, and a few months later at least four of them were here (*Mennonitische Blaetter*, Hamburg). Isaac Van Sintern was a great grandson of Jan de Voss, a burgomaster at Handshooten, in Flanders, about 1550, a genealogy of whose descendants, including many American Mennonites, was prepared in Holland over a hundred years ago. In 1700 also came George Müller and Justus Falkner, a brother of Daniel, and the first Lutheran preacher in the province. Among the residents in 1700 were Isaac Karsdorp and Arnold Van Vossen, Mennonites; Richard Van der Werf, Dirk Jansen, who married Margaret Millan, and Sebastian Bartleson ; in 1701, Heinrich Lorentz and Christopher Schlegel; in 1702, Dirk Jansen, an unmarried man from Bergerland, working for Johannes Kuster; Ludwig Christian Sprogell, a bachelor, from Holland, and brother of that John Henry Sprogell who a few years later brought an ejectment against Pastorius, and feed all the lawyers of the province; Marieke Speikerman, Johannes Rebenstock, Philip Christian Zimmerman, Michael Renberg, with his sons Dirk and Wilhelm, from Mühlheim on the Ruhr, Peter Bun, Isaac Peterson and Jacob Gerritz Holtzhooven, both from Guelderland in Holland, Heinrich Tibben, Willem Hosters, a Mennonite weaver from Crefeld, Jacob Claessen Arents, from Amsterdam, Jan Krey, Johann Conrad Cotweis, who was an interpreter in New York in 1709, and Jacob Gaetschalk, a Mennonite preacher, and 1703, Anthony Gerckes, Barnt Hendricks, Hans Heinrich Meels, Simon Andrews, Herman Dors * and Cornelius Tyson. The last two appear to have come from Crefeld, and over Tyson, who died in 1716, Pastorius erected in Axe's Graveyard at Germantown what is, so far as I know, the oldest existing tombstone to the memory of a German in Pennsylvania. It bears the following inscription in Dutch:

DUTCH.	GERMAN.	ENGLISH.
Obijt Meiy 9, 1716.	Gestorben den 9. Mai, 1716.	Died May 9th, 1716.
Cornelius Tiesen.	Cornelius Tyson.	Cornelius Tyson.
Salic sin de doon	Selig sind die Todten	Blessed are the dead
Die in den Here sterve.	Die in dem Herrn sterben.	Who die in the Lord.
Theibric is haer Kron,	Zahlreich ist ihre Krone,	Numerous is their crown,
Tgloriric haer cvvc.	Glorreich ist ihr Erbe	Glorious is their reward.

On the 28th of June, 1701, a tax was laid for the building of a prison, erection of a market and other objects for the public good. As in all communities the prison preceded the school-house, but the interval was not long. December 30th of that year "it was found good to start a school here in Germantown," and Arent Klinken, Paul Wollf and Peter Schumacher, Jr., were appointed over-

---

* One Herman Dorst, near Germantown, a bachelor, past eighty years of age, who for a long time lived in a house by himself, died there on the 14th instant.—*American Weekly Mercury*, October 18th, 1739.

seers to collect subscriptions and arrange with a school teacher, and Pastorius was the first pedagogue. As early as January 25th, 1694–95, it was ordered that stocks should be put up for the punishment of evildoers. We might, perhaps, infer that they were little used from the fact that in June, 1702, James De la Plaine was ordered to remove the old iron from the rotten stocks and take care of it. But alas! December 31st, 1703, we find that "Peter Schumacher and Isaac Schumacher shall arrange with workmen that a prison house and stocks be put up as soon as possible" (*Rath's Buch*).

February 10th, 1702–3, Arnold Van Fossen delivered to Jan Neuss, on behalf of the Mennonites, a deed for three square perches of land for a church, which, however, was not built until six years later.

In 1702 began the settlement on the Skippack. This first outgrowth of Germantown also had its origin at Crefeld, and the history of the Crefeld purchase would not be complete without some reference to it. As we have seen, of the one thousand acres bought by Govert Remke, one hundred and sixty-one acres were laid out at Germantown; the balance he sold in 1686 to Dirk Sipman. Of Sipman's own purchase of five thousand acres, five hundred and eighty-eight acres were laid out at Germantown, and all that remained of the six thousand acres he sold in 1698 to Matthias Van Bebber, who, getting in addition five thousand acres allowance and four hundred and fifteen acres by purchase, had the whole tract of six thousand one hundred and sixty-six acres located by patent, February 22d, 1701, on the Skippack. It was in the present Perkiomen Township, Montgomery County, and adjoined Edward Lane and William Harmer, near what is now the village of Evansburg (*Exemp. Records*, Vol. 1, p. 470). For the next half century at least it was known as Bebber's Town, or Bebber's Township, and the name, being often met with in the Germantown records, has been a source of apparently hopeless confusion to our local historians. Van Bebber immediately began to colonize it, the most of the settlers being Mennonites. Among these settlers were Heinrich Pannebecker, Johannes Kuster, Johannes Umstat, Klas Jansen and Jan Krey, in 1702; John Jacobs, in 1704; John Newberry, Thomas Wiseman, Edward Beer, Gerhard and Herman In de Hoffen, Dirk and William Renberg, in 1706; William and Cornelius Dewees, Hermannus Kuster, Christopher Zimmerman, Johannes Scholl and Daniel Desmond, in 1708; Jacob Johannes and Martin Kolb, Mennonite weavers from Wolfsheim in the Palatinate, and Andrew Strayer, in 1709; Solomon Dubois, from Ulster County, New York, in 1716; Paul Fried, in 1727, and in the last year the unsold balance of the tract passed into the hands of Pannebecker. Van Bebber gave one hundred acres for a Mennonite church, which was built about 1725, the trustees being Hendrick Sellen, Hermannus Kuster, Klas Jansen, Martin Kolb, Henry Kolb, Jacob Kolb and Michael Ziegler. Their early preachers were Jacob Gaetshalk, Henry Kolb, Claes Jansen and Michael Ziegler.

The Van Bebbers were undoubtedly men of standing, ability, enterprise and means. The father, Jacob Isaac, moved to Philadelphia before 1698, being described as a merchant in High Street, and died there before 1711. He had three grandsons named Jacob, one of whom was doubtless the Jacob Van Bebber who became Judge of the Supreme Court of Delaware, November 27th, 1764. Matthias, who is frequently mentioned by James Logan, made a trip to Holland in 1701, witnessing there Benjamin Furly's power of attorney, July 28th, and had returned to Philadelphia before April 13th, 1702. He remained in that city until 1704, when he and his elder brother, Isaac Jacobs, accompanied by Reynier Hermanns Van Burklow, a son-in-law of Peter Schumacher, and possibly others, removed to Bohemia Manor, Cecil County, Maryland. There he was a justice of the peace, and is described in the deeds as a merchant and a gentleman. Their descendants, like many others, soon fell away from the simple habits and strict creed of their fathers. The Van Bebbers, of Maryland, have been distinguished in all the wars and at the bar, and at the Falls of the Kanawha, Van Bebber's rock, a crag jutting out at a great height over the river, still preserves the memory and recalls the exploits of one of the most daring Indian fighters in Western Virginia.

I have now gone over two decades of the earliest history of Germantown. It has been my effort to give the names of all those who arrived within that time, and as fully as could be ascertained the dates of their arrival and the places from which they came, believing that in this way the most satisfactory information will be conveyed to those interested in them as individuals, and the clearest light thrown on the character of the emigration. The facts so collected and grouped seem to me to warrant the conclusion I have formed, that Germantown was substantially a settlement of people from the lower Rhine regions of Germany and from Holland, and that in the main they were the offspring of that Christian sect, which, more than any other, has been a wanderer (says Loeher in his *Geschichte und Zustände der Deutschen in Amerika*, p. 35: "As the true pilgrims upon earth, going from place to place in the hope to find quiet and rest, appear the Mennonites. They were the most important among the German pioneers in North America"), which endeavoring to carry the injunctions of the New Testament into the affairs of daily life, had no defense against almost incredible persecutions except flight, and which to-day is sending thousands of its followers to the Mississippi and the far West, after they have in vain quest traversed Europe from the Rhine to the Volga*

In the compilation of this article I have been especially indebted to Dr. J. G. DeHoop Scheffer, of the College at Amsterdam, for European researches; to Professor Oswald Seidensticker, of the University of Pennsylvania, whose careful investigations I have used freely, and to Abraham H. Cassel, of Harleysville, Pa., whose valuable library, it is perhaps not too much to say, is the only place in which the history of the Germans of Pennsylvania can be found. In giving the orthography of proper names, I have, as far as practicable, followed autographs (see *S. W. Pennypacker*).

---

* See *Historical and Biographical Sketches*, by Samuel W. Pennypacker.

Mennonite Meeting at Germantown.

DENIS KUNDERS OR CONRAD.—Pastorius had an interview with Conrad at Crefeld, April 12th, 1683, on his way to America. That Conrad was a Mennonite is generally conceded. His wife was a sister of the Streypers and they were Mennonites, and a son of Conrad married a daughter of Willem Streypers in 1710, and Pastorius says: "I talked with Denis Kunders and his wife, and with Dirk, Herman and Abraham Op den Graeff, at Crefeld," and they were Mennonites. The first religious meeting was held at Conrad's house in Germantown, 1683. It is said they first worshiped in private houses, or under the shade of the trees during the pleasant days of summer. Their first minister was Willem Rittinghuysen,* who arrived in 1688† from Broich in Holland, and who in 1690 built the first paper mill in America, on a branch of the Wissahickon Creek, and there was made the paper used by William Bradford, the earliest printer in the middle colonies.

Februry 10th, 1702–3, Arnold Van Fossen delivered to Jan Neuss on behalf of the Mennonites a deed for three square perches of land for a church. The first meeting-

---

* Willem Ruddinghuysen van Mülheim.

† Some historians have it even earlier, but the evidence is merely circumstantial. In 1678 he was yet at Amsterdam and was made a citizen there.

house was built in 1708. It was a log house, neither
large nor costly, but in keeping with those plain people.
The log church was built at the southeast corner of the
lot where the present meeting-house stands, on Main
Street. It was used also as a school-house, and Christopher Dock was for many years the teacher of this
school. Some of the hymns composed by him in German are still preserved. The deed of the meeting-house
bears date September 6th, 1714. It was given by Henry
Sellen to the Mennonite church of Germantown, and is
now in the possession of the author of this work and
reads as follows:

TO ALL PEOPLE to whom these presents shall come
I Henry Sellen of Kriesheim in the Germantownship in
the County of Philadelphia & province of Pensilvania Yeo-
man fend greeting. WHEREAS Arnold van Vofsen of Beb-
bers-township in the sd County Husbandman & Mary his
wife by their Indenture duly executed bearing date the Sixth
day of September Annog. domi 1714, for the consideration
therein mentioned did Grant and Convey unto me the sd
Henry Sellen, & to John Neus late of Germantown deceased, a certain piece of Land fcituate lying & being in
Germantown in the sd County, Containing thirty five
perches of land, to hold the sd piece of land with the appur-
tenances, unto us the sd Henry Sellen & John Neus, and
to the furvivor of us & to the heirs and afsigns of the fur
vivor of us forever, as by the sd Indenture may at Large
appear, Which sd land & premifses wereso as aforesd
convey'd unto us by the direction & appointment of the
Inhabitants in & about Germantown aforesd belonging to
the Meeting of the people called Mennonists (: alias Men-

isten :)   AND the above recited Intenture was fo made or
Intended to us in trust to the Intent only that we or either
of us as should be & continue in unity & religious fellowship with the sd people & remain members of the meeting
of the sd Mennonists (: whereunto we did & I now do belong :) should stand & be feized of the sd land & premifses
in and by the sd Indenture granted.   To the uses & Intents
herein after mentioned & declared & under the conditions
provisos & restrictions herein after limitted & exprefsed &
to no other use Intent or purpose whatsoever, that is to
say, FOR a place to erect a meeting house for the use and
service of the sd Mennonists (: alias Menisten :) and for a
place to bury their dead, PROVIDED always that neither I
nor my heirs nor any other person or persons fucceeding
me in this trust, who shall be declared by the members of
sd Meeting for the time being to be out of unity with them
shall be capable to execute this trust or ftand feized to the
uses aforesd, nor have any right or Intrest in the sd premifses while I or they fhall fo remain.   BUT that in all
such cases as also when I or any fucceeding me in the trust
aforesd shall happen to depart this life, than it shall & may
be lawfull to & for the sd Members of the sd Meeting as
often as Occasion shall require to make choice of others
to mannage & execute the sd trust in stead of such as shall
so fall away or be deceased.   AND UPON this further trust
& confidence that we & the furvivor of us and the heirs
of such furvivor should upon the request of the members
of the meeting of the sd Mennonists either afsign over the
sd trust or convey and settle the sd piece of land and premifses to such person or persons as the members of the sd
meeting shall order or appoint, to and for the uses Intents
and fervices herein before mentioned.

NOW KNOW YE that I the sd Henry Sellen do
hereby acknowledge, that I and the sd John Neus deceased
were nominated in the sd recited Indenture by and on the
behalf of the sd people called Mennonists (: alias Menisten :)
and that we were, and by furvivorship I now am therein
trusted only by and for the members of the sd meeting of
the Mennonists   And that I do not claim to have any
right or Intrest in the sd land & premifses or any part there
of to my own use & benefit by the sd Indenture or Con-
veyance so made to us as aforesd or otherwise howsoever,
BUT only to and for the use Intent & fervice herein before
mentioned under the Limitation and restriction above ex-
preffed and reserved,   And to no other use Intent or fervice
whatsoever.   In witnefs whereof I have hereunto set my
hand & seal, dated the Eight day of December in the year
of our Lord one thousand seven hundred & twenty four.

HENDRICK SELLEN

Signed sealed and delivered
   in the presence of
     MARTIN KOLB
     DIRCK KEYSER

The Mennonites have the honor of being the original
settlers in Germantown.   That claim unquestionably
belongs to them, for they are given that distinction in
every history that details the events pertaining to the
early settlement of Germantown.   They believe in the
doctrine of faith, that it is wrong to take up the sword
against man; such a belief was first expressed by the
Mennonites, and the Quakers followed in their wake.
Certain it is that the Mennonites were the first to champion the cause which had its origin in their conscience,

and it was solely through their efforts and some German Baptists (*Dunkards*) that the Legislature of Pennsylvania intervened and enacted that they and the Quakers should be exempt from military service.*   The passage of such a law was the cause which inspired the Mennonites to forward to the legislators at Harrisburg the following, which is from the original copy, now one hundred and eleven years old, and the only English copy known and now in my possession at Germantown.   It reads as follows:

A fhort and fincere DECLARATION,

To our *Honorable Affembly*, and all others in high or low Station of *Adminiftration*, and to all Friends and Inhabitants of this Country, to whofe Sight this may come, be they ENGLISH or GERMANS.

IN the firft Place we acknowledge us indebted to the moft high GOD, who created Heaven and Earth, the only good Being, to thank him for all his great Goodnefs and manifold Mercies and Love through our Saviour JESUS CHRIST, who is come to fave the Souls of Men, having all Power in Heaven and on Earth.

Further we find ourfelves indebted to be thankfull to our late worthy Affembly, for their giving fo good an Advice in thefe troublefome Times to all Ranks of People in *Pennfylvania*, particularly in allowing thofe, who, by the Doctrine of our Saviour JESUS CHRIST, are perfuaded in their Confciences to love their Enemies, and not to refift Evil, to enjoy the Liberty of their Confcience, for which, as alfo for all the good Things we enjoyed under their Care, we heartily thank that worthy Body of Affembly, and all high

---

* Constitution of Pennsylvania, Article 1, Declaration of Rights, Section 3.

and low in Office, who have advifed to fuch a peacefull
Meafure, hoping and confiding that they, and all others
entrufted with Power in this hitherto bleffed Province, may
be moved by the fame Spirit of Grace, which animated the
firft Founder of this Province, our late worthy Proprietor
William Penn, to grant Liberty of Confcience to all its
Inhabitants, that they may in the great and memorable Day
of Judgment be put on the right Hand of the juft Judge,
who judgeth without Refpeƈt of Perfon, and hear of him
thefe bleffed Words, *Come, ye bleffed of my Father, inherit
the Kingdom prepared for you, &c. What ye have done unto
one of the leaft of thefe my Brethren, ye have done unto me*,
among which Number (*i. e. the leaft of Chrift's Brethren*)
we by his Grace hope to be ranked ; and every Lenity and
Favour fhewn to fuch tender confcienced, although weak
Followers of this our bleffed Saviour, will not be forgotten
by him in that great Day.

The Advice to thofe who do not find Freedom of Confcience to take up Arms, that they ought to be helpfull to
thofe who are in Need and diftreffed Circumftances, we
receive with Chearfulnefs towards all Men of what Station
they may be—it being our Principle to feed the Hungry
and give the Thirfty Drink ;—we have dedicated ourfelves
to ferve all Men in every Thing that can be helpful to the
Prefervation of Men's Lives, but we find no Freedom in
giving, or doing, or affifting in any Thing by which Men's
Lives are deftroyed or hurt.—We beg the Patience of all
thofe who believe we err in this Point.

We are always ready, according to CHRIST's Command
to *Peter*, to pay the Tribute, that we may offend no Man,
and fo we are willing to pay Taxes, *and to render unto Caefar
thofe Things that are Caefar's, and to God thofe Things that*

are God's, although we think ourfelves very weak to give GOD his due Honour, he being a Spirit and Life, and we only Duft and Afhes.

We are alfo willing to be fubject to the higher Powers, and to give in the manner *Paul* directs us;—*for he beareth the Sword not in vain, for he is the Minifter of God, a Revenger to execute Wrath upon him that doeth Evil.*

This Teftimony we lay down before our worthy Affembly, and all other Perfons in Government, letting them know, that we are thankfull as above-mentioned, and that we are not at Liberty in Confcience to take up Arms to conquer our Enemies, but rather to pray to GOD, who has Power in Heaven and on Earth, for *US* and *THEM.*

We alfo crave the Patience of all the Inhabitants of this Country,—what they think to fee clearer in the Doctrine of the bleffed JESUS CHRIST, we will leave to them and GOD, finding ourfelves very poor; for Faith is to proceed out of the Word of GOD, which is Life and Spirit, and a Power of GOD, and our Confcience is to be inftructed by the fame, therefore we beg for Patience.

Our fmall Gift, which we have given, we gave to thofe who have Power over us, that we may not offend them, as CHRIST taught us by the Tribute Penny.

We heartily pray that GOD would govern all Hearts of our Rulers, be they high or low, to meditate thofe good Things which will pertain to *OUR* and *THEIR* Happinefs."

The above Declaration, figned by a Number of Elders and Teachers of the Society of Menonifts, and fome of the German Baptifts, prefented to the Honorable Houfe of Affembly on the 7th Day of November, 1775, was moft gracioufly received.

Among the earliest settlers of Germantown were the Mennonites who came from Holland. Their emigration has been portrayed in a very graphic style by Samuel W. Pennypacker, Esq., in his *Biographical and Historical Sketches*, which is already given in this work. If these articles were read by the residents of Germantown, they would have occasion to feel proud of the early settlers.

It was in 1688 that Willem Rittinghuysen, now Rittenhouse, with his wife and two sons, Klaus (Nicholas) and Gerhard (Garrett), and a daughter, Elizabeth, arrived in Germantown from New York. He was the first Mennonite preacher in Germantown, or in America, as far as known, but he was not yet ordained as Bishop, and the congregation at Germantown had no Bishop, and, according to the discipline of the Church, no one to ordain him, consequently a letter was sent from Germantown to the congregation at Altona for advice.

Miss Anna Brons writes from Holland that said letter was lost, but abstracts of an answer to further correspondence, found in the archives of the Mennonite church at Altona, show that the answer was directed to Claas Behrend, Paul Roosen, Heinrich Van Sintern, Harmen Van Karsdorp and Isaac Van Sintern, all Mennonites, who left the Hamburg Altona Mennonite Congregation and emigrated to America in 1700 and came to Germantown. The Ministers and Deacons of the Altona Congregation took the matter under earnest consideration, and as no one seemed willing at that time to undertake so tedious and dangerous a voyage across the sea to install a Bishop at Germantown, they wrote a letter to the Germantown congregation, authorizing one of the brethren to perform that duty, and admonished them to pray that God may be with them in their undertaking and bless them in performing such an important duty. This letter was signed by four ministers of the Hamburg Altona congregation, viz.: Bishop Gerritt Roosen, aged 90 years, Pieter Van Helle, Jacob Van Kampen and Jean de Lanoi. In consequence of the above instructions, Willem Rittenhouse was installed as Bishop of the first Mennonite church in America, at Germantown, about 1701. In a letter written to Amsterdam, dated September 3d, 1708, from which these particulars are derived, and which was signed by Jacob Gaedschalk, Harmen Karsdorp, Martin Kolb, Isaac Van Sintern and Conrad Jansen, they presented "a loving and friendly" request for "some catechisms for the children and little testaments for the young." Besides, psalm books and Bibles were so scarce that the whole membership had but one copy, and even the meeting-house needed a Bible. They urged their request by saying "that the community is still weak and it would cost much money to get them printed, while the members who came here from Germany have spent everything and must begin anew, and all work in order to pay for the convenience of life of which they stand in need."

Willem Rittenhouse, as stated before, was the first preacher in Germantown, afterwards elected as Bishop, emigrated to Germantown in 1688 and died in 1708, aged 64 years.

Jacob Gaetshalck, also a Mennonite preacher, arrived and settled in Germantown in 1702.

After the death of Bishop Rittenhouse two new preachers were chosen, names not known, but presumably they were Klaus (or Nicholas) Rittenhouse and Dirk

Keyser, because Dirk Keyser officiated at the marriage of Jacob Kolb with Sarah Van Sintern in the year 1710. The same year eleven young people were added to the congregation through baptism, and two new deacons accepted its obligations. From this time there is no regular record of the Germantown congregation until the year 1770. Still it is a well-known fact that the meetings have been kept regular, from the fact that the two new ministers as stated above did officiate at the time. Nicholas Rittenhouse died in 1730. We have also accounts of Jacob Gaetshalk being a preacher at Skippack in 1708, but in 1714 he lived yet in Germantown on the east side of Main Street, on lot No. 7, formerly belonging to Abraham Tunis, drawn in 1689 in the cave of Pastorius, which plan I have and will give in a subsequent chapter. The settlement of Skippack began in 1702, the first outgrowth of Germantown, which had its origin at Crefeld. Van Bebber gave one hundred acres of land on the Skippack for a Mennonite church and burying-ground. The church was built about 1725. Samuel W. Pennypacker says, " One of the oldest communities, if not the oldest of all, was that at Schiebach, or Germantown." So it seems Skippack and Germantown were considered one district, or one community. Many of the members at Germantown moved to Skippack and attended the meeting at Germantown until the year 1725, when the meeting-house at Skippack was built. Afterwards ministers were chosen at Skippack, among whom were mentioned Martin Kolb, Henry Kolb, Claus Jansen, Michael Ziegler and Isaac Kassel. They are also mentioned as preachers at Germantown. Also Heinrich Hunsicker, who rode on horseback from the Perkiomen to Germantown on a Sunday morning to preach.

Watson, the annalist, says that in 1740 Christopher Dock taught school in the old Mennonite log church in Germantown. Dock was also a Mennonite and lived in Salford, Montgomery County.

In 1770, at a congregational meeting, the following petition was prepared and agreed upon. It reads as follows : "Memorandum of the cost and charges and proceedings of the Building of the Baptists or Mennonists Meeting-house in Germantown. When, on the 20th day of January one thousand seven hundred and seventy, met a number of the Inhabitants of Germantown and People called Mennonists, and Unanimously agreed on a plan thereof, and appointed Jacob Keyser, sr., Nicholas Rittenhouse, Abraham Rittenhouse, and Jacob Knor, Managers of said Building &c. The following is a copy of the subscriptions & subscribers names, and also the cost of each particular of the aforesaid Building and the amount of sale of sundry old roofs &c."

Then follow the names of fifty-eight subscribers, with the respective amounts. The lowest was 7s. 6d., and the highest £11. The whole amount raised by subscription was . . . . £195 2s. 7d.
From sale of roof, etc., of the old house, 9 2 3

Total amount of money raised, £204 4s. 10d.
Whole cost of new house, . . 202 5 0

Balance left after expenses paid . £1 19s. 10d.

I have also in my possession the accounts of expenses for the maintenance of their poor, from year to year, to 1838.

The records also show that Communion was held by

Bishop Andrew Ziegler in 1780, when twenty-six members communed; in 1783, thirty-one members; in 1784, thirty-four members; in 1785, twenty-nine; in 1786, twenty-four, and in 1789, thirty members, and sixteen members being absent. There were twenty-five members in the Germantown congregation in 1770 when the new house was built; fifty-two new members were added in the following nineteen years, according to the Church records of those years, now in my possession. Andrew Ziegler officiated as Bishop at Germantown, how long afterwards the records do not show.

The first record that we find of Jacob Funk is in 1774, and reads as follows: "In 1774 Jacob Funk, Preacher, joined, and Ann his wife. joined, and Catharine Funk joined." According to the above he was a preacher when he joined the Germantown congregation. He was the great-grandfather of the author of this work. His father was a nephew of Bishop Heinrich Funk, who settled at the Indian Creek in Franconia Township, Montgomery County, in the year 1719. They came either from Holland or the Palatinate. He was a fluent and earnest speaker and accomplished a great deal of good. He died March 11th, 1816, in the 86th year of his age, and is buried in the Germantown Mennonite burying-ground near the church door. It is also said by some of the older Friends that his father was a preacher, but nothing definite is known or on record. Jacob Funk was quite a prominent man in his day. He owned a farm on Willow Grove Road, about two miles east of Germantown. The house in which he dwelt remains there to this day, and is in good condition. It is a quaint structure. The front room was used as a reception room, and the back room was used as a horse stable in Revolutionary times; later it has been renovated and utilized as a parlor. To the right of the reception room is a capacious room, which was used by Mr. Funk as his library and study, and in the rear of this room is another large room, which was cemented and used for storing produce, cabbage, potatoes, etc.

Mr. Funk was also a great financial loser by the depredations of the British at the time of the battle of Germantown. They took from him all his live stock, of which he had a great quantity, and whatever else they could lay their hands on; what they could not take away they destroyed, and about all they left was the farm itself. They wanted that portion of the earth, but could not very well take it along. His daughter Elizabeth happened to be in Germantown at the time of the fight, and could not get away in time, and hid in a cellar until the battle was over; she was twelve years of age at that time. She afterwards in mature years became the wife of Daniel Kulp, and was the grandmother of the writer of this work.

No indemnity was ever paid to Mr. Funk for these depredations, probably for the reason that he never asked for it. He lost pretty near all he had, but he managed to purchase a yoke of oxen, with which he did his farming, and in spite of his great reverses he again prospered very substantially.

There is another bit of Revolutionary history attached to this farm. It is a well-known historical fact that General Murray was killed at the battle of Germantown. It is not generally known, however, that a vault was built on Mr. Funk's farm wherein to place the General's body.

Such a vault was built, and it remains on the farm to-day; it is a great curiosity even now. This farm was in the Funk family about one hundred and ten years. Prior to the building of the present church edifice, the Quakers and Mennonites frequently worshiped together, and most amicable feelings existed between them until the time when the Quakers rather presumed too much upon the generosity of the Mennonites, by claiming the honor of consummating such a thing as we have hereinbefore briefly referred to, viz.: the honor of being the authors of the protest against slavery, when it cannot be shown that one of the signers was a Quaker. The two Op den Graeffs (says S. W. Pennypacker) were Mennonites. It is also presumed that Hendricks was a Mennonite. Daniel Francis Pastorius calls the Pietists his friends even nine years after the signing of the protest; he wrote a pamphlet to his friends the Pietists in Germany, which was published at Amsterdam in 1697.* In the matter of the proclamation against slavery, it is pretty conclusive that the document does not bear a single Quaker signature, while it is known that at that time a number of the Quakers were slaveholders.

The ministers up to the present time, after Jacob Funk and Andrew Ziegler, were John Minnick, Mr. Hellerman, Abraham Hunsicker, Henry A. Hunsicker, Frank Hunsicker, Israel Beidler, John Haldeman, A. H. Fredericks, Albert Funk and Nathaniel Bartolet Grubb, the present pastor.

The membership of the Germantown church at the present time numbers about twenty, nearly the same

---

* *Pennypacker's Historical and Biographical Sketches*, p. 49.

number that communed in the new church for the first time, December 10th, 1770. Rather a remarkable coincidence, is it not? The small membership of the church may be considered extraordinary; but there is nothing so extraordinary about it when all the facts are considered. We have stated that the Mennonites are a farming people—tilling the soil is their favorite avocation. When property in Germantown became very valuable, a great number of the then Mennonite residents disposed of their farms at almost fabulous sums, and purchased farms in Montgomery, Bucks and Lancaster Counties, where many of them still reside. Those who have gone before have left a posterity who still cling alike to the farm and to the old faith.

The *Germantown Independent*, of July 28th, 1883, has the following: "Of the doings of these early Mennonite settlers we have but scanty materials from which to draw." But Samuel W. Pennypacker, in his "Sketch of the Settlement of Germantown," has brought forth a document which "time has shown to have been the echo of the great wave that rolls around the world." It was the first public protest ever made on this continent against the holding of slaves; it is dated April 18th, 1688, and is signed by Francis Daniel Pastorius, Gerret Hendricks, Dirk Op den Graeff and Abraham Op den Graeff. The last two were Mennonites, and it is held quite probable that Hendricks was also of that faith. The protest was sent to a Friends' meeting; a copy of the protest is given in a former part of this work.

The *Schwenksville Item*, of November 2d, 1883, says: "The Crefeld colonists, who landed at Philadelphia and established themselves in German township, afterward a part of Germantown, in October, 1683, transplanted from the valley of the Rhine the spirit of the Mennonite fathers, who had struggled for centuries against the persecutions of the Church and State.   These same Mennonites formulated the doctrine of American freedom in a protest against slavery as early as 1688, or almost a century before the Declaration of Independence.   In fact, the history of the Mennonites of Pennsylvania is the history of a symmetrical superstructure of real liberty and religion, reared upon the foundation laid by St. Paul, and whose doctrines were handed down in unbroken succession."

Pastor S. F. Hotchkin says in an article in the *Germantown Telegraph*, under date February 24th, 1886: "Stockings had been made on hand frames in the Germantown homes from 'the settlement of Germantown by the Mennonites.'"   Also in the same paper, under date of June 2d, 1886, when speaking of the Axe's graveyard, a short distance above the Mennonite- church, afterward called the Concord burying-ground, he says: "When Germantown was settled in 1683 to 1695, the Mennonites and Quakers were the two religious bodies of the town.   At first their meetings were held in private houses, and it is supposed that at times they worshiped together in the same house till the building of their meeting-houses.   It is not known that they had a special burying-place, and the dead were probably buried in their own ground. When the Mennonite church was built in 1708 it had its graveyard adjoining it for the burial of their members."

In regard to the Axe's, afterward Concord, graveyard, he says: "The front wall on the main road was begun in May, 1724, by Dirk Johnson and John Frederick Axe." A list of those who aided the work is added, which should interest ancient Germantowners. We find the names of Paul Engel, Garret Rittinghausen, Hans Reyner, John Streepers, Johannes Jansen, Dennis Cunrads (Tunis Kunders), Peter Keyser, John Gorgas, Peter Shoemaker, Christopher Witt, Frantz Neff and many others. The work cost £40 8s. 6d.

Dirk Jansen and his wife Katrina were one of the thirteen families who settled Germantown. They were the ancestors of this family as well as of the other Johnsons already noted, and were Mennonites. Paul Engel, above mentioned, also a Mennonite, is buried at Skippack, and the date on his grave-stone is 1723. In 1703 he declined to be a burgess in Germantown for conscientious reasons.

Elizabeth Engel, wife of Charles, saw the wounded General Agnew carried past her house on a door. One of the family's horses was taken by the English and a poor one put in its place.

It was from behind a wall which separated the Mennonite burying-ground from the street that the British General Agnew was fired upon while at the head of a column of his soldiers and mortally wounded, during the Revolutionary War. The name of the perpetrator of the deed is carefully guarded to this day by the only person who knows the truth. Hans Boyer, a half-witted fellow of that day, claimed the credit of the deed, but it is said to have not rightfully belonged to him. General Agnew is buried in the Lower burying-ground, now Hood's Cemetery, Germantown.

8

Names of the Members of the Mennonite Church at Germantown in 1708 when the first house was built.

Pastor Jacob Godshalk,	Barbara Kolb,
Bishop Willem Rittenhouse,	Ann Bowman,
Herman Carsdorp,	Margaret Huberts,
Martin Kolb,	Mary Sellen,
Isaac Van Sintern,	Elizabeth Kuster,
Conrad Johnson,	Margaret Tuysen,
Henry Kassel, and their wives,	Altien Revenstock,
Herman Teyner,	John Nise,
John Fry,	Hans Nise,
Peter Connerts,	John Lensen,
Paul Klumpkes,	Isaac Jacobs,
Arnold Van Vossen,	Jacob Isaacs,
John Kolb,	Hendrick Sellen,
Jacob Kolb,	John Connerts,
Wynant Bowman,	Peter Keyser,
John Gorges,	Herman Kuster,
Cornelious Classen,	Christopher Zimmerman,
Arnold Kuster,	Sarah Van Sintern,
Mary Tuynen,	Civilia Connerts,
Helena Frey,	Altien Tysen,
Gertrude Conners,	Catharine Casselberry,
Mary Van Vossen,	Civilia Van Vossen.

The above is taken from Morgan Edwards' History, 1770.

Names of the Members in 1770 when the present house was built as they appear on the Records.

Jacob Keyser, Sen.,	William Hendricks
& Margaret his wife,	& —— his wife,
William Rittenhouse, Sen.,	Mary Penninghausen,
Nicholas Rittenhouse	Abraham Rittenhouse
& Sarah his wife,	& Ann his wife,
Susanna Nice, grany,	Jacob Rittenhouse, carpenter,
Catharine Rife,	& Susanna his wife,
Mary Stoneburner,	Nicholas Johnson
Ann Heisler, grany,	& Ann his wife,
Barbara Bergman,	Ann Houpt,
Margaret Smith,	Jacob Rittenhouse, paper-maker,

William Van Aiken,
John Rittenhouse
  & Margaret his wife.
    1771
John Keyser, cordwainer,
  & Elizabeth his wife,
Jacob Knorr
  & Hannah his wife,
Isaac Rittenhouse,
Susanna Knorr,
Isaac Kolb
  & Barbara his wife,

Henry Roosen
  & ——— his wife.
    1774
Jacob Funk preacher joined
  & Ann his wife joined,
Catherine Funk joined
    1775
Cornelius Engle baptized
  & Teen his wife do
Susanna Keyser   do

Continued on to 1789.

He also says : " In about sixteen years (1727) this church had branched out to Skippack, Conestoga, Great Swamp and Manatany, and become five churches, to which appertained sixteen ministers, namely, Jacob Godshalk, Henry Kolb, Martin Kolb, Nicholas Johnson, Michael Zigler, John Gorgas, John Conrads, Nicholas Rittenhausen, Hans Burgholser, Christian Herr, Benedict Hirschy, Martin Baer, Johannes Bowman, Velti Clemmer, Daniel Langenacker and Jacob Beghtly."

Hupert Cassel, born and raised in Towamencin Township, now Montgomery County, was also a Mennonite. He was the grandfather of Abraham H. Cassel, the great antiquarian of Harleysville, and lived to the age of about ninety years. He was for quite a number of years a deacon in the Mennonite congregation in Hatfield, Montgomery County, Pa.

On Sunday, July 16th, 1876, Pastor N. B. Grubb, of Schwenksville, preached a Centennial sermon in the Germantown Mennonite church, from the text Psalm 97 : 1. Among the audience were persons from different parts of this State, also from Massachusetts, New York, New Jersey, Connecticut and Rhode Island.*

---

* Church Records, p. 48.

October 6th, 1883, Holy Communion was celebrated in the morning, Pastor Albert Funk officiating, this being Bi-Centennial day, or the two hundredth year since the organization of the Mennonite church at Germantown. In the afternoon a meeting was held in commemoration of the *first* meeting held in Germantown in the house of Thonis Kunders in 1683, when a small band of those early Christians assembled to give praise unto the Lord. This was the first Mennonite meeting known to have been held in America.

Upon this occasion appropriate addresses were made by Samuel W. Pennypacker, giving sketches of the early history of the Mennonites in America, more particularly of them at Germantown, and was followed by Pastor John Oberholzer in the German language.

On the same day, as mentioned above, religious service was also held in Crefeld, Prussia, from whence the first thirteen families came to settle Germantown. This service was held for the purpose of celebrating the first Mennonite meeting in America, which took place two hundred years ago.

An Address

At the Bi-Centennial Celebration of the Settlement of Germantown, Pa., and the Beginning of German Emigration to America.

By Samuel W. Pennypacker.

In the Philadelphia Academy of Music, on the evening of October 6th, 1883.

Ladies and Gentlemen:

The Teutonic races since the overthrow of the power of ancient Rome, which they brought about, have been in the van of thought and achievement. The only rival of the German and the Dutchman, in those things which mark broadly the pathway of human advancement, came from the same household. In the sixth century a tribe of Germans found their way across the North Sea to an island which in time they made their own, and to which they gave the name of Angleland. Like all of their stock, the men of this colony grew in substance and developed in intelligence, but they have ever since, in times of trial and difficulty, looked back to the Fatherland for guidance and support. In 1471 a man named Caxton was in Cologne learning the art of printing. He returned to England to impart to his countrymen a

(117)

knowledge of the new discovery, and the literature of Chaucer, Shakespeare, Scott and Dickens became a possibility. The impulse which Martin Luther gave to human thought, when he nailed his propositions to the church-door at Wittenberg, beat along the shores of the Atlantic, and the revolution of 1688, bringing with it the liberty of Englishmen, was one of the results. For the attainment of that liberty, England drove her own royal line beyond the seas and made the Stadtholder of Holland her king. From this day down to the present time every king of England has been a German.

Early in the seventeenth century an English admiral went to Rotterdam for a wife. According to Pepys, who described her later, she was "a well-looked, fat, short old Dutch woman, but one that hath been heretofore pretty handsome, and I believe, hath more wit than her husband." The son of this woman was the Quaker William Penn. He who would know the causes for the settlement of Pennsylvania, the purest and in that it gave the best promise of what the future was to unfold, the most fateful of American colonies, must go to the Reformation to seek them. The time has come when men look back through William Penn and George Fox to their masters, Menno Simons, the Reformer of the Netherlands, Casper Schwenkfeld, the nobleman of Silesia, and Jacob Boehm, the inspired shoemaker of Görlitz. In that great upheaval of the sixteenth century there were leaders who refused to stop where Luther, Calvin and Zwinglius took a successful stand. The strong, controlling thought which underlay their teachings was, that there should be no exercise of force in religion. The baptism of an infant was a compulsory method of bringing it into the

Church, and they rejected the doctrine; an oath was a means of compelling the conscience, and they refused to swear; warfare was a violent interference with the rights of others, and they would take part in no wars, even for the purpose of self-protection. More than all in its political significance and effect, with keen insight and clear view, hoping for themselves what the centuries since have given to us, they for the first time taught that the injunctions of Christ were one thing and the power of man another, that the might of the State should have nothing to do with the creed of the Church, and that every man in matters of faith should be left to his own convictions. Their doctrines, mingled as must be admitted with some delusions, spread like wildfire throughout Europe, and their followers could be found from the mountains of Switzerland to the dykes of Holland. They were the forlorn hope of the ages, and, coming into direct conflict with the interest of Church and State, they were crushed by the concentrated power of both.

There is nothing in the history of Christendom like the suffering to which they were subjected, in respect to its extent and severity. The fumes from their burning bodies went up into the air from every city and village along the Rhine. The stories of their lives were told by their enemies and the pages of history were freighted with the records of their alleged misdeeds. The name of Anabaptist, which was given them, was made a byword and reproach, and we shrink from it with a sense of only half-forgotten terror even to-day. The English representatives of this movement were the Quakers. Picart, after telling that some of the Anabaptists fled to England to spread their doctrines there, says: "The Quakers owe their rise to these Anabaptists."* The doctrine of the inner light was an assertion that every man has within himself a test of truth upon which he may rely, and was in itself an attack upon the binding character of authority. The seed from the sowings of Menno, wafted across from the Rhine to the Thames, were planted on English soil by George Fox and were brought by William Penn to Pennsylvania, where no man has ever been molested because of his religious convictions. Three times did William Penn, impelled by a sympathetic nearness of faith and methods, go over to Holland and Germany to hold friendly converse and discussion with these people, and it was very fitting that when he had established his province in the wilds of America, he should urge and prevail with them to cross the ocean to him. On this day, two hundred years ago, thirty-three of them, men, women and children, landed in Philadelphia. The settlement of Germantown has a higher import, then, than that thirteen families founded new homes, and that a new burgh, destined to fame though it was, was built on the face of the earth. It has a wider significance even than that here was the beginning of that immense emigration of Germans who have since flocked to these shores.

Those thirteen men, humble as they may have been individually, and unimportant as may have been the personal events of their lives, holding as they did opinions which were banned in Europe, and which only the fulness of time could justify, standing as they did on what was then the outer picket line of civilization,

---

* Picart was here cited because he makes the statement directly and in few words. Upon this subject consult Barclay's " Religious Societies of the Commonwealth," Hortensius' " Histoire des Anabaptistes," and " Pennsylvania Magazine," Vol. 4, p. 4.

best represented the meaning of the colonization of Pennsylvania and the principles which lie at the foundation of her institutions. Better far than the Pilgrims who landed at Plymouth, better even than the Quakers who established a city of brotherly love ; they stood for that spirit of universal toleration, which found no abiding place save in America. Their feet were planted directly upon that path which leads from the darkness of the middle ages down to the light of the nineteenth century, from the oppressions of the past to the freedom of the present. Bullinger, the great reviler of the Anabaptists, in detailing in 1560 their many heresies, says they taught that "the government shall and may not assume control of questions of religion or faith."*

No such attack upon the established order of things had ever been made before, and the potentates were wild in their wrath. Menno went from place to place with a reward upon his head ; men were put to death for giving him shelter, and two hundred and twenty-nine of his followers were burned and beheaded in one city alone. ·

But two centuries after Bullinger wrote there was put into the constitution of Pennsylvania, in almost identical language: " No human authority can, in any case whatever, control or interfere with the right of conscience."†
The fruitage is here, but the planting and watering were along the Rhine. And to-day the Mennonites and their descendants are to be found from the Delaware River to the Columbia. The Schwenckfelders, hunted out of Europe in 1734, still meet upon the Skippack on the 24th of every September, to give thanks unto the Lord

---

* " Die Oberkeit solle und moege sich der Religion oder Glaubens sachen nicht annemmen." *Der Widertoufferen Ursprung*, p. 18.

† Constitution of the Commonwealth of Pennsylvania, Article 1, Section 3.

for their deliverance. This is the tale which Lensen, Kunders, Lucken, Tyson, Opdengraeff and the rest, as they sat down to weave their cloth and tend their vines in the woods of Germantown, had to tell to the world. A great poet has sung their story, and you Germans will do well to keep the memory of it green for all time to come. It cannot be gainsaid that the influence upon American life and institutions of that German emigration which began with thirty-three persons in 1683, and had swollen in 1882 to 250,630, has fulfilled the promise given by its auspicious commencement. The Quakers maintained control of their province down to the time of the Revolution, and they were enabled to do it by the support of the Germans. The dread with which the Germans inspired the politicians of the colonial days was exces sive. In 1727 James Logan wrote to the Proprietary: " You will soon have a German colony here, and, per haps, such a one as Britain once received from Saxony in ye fifth century."

Said Thomas Graeme to Thomas Penn in a letter in 1750 · " The Dutch, by their numbers and industry, will soon become masters of the province." Many were the devices to weaken them. It was proposed to establish schools among them where only English should be taught; to invalidate all German deeds ; to suppress all German printing presses and the importa tion of German books, and to offer rewards for inter marriages. Samuel Purviance wrote to Colonel James Burd, in 1765, that the way to do was "to let it be spread abroad through the country that your party intend to come well-armed to the election,   and that you will thrash the sheriff, every inspector, Quaker and Mennonist to a jelly." But, as a disappointed manager wrote from Kingsessing the same year : "All in. vain was our labor. . . . Our party at the last election have loosed (lost) all."

The Speaker of the first Federal House of Representatives was a German, and with Simon Snyder, in 1808, began the regime of the eight German governors of Pennsylvania. To represent her military renown during the Revolutionary War, Pennsylvania has put the statue of Muhlenberg in the Capitol at Washington. The terrific and bloody struggle with slavery in this country, which ended at Appomattox in 1865, began at Germantown so long ago as 1688. The Murat of the Rebellion, he who afterwards so sadly lost his life among the savages of the West, had traced his lineage to the Mennonite, Paul Kuster, of Germantown, and if the records were accessible, it could, it may be, be carried still further back to that Peter Kuster who was beheaded at Saardam in 1535. Another of the descendants of those earliest emigrants, the youngest general of the war, planted his victorious flag upon the ramparts of Fort Fisher.

The Schwenkfelder forefathers of Hartranft, Major-General, Governor, and once urged by this State for the Presidency, lie buried along the Perkiomen. He who reads the annals of the war will find that among those who did the most effective work were Albright, Beaver, Dahlgren, Heintzleman, Hoffman, Rosecrans, Steinwehr, Schurz, Sigel, Weitzel and Wistar.

The liberties of the press in America were established in the trial of John Peter Zenger. Man never knew the distance of the sun and stars until David Rittenhouse, of Germantown, made his observations in 1769. (He was born in Roxborough Township, near Germantown, in 1732.) The oldest publishing house now existing on this continent was started by Sauer, in Germantown, in 1738. The first paper mill was built by Rittinghuysen upon the Wissahickon Creek, in 1690. (It was on a branch of the Wissahickon.) The German Bible ante-dates the English Bible in America by nearly forty years, and the largest book published in the colonies came from the Ephrata press in 1749. From Pastorius, the enthusiast, of highest culture and gentlest blood, down to Seidensticker, who made him known to us, the Germans have been conspicuous for learning. To the labors of the Moravian missionaries, Heckewelder and Zeisberger, we largely owe what knowledge we possess of Indian history and philology. Samuel Cunard, a descendant of Thonis Kunders, in the fifth generation, established the first line of ocean steamers between America and England, and was made a British baronet.

If you would see the work of the American Germans of to-day, look about you. Is there a scientist of more extended reputation than Leidy? Is there a more eminent surgeon than Gross? Who designed your Centennial buildings, and in whose hands did you trust the moneys to pay for them? The president of your University, the most enterprising of American merchants, and the chief justice of your State are alike of German descent. The great bridge just completed, after years of labor and immense expenditures, which ties Brooklyn to New York, was built by a German. The financier of the nation during the Rebellion undertook to construct a railroad from the greatest of the inland seas to the widest of the oceans. He fell beneath the weight of the task; a German completed it.

But the time allotted to me does not permit me to more than suggest a few points in the broad outlines of German achievement. The hammer of Thor, which at the dawn of history smote upon the Himalayas, now resounds from the Alleghenies to the Cascades.

The Germanic tide which then began to pour into Europe has now reached the Pacific. In its great march, covering twenty centuries of time, it has met with no obstacle which it has not overcome; it has been opposed by no force which it has not overthrown, and it has entered no field which it has not made more fruitful. America will have no different story to tell. The future cannot belie·the past. Manners and institutions change; the rock crumbles into dust; the shore disappears into the sea, but their is nothing more permanent than the characteristics of a race.

Already the rigidity and angularity which Puritanism has impressed upon this country have begun to disappear; already we feel the results of a broader scope, a sterner purpose and of more persistent labor. And in the years yet to be, America will have greater gifts to offer unto the generations of men, will be better able to attain that destiny which, in the providence of God, she is to fulfil because she has taken unto herself the outpourings of that people, which neither the legions of Cæsar, nor Papal power, nor the genius of a Bonaparte were able to subdue.

[The above address was delivered in the Academy of Music on the evening of October 6th, 1883, by Samuel W. Pennypacker, member of the Philadelphia Bar, and great-grandson of Matthias Pennypacker, first Mennonite minister and bishop of the Mennonite congregation at Phœnixville, Chester County.]

Report of the Indian Mission

Conducted under the Auspices of the General Conference of the New School Mennonites.

BY PASTOR S. S. HAURY.

CANTONMENT, INDIAN TERRITORY, May 4th, 1886.

The Mennonite Mission in Darlington, Indian Territory, was established in 1880, in the Spring, among the Arapahoe Indians. One year later we erected a mission house and began with a mission and boarding school, having eighteen pupils, boys and girls, at the commencement. The mission house had just been finished when it was destroyed by fire on the 19th of February, 1882. In this trial we lost our only child, nine months old, and three Indian children. We carried on our school in hospital tents until the fall of that year, when our mission house had been rebuilt to double the capacity of our first house.

This same year a military post, fifty-six miles northwest of Darlington, was vacated, and we were urged by the Indian agent, John D. Miles, to take charge of these military buildings at Cantonment and make use of them in educating, Christianizing and civilizing the Arapahoe and Cheyenne Indians located in that vicinity, believing that our Lord and Master had opened for us a new and wider door.

(126)

Brother H. R. Voth having received charge of our mission work at Darlington, I moved with my family to Cantonment in February, 1883, to raise up the Cross of Christ, bringing the Gospel of goodwill to men in a place where shortly before the ensigns of an army signalized war and bloodshed.

In the Fall of 1883 we began at this place a mission and boarding school for both the Arapahoe and Cheyenne Indians. The school was begun with fifteen children of both sexes. The school work, however, is not our only mission work, although it gives us for the present our strongest hold with our people to bring the Gospel near their understanding and near their heart. We have Sunday-schools and regular meetings for our older Indians. As the children are encouraged to learn and to talk English, and as they are taught only in this language, we have to speak to their people through interpreters in their own tongue.

I also wish to say here that our school work centres in teaching our children the contents of the Bible and in trying to lead them to Christ. As we teach our children to read and to write, and as we daily and continually point them to Christ as their only Redeemer, we do not and dare not neglect to teach them to work. We preach the Gospel in season and out of season, but unless we convince our Indians by a true Christian life, daily and continually exhibited before them, that to eat their bread in the sweat of their brow is no curse and no shame, but a blessing and honor for them as well as for the white man, they will not be Christianized. In getting the Indians to work, to provide for themselves, and to leave their life of sluggishness and indolence, we are trying to colonize them and get them located in houses. We have now eighteen families living in houses at this place, and several are building houses for themselves this Spring.

As to the success of our missionary work, I can say that it has not been in vain ; I can see how the Indians have advanced in all respects very distinctly. But they will not be Christianized in a few years; it will take many years of hard work, much patience and perseverance, and a life of prayer. And not always that which seems success is such, whilst often that which is real success appears to be just the reverse at the time. Our school at Darlington has an enrolment of forty-eight, and the school at this place of sixty-eight children. In Kansas we have now twenty children in school.

S. S. HAURY.

Virginia.

A Historical Sketch of the Early Mennonites in Virginia, communicated by Abraham Blosser, Editor of the "Watchful Pilgrim."

I WILL now give you some items and facts concerning the Mennonites in Virginia, but the difficulty in getting the exact dates of the first Mennonite settlers in the Valley of Virginia is due to the fact that few, if any, of the first Mennonite emigrants kept any records of either their family or churches. Their education generally was meagre and almost exclusively German, and in course of time the mother tongue ceased to be taught in the schools, and the English language almost entirely introduced in the schools and generally spoken, so that few could read German, and old records, account books and other papers containing historic facts or records of the early Mennonites, were no longer saved or cared for. For this reason we know so little of the early emigrants in this valley. The following is an extract from a book entitled *Kercheval's History of the Valley of Virginia*, by Samuel Kercheval, printed by John Gatewood, at Woodstock, Va., in 1850, second edition, chap. 5, p. 50 : " A large majority of our first emigrants were from Pennsylvania, composed of native Germans and German descent. There were, however, a number directly from Germany, some

9   (129)

from Maryland and New Jersey, and a few from New York. These emigrants brought with them the religious habits and customs of their ancestors. They were composed generally of three religious sects, viz.: Lutherans, Mennonists and Calvinists, with a few Dunkards. They generally settled in colonies, each sect pretty much together."

The Valley of Virginia is composed of all that scope of country lying between the Blue Ridge and the Allegheny range, varying from thirty to fifty miles in width and about two hundred miles in length. The territory now comprising the Counties of Page, Powel's Ford and the Woodstock Valley, between West Fort Mountain and North Mountain, extending from the neighborhood of Stephensburg for a considerable distance into the County of Rockingham, was settled almost exclusively by Germans. They were very tenacious in the preservation of their language, religion, customs and habits. In what is now Page County the inhabitants were almost exclusively of the Mennonite persuasion; but few Lutherans and Calvinists settled among them in other sections of the territory. The Mennonites were remarkable for their strict adherence to all the moral and religious observances required by this sect. Their children were early instructed in the principles and ceremonies of their religion, habits and customs. They were generally farmers, and took great care of their stock; and with few exceptions they strictly prohibited their children from going to the dance or juvenile amusements, so common to other religious sects of the Germans."

On page ninety of the above named book, among other accounts of Indian massacres is a statement of the massacre of John Roads, a Mennonite minister, in the latter part of August, 1766, by a party of eight Indians and a white villain, who crossed Powel's Ford to the south fork of the Shenandoah River, where Roads resided, and shot him standing in his door. His wife and one of his sons were killed in the yard, another of his sons in the cornfield. Elizabeth, his eldest daughter, picked up her little sister, sixteen or eighteen months old, and ran into the barn and through a hempfield to the river, which she crossed and escaped. One of his sons running away was shot and killed when nearly across the river. Two of his daughters and two sons were captured, but one of the boys, the youngest, was sickly, and as he could not travel fast enough they killed him; the two daughters refused to go further, and they also were killed. The other son got away from the Indians after three years of captivity, and came home to his friends. This was the last Indian massacre in the Page Valley.

For a while the Mennonite Church was prosperous in what is now the Page County (formerly part of Shenandoah and Rockingham Counties), but in course of time some dissensions took place and some of their children joined the Baptist and other societies more popular in the eyes of the world than the Mennonites. In later times there were no ministers there, and the Church was waited on by the ministers from Rockingham County, and it is said that there were not over five members of the Mennonite Church in Page County. In former times there were a number of Mennonite families in the vicinity of Woodstock, and northward towards Strasburg and Stevens City (formerly Newtown)—Stauffer and Graybill were preachers there—but these have nearly all been swallowed up by other societies, as is so apt to be the case in this our progressive age (progressive in worldly popularity). There are yet some members in Shenandoah County, but the Mennonites at present have no meeting-house in either Page or Shenandoah Counties. As in former times the Mennonites of the Valley of Virginia had no meeting-houses, but held their meetings in private houses, so there never were any built in what is now Page County, nor in Shenandoah County, and by the time building meeting-houses came more into vogue, the Church in these two counties dwindled down almost to nothing, while the Church in Rockingham and Augusta Counties increased. The first meeting-house in Rockingham was Frissel's, built in 1822 and rebuilt in about 1859. The one at the Pike was built in 1825 and rebuilt in 1878; 40 feet wide and 50 feet long. The one at Brenneman's was built in 1826 and rebuilt in 1875; 40 feet wide and 50 feet long. The one at Weaver's was built in 1827 and rebuilt in 1880; 50 feet wide and 70 feet long. That at Mt. Clinton was built in 1873; 30 feet wide and 40 feet long. The one at the Bank was built in 1849, and the one at Zion in 1885. There are several other meeting-houses in this county, which have been built since the war, owned partly by the Mennonites, as that at the Plains, New Dale, White Hall, North River and Dry River. Besides, meetings are held in school-houses in different parts of the county. There are three meeting-houses in Augusta County, viz.: Kindig's, Hildebrand's and Mt. Pleasant. There were Mennonites in this vicinity as early as 1816, when a person by the name of Bishop was officiating as Bishop, and John Shenk and John Fauver were ministers. (This is the statement of the present Bishop, Jacob Hildebrand.)

Formerly the Mennonites held their meetings in private houses. In what year Kindig's meeting-house was first used by the Mennonites my informant could not tell; but it was bought by the Mennonites many years ago. Formerly it was used as a school-house, called Hall's school-house. It was then remodeled and used as a meeting-house until the year 1885, when the whole structure was taken down and a new one built in its place, which is now completed, and the first· meeting in the new house was held May 30th, 1886. The meeting-house at Hildebrand's was built many years ago, and rebuilt in 1876. The house at Mt. Pleasant is a large one, built about 1870. There is a meeting held also at Union Chapel.

In Frederick County there are three regular places of meeting, viz.: Keurstown Church, a large new house, built in 1875 ; the other two places are school-houses, Kauffman's and Macedonia. In Pendleton County, West Virginia, there was a new meeting-house built in 1885, 32 by 38 feet, called Miller's Meeting-house. As there is no minister in Pendleton County yet, the Rockingham and Augusta County ministers have charge of that congregation.

There are also meetings held by the Mennonites at a place called Lost River, in Hardy County, West Virginia.

There are also meetings held by the Mennonites in Shenandoah County, at Haldeman's Creek school-house. In former times there was a small community of Mennonites in Greenbriar County, West Virginia. A few members live there yet, but they have had no resident minister for probably fifty years. Coffman was their last minister. They are occasionally visited by other ministers.

Trials and Afflictions of the Virginia Mennonites During the Late Civil War.

When the war of 1860 broke out the Mennonites, as an anti-slavery party or society, were in danger of being somewhat roughly treated or imposed upon, as this was a war for slavery by the seceeded States. But fortunately the Mennonites did not, comparatively speaking, cover much of the seceded territory, and the extreme South knew very little about them, while that of the Friends, or Quaker denomination, was principally in the Northern States. The principal body of the Mennonites within the then so-called " Confederate States " was in the Valley of Virginia ; so, also, were the Dunkers, or Brethren, as they style themselves. Though many of the more rigid war men among the Secessionists angrily denounced these non-resistant anti-slavery societies in the most distasteful manner imaginable, yet, strange to say, most of the principal officers among those who knew them personally, and their religious teachings, their modest, upright, honest and inoffensive deportment,. were inclined to favor them, though some of the unintelligent officers were harshly against them.

There was a militia draft made in May, 1861, and a number of the Mennonites and Dunkers, and their sons over eighteen years of age, were drafted, and from the way the draft took in these non-resistants in several places it looked very suspicious of fraud. They were taken into the army, then near Harper's Ferry, Va., and though they were brought into ranks, they could. not, under the severest threats, be made to fire a musket. So they were a dead drag in the army, and only in the way, or rather a hindrance there.

About the middle of July, 1861, a call was made by the Confederates for the entire force; i. e., every able-bodied man between the age of eighteen and forty-five years was called into the service of the government. Upon this many of the members of these societies, and their sons, kept themselves hid, and many secretly crossed the picket lines and came to the Northern States. Some time in August or September about seventy men crossed the mountains into West Virginia, intending to go to the Northern States by that route, under the guidance of Brother Daniel Suters, but they were captured by the Confederate pickets near Petersburg, in what is now called Grant County, West Virginia. They were taken to Castle Thunder, in the city of Richmond, Va., as prisoners for attempted desertion to the enemy. And as regards myself, I escaped the aforenamed draft, but expected that another would soon follow, and was determined not to be dragged into the army if it could possibly be avoided. I did not want to go to the North and leave my family, consisting of my wife and four small children, in a land of terror. Though I could not stay with them all the time, I thought I wanted to be, if possible, where I could at chance times, perhaps, render them aid and assistance, so I immediately began to make preparations to hide in a secluded place in a deep hollow, some distance up the mountains, about sixteen miles away from home, which distance I could go and come in a night, being brisk of foot. But no one knows what a trying crisis this was to me. One night I carried some provisions to this hiding place and stayed about three days.

Living now away from all human beings, I earnestly sought the aid and assistance of the Most High, with fasting and prayer. I trust the Lord heard me, and it seemed a way was opened for me. It was in July, 1861. When I got home again word came to me by a friend that a way to escape military duty was open through a certain lame Methodist preacher, George W. Stanly, who had been selling Bibles for the Bible Society before the war. He was a poor man, with a family to support; but as his business was stopped when the war commenced, he applied for and sent in a bid for a certain mail route, and it was awarded to him at $199 per year, but after carrying it a short time he found it a task too great for his capacity, and was advised by a friend of his, who imagined he saw a chance for him to sell his mail route to one of us non-resistants, as an exemption from military duty. This information was brought to me just at the time I came home, and I immediately went to see Mr. Stanly in Harrisonburg, our county seat, and offered him $1,000 for his route on condition that it exempted me from military duty, which he accepted, and an instrument of writing was prepared and signed to this effect. On the same day a call was issued for every able-bodied man to be pressed into the Confederate army. The excitement then was great, and the news that the crippled preacher sold his mail route and that a sound man was taking his place, to be exempt from military duty, was raised and spread over the town in a very short time after the bargain was made, and finding that it aroused public disapprobation, I immediately applied for and got another mail route of the Confederate Government, as a continuation of the route that had been let out to Stanly. The Post Office Department having a few days before concluded that the two routes 'could and should be carried by one carrier, I went right in and got orders to take charge of the two routes next day, and as soon as the indignant public was aware that I had the two routes to carry, in place of one by Mr. Stanly (who had a good reputation and the sympathy of the public), which he could barely have carried; all was right and everybody was satisfied and became my friends, being pleased that the poor crippled preacher had got one thousand dollars. I now had an opportunity to be out in public, instead of keeping hid (as I imagined I would have to do during the war). I was not compelled to go with the mail where there was danger, which I regarded as a favor in war times, and people along my route expected me to bring the latest and most reliable news for which they were very anxious, which I gave as I got it, sometimes adding my opinion as to its correctness and tried to avoid giving occasion to dangerous questions regarding my sentiments. Thus I carried the mail for nearly four years, by the help of the Most High, without meeting with any serious difficulty, not considering the depredations on my premises usual in times of war.

I will now give the reader a further statement concerning the seventy men who were captured in the attempt to cross the mountains into West Virginia under the guidance of Daniel Suters, as above referred to. The party consisted of a number of our Mennonite brethren and some of the non-resistant Dunkards. They were taken to Richmond as prisoners for attempted desertion. Their time of imprisonment was about six weeks from the time they left home until they reached home again.

But this was a serious and solemn time, and during this
time they, as well as their loved ones at home, offered
many prayers to the throne of grace in their sore trials
and afflictions.   Though the Lord suffered them to be
severely tried, which will show that the Lord cares for
his people as for the apple of your eye, He was yet merciful unto them ; though they were threatened to be'
taken out and shot, yet the hand of the Almighty did not
permit their enemies to do so.   The Lord undoubtedly
had let all this to come to pass for a wise purpose, as the
inspired Word tells us, " All things work together for
good to those who love God."   Their prayers were heard
and answered in due time.   About one-half of the above-
mentioned prisoners were Dunkards.   They became very
friendly to us at the time the prisoners were tried.   They
had no published discipline or confession of faith, as they
say the Bible is their discipline and confession of faith,
and when our confession of faith was brought into court
at Richmond by Algernon S. Gray, Attorney at Law,
the Dunkards claimed to hold exactly the same non-
resistant doctrine that we do in respect to war.   And if
these seventy prisoners had not been captured and taken
prisoners to the Confederate Capital, and their doctrine
and belief been made known by this exciting occurrence,
and explained demonstratively by a high Confederate
official in a way that gave them credit, the non-resistant
anti-slavery societies would certainly never have gotten
the golden privilege of staying at home on their farms
with their loved ones in such a terrible war time, but
would most certainly have been very severely dealt with
as anti-war and anti-slavery men.   What wonderful ways
the Lord has to protect those who love Him !   Later, a

bill was introduced in the Confederate Congress concerning these non-resistant societies, and it happened that one of the members of the Confederate Congress was the above named lawyer, Algernon S. Gray, who came right from their neighborhood, viz.: Harrisonburg, Va., who knew all about these defenseless people, and it seemed the Lord guided his tongue in explaining the case satisfactorily to his fellow-members of the Confederate Congress. He showed them a copy of their confession of faith, a copy published by Bishop Peter Burkholder, of Virginia, in 1857. He showed to them clearly that these people were honest in their way of thinking. Besides, they were frugal, industrious, and generally farmers, who have the best land in the renowned Valley of Virginia in their possession, and that they were thus the producers of a great source of provisions to feed the army. " Let them," said he, " stay unmolested on their productive farms, and they will continue to produce provisions that we need and must have to keep up the army. But if you take these non-resistants away from their farms, and force them in the army, they are utterly useless in the militia. We have already tried them, and they were a dead drag there. They would suffer death before they would fight. But let them stay on their farms and they will do their duty promptly in support of the army, in producing provisions more abundantly than any other people put in their place would do; we are badly in need of just such farmers as these people are." This argument prevailed; and the Confederate Congress passed an act that the Mennonites, Dunkards Quakers and Nazarites should be exempted from military duty by paying five hundred dollars Confederate money into the treasury. This these non-resistants gladly accepted, and those who had not already left the country stayed on their farms up to near the close of the war, when some of them left, when many of their homes were desolated by the torch. But strange to say, and something I cannot account for, a much greater percentage proportionately of the property belonging to the non-resistants in the Valley of Virginia was desolated by fire than that of the secessionists. At one time General Sheridan gave orders that every building within a circuit of ten miles around should be burned, in revenge for the supposed assassination of his Chief Engineer, Meigs, near Dayton, in Rockingham County, Va., and part of this order was already executed when General Sheridan learned that Meigs had been killed in a fair hand-to-hand fight, and revoked the order. Nearly all the burned property was that of non-resistants. The principal part of the burning was right in a neighborhood where these non-resistant people were most thickly settled. But when General Sheridan's army fell back again in 1864 they burned the mills, barns, etc., for the purpose of destroying provisions, so that the country was much devastated through this valley, and a much greater percentage of this burning proportionately, as referring to non-resistants and rebels, was the property of non-resistants, as also in the case of the stock driven away and destroyed. There were many non-resistants in this valley, as the conservative Dunkards numbered, perhaps, about five members to our one, and many of them had much property. They owned many of the mills that were burned.

The Mennonites of Virginia all belong to one General

Conference, which is held semi-annually in the following manner: First, those in Augusta County, or Upper District, consists of the following members: Jacob Hildebrand is their Bishop, and their ministers are Jacob R. Hildebrand, Isaac Grow, Jacob N. Driver; their deacons are Jacob Landis, Martin Brunk, A. P. Heatwole and Samuel Weaver.

Those in the Middle District in Rockingham County: Bishop, Samuel Coffman; ministers, Daniel Heatwole, Gabriel D. Heatwole, Peter S. Heatwole, Joseph F. Heatwole, Solomon Beery, Abraham B. Burkholder, David H. Landis and Samuel Weaver; the deacons are Frederick A. Rhodes, Simeon Heatwole, Christian Good, Daniel H. Good, David H. Rhodes and Jacob Showalter.

In the Lower District in Rockingham County are Abraham Shank and John Geil, Sr., Bishops; the minister are Samuel Shank, George Brunk, Daniel Showalter, Henry Wenger, Lewis Shank and John Geil, Jr.; the deacons are Jacob Good, Jacob Geil, Peter Blosser and Christian Shank.

There is no Bishop in Frederick County at present; the ministers are Daniel Mellinger and Christian Brunk; deacon, John Witmer.

In Hardy County, West Virginia, is but one minister, viz.: Jacob Teeds.

There is no record kept in Virginia as to communicant members, consequently the exact number of their membership cannot now be given, but having consulted some of those likely to be well informed, we estimated as follows by counties: Augusta County, about 60 members; Rockingham County, 500; Pendleton, Randolph and

Tucker Counties, West Virginia, 35 ; Hardy County, West Virginia, 40; Shenandoah County, Virginia, 8 ; Page County, 5 ; Frederick County, 25 ; or, in round numbers, say about 700. I think this will not be very far from the truth.

The above, as given under date of 26th day of April, 1886, by Abraham Blosser, of Dale Enterprise, Virginia.

Mennonites in West Virginia.

WHEREAS we have been in Pendleton County, West Virginia, engaged in building a church, and having had many inquiries about the Church there, I thought that a brief sketch of the rise and progress of that branch of the Church might be read with interest and probably with profit by many of our readers. During the late war, while many of our people from the valley were seeking shelter from military service by crossing the Federal lines, some concluded to stop there, as they felt safe and were not far away from home. Among them was a brother who became somewhat attached to these people by the kind treatment he received from them ; he concluded to make his home there for a while. Through him they learned some of our doctrine and also secured our Confession of Faith, which seemed to be read with interest and we hope with profit. They also became desirous of having some of our ministers preach. In the Fall of 1865 or '66, Bishop Samuel Coffman and Pre. Christian Brunk, from this county, took a trip to Upshur County, West Virginia, where Brother Coffman was called to receive a man into the Church. On their way home they came through Pendleton County and filled an appointment there, which was well attended and seemed to interest the people; and through their persuasion and the kindness with which they (our ministers)

were treated, and also seeing the necessity of spiritual
labor there and the desire for spiritual food, they concluded
to visit them again and preach for them, which they did,
and still extended their labors further by filling appointments at different places. In the course of time they
began to receive members into the Church; the work
seemed to progress slowly at first, but through the faithful labors of the brethren there have been since that time
thirty-four members added to the Church, scattered
through Pendleton, Randolph and Tucker Counties.
But of this number seven have since passed away; two
have fallen from the Church, leaving twenty-five members, and at present there are three applicants for membership.

Last Fall the brethren and sisters there began to
consider the necessity of building a house of worship.
Previously services were held in school and dwelling
houses, but the members there were not in a condition
financially to undertake the building of a meeting-house,
and the congregation in the valley under the charge of
Bishop Coffman assisted in the work. They also received
aid from friends outside and contributions from Maryland
and Pennsylvania; so they succeeded in getting a house,
32 by 38 feet, situated on North Fork, near the mouth of
Seneca River, Pendleton County, West Virginia. The
house was finished August 11th, and the first meeting
was held in it on the evening of August 28th, by Pre.
Joseph N. Driver, Gabriel D. Heatwole and Joseph F.
Heatwole. Services were also held by the above-named
brethren on Sunday, August 30th. The brethren labored
faithfully and endured many privations for the benefit of
this congregation; the distance and the roads they had

to travel made it very tiresome. I accompanied several of the brethren on one occasion, and we traveled about two hundred miles and filled thirteen appointments in twelve days. They are generally gone from ten to fourteen days; sometimes one brother goes two or three times in a summer. Brother Joseph N. Driver, of Augusta County, has made two trips this Summer and his distance is over two hundred and fifty miles. They make no appointments for the Winter, as the country is very mountainous through which they have to travel, and the roads sometimes almost impassable on account of snow and ice. They travel mostly on horseback, sometimes in carriages. There are four considerable mountains to cross, which also makes the labor on a horse very hard. Bishop Coffman is on one of these visits now, September 20th. This is the fifth trip for the brethren this Summer. He expects to receive some members into the Church, and also to hold Communion meeting with them before he gets back.

Truly the labors of the brethren seem great, but when we consider the reward which is sure to follow if they prove faithful to their Master to the end of their pilgrimage, it admits of no comparison with their labors; for Paul says: "For I reckon the sufferings of this present time are not worthy to be compared with the glory which shall be revealed in us." Romans 3: 18. Could they in all their travels but have been the means of saving one soul, they would have accomplished a great work; but we hope many souls have been gathered by them into the fold of God. And the Apostle Paul says, Gal. 6: 9: "And let us not be weary in well-doing, for in due season we shall reap, if we faint not." James says:

10

"Let him know that he who converteth the sinner from the error of his way shall save a soul from death and shall hide a multitude of sins." James 5 : 20. When we look around us are there not many doors open? Are there not many places where there is much spiritual labor needed, which by a little more energy on the part of our churches could be supplied? There is much special work needed, and it is indeed a lamentable fact that our Church is so slow in spreading the Gospel. There are many places close around us where our doctrine is but little known. Then, is it not high time that we awake out of our drowsiness and work more effectually for our Master's cause? Let us therefore labor that we may enter into that rest which is prepared for the children of God.   S. M. BURKHOLDER.

Taken from the *Watchful Pilgrim* of October 1st, 1885.

Shenandoah, and Rockingham Counties in Virginia were settled by Germans from Pennsylvania prior to 1746. Many of their descendants still speak the German language. Shenandoah Valley, in the vicinity of Harrisonburg, was almost exclusively settled by Germans from Pennsylvania prior to 1748. A traveler through this part of Virginia, during the French and Indian war, writes: "The low grounds upon the banks of the Shenandoah River are rich and fertile They are chiefly settled by Germans, who gain a sufficient livelihood by raising stock for the troops, and sending butter down into the lower parts of the country. I could not but reflect with pleasure on the situation of these people, and think, if there is such a thing as happiness in this life, they enjoy it. Far from the bustle of the world, they live in the most delightful climate and richest soil imaginable. They are everywhere surrounded with beautiful prospects and sylvan scenes—lofty mountains, transparent streams, falls of water, rich valleys and majestic woods, the whole interspersed with an infinite variety of flowering shrubs constitute the landscapes surrounding them. They are subject to few diseases, are generally robust, and live in perfect liberty. They know no wants, and are acquainted with but few vices. Their inexperience of the elegancies of life precludes any regret that they have not the means of enjoying them; but they possess what many princes would give half their dominions for—health, contentment and tranquillity of mind." (Rupp's *Thirty Thousand Names*, p. 460.)

In 1786 the community in Virginia is also specially mentioned on the records in the archives at Amsterdam. They have a Name List of the Mennonite Preachers in North America, up to about 1800.

ADDITIONAL STATISTICS OF BISHOP BURKHOLDER AND HIS FAMILY.

Said Bishop Peter Burkholder was born in Pennsylvania, on the 27th day of August, 1783, and while yet quite young his father emigrated to Rockingham County, Virginia, with his family, where he spent the remainder of his days. He was married, October 11th, 1803, to Elisabeth Coffman, who was born February 24th, 1775; was called to the ministry, October 27th, 1805; lost his consort, April 26th, 1846; died himself, December 24th, 1846. He had nine children, as follows:

1. Margaret, born September 26th, 1804, who was married to Jonas Blosser.

2. Esther, born August 21st, 1806, who was married to John Hildebrand.

3. Christian, born November 30th, 1807, who was married to Frances Lehman.

4. Abraham, born February 20th, 1809, who was married to Susanna Zimmers.

5. Peter, born July 20th, 1812, who died in his minor year.

6. David, born March 3d, 1814, who was married to Anna Beery.

7. Elisabeth, born October 10th, 1815, who was married to David Hartman.

8. Martin, born February 7th, 1817, who was married to Rebecca Shank.

9. Maria, born March 26th, 1818, who was married to Henry E. Rexroad.

They all belonged to the Mennonite Church, also their consorts, except Peter, who died in his minor' years.

Besides the foregoing, the said Peter Burkholder compiled the Confession of Faith of the Christians known by the name of Mennonites, in thirty-three Articles, with a short extract from their catechism translated from the German, and accompanied with notes, to which is added an introduction. Also Nine Reflections, from different passages of the Scriptures, illustrative of their Confession, Faith and Practice, by said Peter Burkholder, pastor of the Church of the Mennonites, written by him in the German language, and from his manuscript translated, together with the foregoing Articles, by Joseph Funk. Printed by Robinson & Hollis, Winchester, Va., in 1837.

DIED.

HEATWOLE.—On September 4th, 1886, near the Mole

Hill, Rockingham County, Va., of an inward rupture, after a severe illness of nine days, Joseph Heatwole, aged 68 years, 5 months and 10 days. He was buried at Weaver's Church on the 6th. Funeral services by Bishop Samuel Coffman and John Geil, Jr., from Job 14, in the presence of a very large audience. Said John Geil, Jr., was once a fellow-prisoner with the deceased—they were captured with about seventy other Mennonites and Tunkers, in the Fall of 1861, near Petersburg, in what is now called Grant County, West Virginia, in the time of the war of the Rebellion, in an attempt to cross the picket lines to the Northern States, by the Churchville cavalry (rebels), who were then on picket in those mountain regions, of whose position and whereabouts these refugees were not minutely posted. At this instant, when the enemy closed in upon them, the said deceased, who was then in front of this defenseless company, turned to his fellow-prisoners and said: "Brethren pray mightily unto God." This remark of the deceased Bro. Geil said he remembered as clearly as if spoken but yesterday, the words having made a deep and solemn impression on his mind the instant they were uttered. Although about a quarter of a century has passed since this remark was made by the deceased brother, I think it ought to be put on record on the page of history for his posterity and those of his fellow-prisoners, and also many other persons to read and know that the deceased was one of those who had put their trust in God, and that God was his first thought when caught in danger.

The deceased was a consistent member of the Mennonite Church for many years. He leaves seven children and many relatives and friends to mourn his loss.

ABRAHAM BLOSSER.

Christian Funk.

The Schism among the Mennonites in 1777.

CHRISTIAN FUNK was born in 1731; was married in 1757. About the same time, or shortly after, he was called to the ministry by the congregation at Franconia, where he worked faithfully, as far as known, until the year 1774, at which time the American war was about commencing with England. The Mennonites as a body never had any disposition to take part in civil government, so when in the year 1774 a meeting was held for the purpose of choosing three men who were to attend a delegation from other parts of the Province, to deliberate whether Pennsylvania should join the other Provinces which were already fully engaged in the Revolutionary contest, there was a stormy time, many of the Mennonites being still somewhat anxious to be loyal in their allegiance to the King of England. The meeting was largely attended, and there was every indication that there would be serious trouble and probably serious dissension in the ranks of the Mennonites. Happily, at this time, Funk arrived. He asked if anything had been done at the meeting, and being answered negatively, he said that it was no business of the Mennonites to interfere in the matter. After much debating it was decided not to oppose the joining of

Pennsylvania to the other Provinces, in the work of free-ing this country from hateful and despotic rule.

A tax of £3 10s. was now laid, payable in Congress paper money. Many of the ministers and members were opposed to paying this tax. Funk, however, said they ought to pay it, because they had taken the money issued under the authorities of Congress and paid their debts with it. The dispute continued until about the year 1777, when the division took place. (Funk's *Mirror*.)

This schism lasted about twenty-five years, when its members returned to the original faith of their fathers.

Manitoba Mennonites.

BRO. JACOB Y. SCHANTZ, of Berlin, Ontario, the Mennonite immigration agent, when examined before the Immigration and Colonization Committee at Ottawa, in April, 1886, said that when the Mennonites first came into Southern Manitoba they lived in small villages of say about twenty-four families, and worked land together as a common hólding, each sharing in the proceeds. They, however, discovered that they had made a mistake, and now took up homesteads and settled the same as farmers did. Some of the younger people were now speaking English, and a few were attending English schools. The Government had loaned the Mennonites $96,400 to tide over their difficulties, getting security for the money from the people resident in that locality. Of that sum there was some $65,000 paid back, and he was in a position to say, being Secretary of the Committee, that upwards of $20,000 would be paid in the course of two or three months. There was little prospect of further immigration, as young men could not get away owing to Russian war troubles. Some few families had left and had gone to Kansas. Speaking of Southern Manitoba, he said about 1,336 families located there, who were pretty successful. They were more temperate in their habits than when they first came into the country. Mr. Trow, in seconding a vote of thanks to Bro. Schantz, paid a high tribute to that gentleman's energetic efforts on behalf of the Mennonite settlers.

In Manitoba, British America, are living at present 12,000 Mennonites, who are all in good circumstances. They generally follow farming and find a good market for their products, which they can ship at very low freight rates on the Canada Pacific Railroad, which is greatly in their favor. The first Mennonites in Manitoba came from the southern part of Russia in the year 1874.

The Herrites (or Herrenleute).

THE Herrites (*Herrenleute*) of which we are now to speak, is a schism of the Mennonite Church, and was led by John Herr, of Lancaster County. They have at present one congregation in Worcester, Montgomery County. Their ways and views are so peculiar that some of them are appended · " They do not or dare not, for fear of the ban of separation (a sort of penance), hear the ministers of another denomination preach. When one of their members commits a sin or breaks their rules, he or she is put under the ban, and is kept in avoidance ; then they do not eat or sleep with him or her, nor sit at the same table under pain of like censure." The " Herrites" originated from the second schism of the Mennonite Church, in about 1811. (The first was Christian Funk's.) The portion that withdrew erected for themselves a small one story stone meeting-house over the Franconia line in Salford Township, near the present turnpike leading to Souderton. By 1850 they had diminished, so that the building was used only for a school-house. In 1855 they built a house just in Franconia, several hundred yards north of the Harleysville and Souderton turnpike, near a private burying-ground, usually called Delps' Graveyard. Of those who sleep there, the stones give the family names of Yoder, Moyer, Kratz, Booz, Landis, Funk, Delp, Kline, Wisler, Godshall, Cassel and others ; Jacob Landis, 1807 ; Christian Funk, aged 80 years ; Valentine Kratz; 95 years, and Abraham Delp, 81 years.

This old graveyard is certainly an object of interest. It contains about a quarter of an acre, enclosed with a substantial board fence, situated on elevated ground, with a beautiful glimpse of the surrounding country into the quiet valley of the Indian Creek.

Mennonites in Missouri.

I WILL now try and give you some information about the Mennonites in Missouri, and I shall truly rejoice if I can assist you in your undertaking to write a history of the Mennonite Church, a work requiring much labor to get the necessary material.

There were, according to my knowledge, no Mennonite organizations in Missouri anterior to the great Civil War, unless it be of the so-called Amish Mennonites, about which I am not sufficiently informed to furnish anything like a history. There are, to my knowledge, Amish Mennonites in Hickory, Cass and Gentry Counties, no doubt also in other counties. In Cass County there is a very large congregation of Amish Mennonites; a man by the name of Knaege is the Bishop.

Of the congregations going by the name of Mennonite Churches, there are five organized congregations. Three of them are connected by conferential ties to the Mennonites represented by the *Herald of Truth* (or Old School Mennonites), and two have united themselves to the General Conference (or New School Mennonites). Of the former, one is in Jasper County, one in Shelby County and one in Morgan County. Of the latter, one is in Moniteau and one in Hickory County. The church in Shelby County was organized soon after the war, perhaps in 1867 or 1868, of which the following is an account.

(156)

Among the first settlers were persons by the name of Lapp, one of whom was a preacher. Bishop Benjamin Hershey moved there and has been their Bishop ever since. A man by the name of John Brubacher was chosen to the ministry since. The congregation is small, hardly numbering over twenty-five members. The congregation in Jasper County is still smaller, having a membership not exceeding fifteen. Mennonites had settled there soon after the war, but no organization took place until the year 1877. The first Mennonite settler was Dr. Jacob Blosser. They have no church building. Jacob Brennemann and Joseph Weaver were elected to the ministry. The congregation in Morgan County, called the Mt. Zion Church, has a somewhat larger membership than either of the two last referred to. The present preachers are D. D. Kauffman, Bishop, and Daniel Driver. It originated as follows: A number of Mennonites moved to Moniteau and Morgan Counties, Missouri, in the year 1867, and later from Ohio, Indiana, New York, Virginia, Michigan and other places. They settled near the county line, between the above-mentioned counties. The first communion was held by Bishop John Schmitt, of Summerfield, Illinois. But these people, coming from different places, had different views and customs also in church matter, and when they came to form a more complete organization, if they would unite into one body, they had to learn to tolerate one another's views. This they agreed to do. This was especially the case with feet-washing, which some regarded as a ceremony, while others gave it a spiritual interpretation, or regarded it as an act of hospitality; but the great zeal of a few to bring about a unity of views, and, if necessary, by power, authority and dis-

cipline, produced a lively discussion of this point of differ
ence and resulted in a split, and each party has since its
own organization, though there is not that animosity between the parties which we sometimes find where such
schisms take place. The party practicing ceremonial
feet-washing is organized under the name of Mt. Zion
Congregation, while the other is called the Bethel Congregation; the former is united with the Mennonites
represented by the *Herald of Truth*, while the Bethel
Congregation has united with the " General Conference."
Their united membership may be about one hundred and
thirty-five members. There was no ministerial election
before the separation, but Daniel Brundage, now living in
the State of Kansas, who moved from Indiana to Missouri as a minister, was ordained as Bishop. The Mt.
Zion Congregation since elected David D. Kauffman and
Daniel Driver, and the Bethel Congregation elected P. P.
Lehmann.

M. S. Moyer, who was elected to the ministry in Ohio,
moved to Morgan County, Missouri, in the year 1878,
and was accepted as minister and afterwards, with P. P.
Lehmann, ordained as Bishop. The two churches are
five miles apart, Mt. Zion in Morgan and Bethel in
Moniteau County. Another congregation is in Hickory
County; Peter S. Lehmann, who moved there from Indiana, is its preacher. The members came there from
Ohio, Indiana and other States. The membership may
be about forty. They have also sent their delegate to
the General Conference and are regarded as a part of
that body.

Early Settlement of the Mennonites in Elkhart County, Indiana.

In 1843 John Smith came from Medina County, Ohio, and purchased the farm now occupied by Martin Hoover, near Harrison Centre, in Harrison Township. Two years later, in the spring of 1845, Bishop Martin Hoover, then already 85 years old, with his son, John, settled on the farm now occupied by Joseph Rohrer, a short distance north of South West. In the fall of the same year John Smith, his son, Joseph, and Christian Henning, with their families, arrived on the 3d of October from Medina County, Ohio, and settled in the same township; Jacob Strohm also was here when they came. In the spring of 1848 Christian Christophel, Jacob Christophel and Jacob Wisler, with their families, from Columbiana County, Ohio, joined the little colony; the latter two were ministers of the Gospel, and on Ascension Day in that year they appointed and held their first meeting, in the old log school-house, on the northwest corner of the farm on which Joseph Rohrer is now living, opposite to the Dunker meeting-house, built a few years ago. The three ministers were present. The principal discourse was delivered by Jacob Wisler. Bishop Hoover was then 85 years old, and only made a few remarks sitting. No hymn was sung, because no one present was able to lead the singing.   The meeting was attended by only sixteen persons.   From this time forward, however, regular services were held every two weeks, sometimes, no doubt, in the school-house, and sometimes in barns, private dwellings, etc.   During the summer of 1848, twenty-four families more arrived from Wayne, Medina and Columbiana Counties, Ohio, among whom were the Hartmans, Holdemans, Moyers, Smeltzers and others.   In the summer of 1849 a log meeting-house, 26 feet square, was built on the same ground now occupied by the Yellow Creek meeting-house.   This building once took fire from the stove-pipe, burned four of the ceiling boards and charred the girder to coals half the length of the building, but of its own accord went out again and did no further damage.   An addition of 24 feet in length was afterwards made to this house, and in 1861 the old house was moved away and the new frame house, now standing, 40 by 60, put in its stead.

In 1850 Benjamin Hershey came from Canada and settled here.   He also was a minister and afterwards removed to Whiteside County, Illinois, and from there to Shelby County, Missouri, where he was ordained a Bishop and still resides there.   Daniel Moyer was chosen to the ministry and served in that capacity for a number of years.   He was an earnest preacher, but his earthly labors were brought to a sudden close by a collision on the railroad, through which he lost his life while on his way with two other ministers to visit the churches in Canada, in December, 1864.   In 1853, R. J. Schmidt and N. J. Sijmensma, two ministers, and their families and a number of their brethren and their families, on account of their faithful adherence to the doctrine of non-resistance, were compelled to emigrate from Holland, and settled in this county, where Bro. Sijmensma died a few years afterwards, leaving the care of the charge to Bro. Schmidt, who still holds services, at stated periods, in the Holland language. Daniel Brundage, who was called to the ministry in Canada, emigrated from there to this county, and, after serving the church here for a time, removed to Morgan County, Missouri, in the spring of 1869, if our information is correct, where he was advanced to the office of Bishop on the 28th of May, 1870, and later went to McPherson County, Kansas, where he resides at the present time. Jacob Freed came from Holmes County, Ohio, to Elkhart County, where he died in April, 1868, in the 72d year of his age. He served as a minister in the Church over thirty years. He was born in Virginia, and probably was elected to the ministry in Ohio. David Good was a deacon and came to Elkhart County from Canada at an early date. He was a man of excellent abilities, and faithful and zealous in the performance of his duty. He died on the 16th of March, 1864, in the 60th year of his age. Benjamin Huber, also formerly from Canada, was a deacon, and died December 19th, 1866, aged 88 years. Henry Newcomer filled the same office for a number of years, and died in November, 1867.

A meeting was also organized in Clinton Township, east of Goshen, and for a time maintained by the ministers in Harrison Township, until it could be supplied from their own congregation. John Nusbaum, who is still pastor of this church, came to Clinton on the 4th of September, 1860. He was chosen and ordained to the ministry in Ashland County, Ohio, in 1827.

The church in Elkhart County, in her earlier years,

enjoyed a good degree of prosperity, receiving large accessions, both by immigration and new converts; on one occasion forty-eight were baptized on the same day; but within the last several years this church has been called to pass through a most severe trial, in which the faith of many was brought to a severe test, and though she lost some in numbers, there is no doubt she has been confirmed and established in the faith; and we trust, by the grace of God, she may in years to come be a bright and shining light and lead many unto righteousness.

There are now in Elkhart County six congregations, and religious services are regularly held in eleven different places (Funk's *Mennonite Almanac*).

There are now in the State of Indiana thirteen congregations, as follows ·

The church in Owen County, in charge of Daniel Royer, Bishop,

The church in Adams County, in charge of Christian Augspurger, minister.

The church in De Kalb County. The ministers in this church are James Coyle and Eli Stofer.

The churches in Elkhart County are as follows:

The Clinton Church, ministers John Gnagy and Peter Y. Lehman.

The Yellow Creek Church, ministers Noah Metzler and Jonas Loucks.

The Holdeman Church, of which Amos Mumaw and Jacob Loucks are the ministers.

The Shaum Church, of which Henry Shaum is the minister.

The Elkhart Church, in the city of Elkhart. The ministers here are John F. Funk, John S. Coffman and Samuel Yoder.

All the churches in Elkhart County are under the care of Henry Shaum as Bishop, except the Clinton Church, which is under the oversight of Henry A. Miller, Bishop, of Lagrange County.

The Blosser Church, supplied by ministers from the surrounding districts.

The Christophel Church, including the Holland brethren, under charge of R. J. Schmidt.

The Nappanee Church, of which David Burkholder is the minister.

Besides these there are several places of meeting in the surrounding districts supplied cheerfully by the ministers of this county. J. S. Coffman, also one of the ministers of the Elkhart City Church, devotes a large portion of his time to evangelistic work among the smaller churches and scattered members, having his expenses met, partly from voluntary contributions and partly from the evangelizing fund. This fund was established by the Conference of the State of Indiana, and is maintained by voluntary contributions from all parts of the United States, where Mennonite settlements are found. Joseph Summers, of Elkhart, is the treasurer, and all disbursements are made through a committee elected annually. The means are supplied to any minister who goes out to preach the Gospel and labor for the Church, at the discretion of the committee.

The Shore Church, in Lagrange County, where Rev. J. J. Weaver and Bishop Henry A. Miller are the ministers in charge.

There is also a small number of members in Allen County, which is supplied by the ministers in De Kalb County.

There is also a church in Branch County, Michigan, in charge of Harvey Friesner. Also one known as the Barker Street Church, near the State line.

The Caledonia Church, in charge of Christian Wenger, and the Bourie Church, in charge of John P. Speicher and Peter Keim; the two last mentioned are in Kent County, Michigan, all of which are under the care of the Conference of Indiana.

Besides these, there are in the State of Indiana some ten or twelve congregations of Amish Mennonites.

The Conference of Illinois includes the church in Livingston County, where the ministers are: Henry L. Shelly, Peter Unzicker and Christian Schantz; the church in Tazewell County, under charge of Emanuel Hartman, Bishop; the church near Morrison, in Whiteside County, where the ministers are Bishop Henry Nice and minister John Nice; the church near Sterling, in the same county, where the ministers are Abraham Ebersole and —— Riesner; the church near Freeport, in Stephenson County, where the ministers are —— Snavely and Joseph Lehman.

Biographical Sketch of Jacob Christophel.

JACOB CHRISTOPHEL was born in Redenbach, in the Palatinate on the Rhine, in Europe, from which place he emigrated and came to America in 1818. He settled in Westmoreland County, Pa., where he lived three years, after which he removed to Allegheny County. He was a member of the Mennonite Church, and in 1827 he was here chosen and ordained to the ministry. He was ordained by Bishop David Funk.

From Allegheny County he removed to Columbiana County, Ohio, and afterwards to Elkhart County, Indiana, arriving there with his family on the 5th day of June, 1848. He bought a farm in Jackson Township, with a small clearing, where he lived to the time of his death, which occurred on the 3d of December, 1868. He was in the ministry about forty-one years, though for several years before his death he was not able, on account of his bodily infirmities, to attend to the duties of his office. He suffered with palsy for about three years, during which time he was unable to walk and almost helpless. About twenty-four hours before his death he was attacked with a severe pain in the bowels. He died calmly and peacefully, as one lying down to pleasant dreams, and was gathered to his fathers, as had been his desire for a long time, at the advanced age of 85 years 11 months and 3 days. He was faithful in the performance of his min-

isterial duties as long as his bodily health permitted him
to do so, and after he was no longer able to labor in the
ministry, it still seemed to be his delight to attend public
worship as often as he could.   He was buried in the graveyard at Yellow Creek meeting-house, where his funeral
services were performed by J. Weaver and J. M. Brenneman from the text Luke 2 : 29, 30.

First Amish Settlement in Elkhart County, Indiana.

THE first Amish Mennonite settlement in Elkhart County, Indiana, was made in the year 1841. At that time Daniel and Joseph Miller, with Joseph and Christian Borntreger, with their families, emigrated from Somerset County, Pa., to Elkhart County, Indiana, and settled about four miles east of Goshen.

The first meeting for religious worship held by these new settlers occurred in August of the same year, at the house of Joseph Miller. He was their Bishop. In the winter of 1842 Emanuel Miller and family settled in the same place. The church then consisted of five families. Later in the same year seven other families came also from Somerset County, Pa., and settled in the same neighborhood. This was the beginning of the extensive settlements of the Amish brethren now found in that vicinity (*Funk's Almanac*, 1875).

Mennonites in Colorado.

JACOB ROTH writes from Harrisburg, Arapahoe County, Colorado : " Our community here numbers ten brethren. We have taken up homesteads and pre-emption lands, and there is still land here to be taken up. This seems to be a healthy place and the settlement is entirely new. We expect to organize a Sabbath-school next Sunday, as we hold meetings on the intervening Sundays. We trust the brethren will pray for us that the Lord may bless us and we may at last be found among the redeemed of the earth " (*Herald of Truth*, April 1st, 1888).

In Yuma, Colorado, is a settlement of Mennonites.

A number of Mennonites by the name of Wiens, of Nebraska, have in contemplation the founding and building of a city, about forty-five miles south of Yuma. They can obtain the land on very reasonable terms (*Patriot and Reformer*, August 18th, 1886).

Mennonites in New York State.

THE first Mennonite who settled in Western New York was Johannes Roth, who came from Lancaster, Pa., before the Revolutionary war, and settled four miles west of Williamsville. No more of the same persuasion arrived until 1824; then came C. Leib, shortly afterwards A. Leib, D. Lehm, Johann Scherer, P. Lehman, S. Martin and his sons, A. Diller, Johann Diller, Walter J. Frick, J. Metz and others, all from Lancaster, Pa. In 1828 came John Lapp; then a Mennonite congregation was organized and a new meeting-house was built, and John Lapp was chosen as their first minister and John Martin as their first deacon. In 1831 arrived Jacob Krehbiel with his family, a preacher in the Mennonite congregation at Meyerhof, Rheinpfalz, Germany, so the congregation increased by immigration and new converts who were added by baptism, and became a pretty large congregation. Abraham Lapp and Peter Lehman were chosen as their ministers, and Frederick Krehbiel and Abraham Leib as deacons. Now (1888) all have gone to their eternal home.

At the present there are two congregations, one in Clarence Centre, with Jacob Krehbiel (grandson of the above-named Jacob Krehbiel) as their pastor and J. Eberhard as their deacon; the other is three miles south-

west of the former, with Jacob Hahn as their pastor and
A. Metz as their deacon.

The first Mennonites who settled at the Falls, in Niagara County, were Hans Wittmer, in 1810, and his
brother, Abraham Wittmer, in 1811, both from Lancaster, Pa. Soon after more of their brethren came from
Lancaster and settled in Niagara County, and a congregation was organized and the ministers from Clarence
Centre, Lapp and Krehbiel, had charge of the Falls congregation. They held their meetings, presumably, in
private houses, as they had no meeting-house until shortly
after 1830, when a meeting-house was built and David
Habecker was chosen as their minister and J. Dreichler
as their deacon. Pastor Habecker is yet living, but not
able to perform the duties as pastor, on account of old
age, being nearly one hundred years old. The congregation, with U. Linkele as deacon, is at the present time in
charge of Jacob Krehbiel, of Clarence Centre.

JOHN KREHBIEL.

Clarence Centre, N. Y., March 20th, 1888.

Maryland.

In Washington County are four congregations of Mennonites, viz.: Reiff's Congregation—Michael Horst, Bishop, Jacob Risser, minister, and Christian W. Eby, deacon; Stauffer's Congregation—Adam Bear, minister, and Peter R. Eshleman, deacon; Clear Spring Congregation—Daniel Roth, Josiah Brewer, Abraham Ebersole, ministers, Isaac W. Eby, deacon; Miller's Congregation —John Martin, Adam Bear, ministers, Peter R. Eshle man, deacon.

Russian Settlements in the West.

THE readers of this sketch, no doubt, have all heard much about the emigration of the Mennonites from Russia on account of their religious freedom, and their settlement on the great prairies of the West. Settlements have been formed in Manitoba, Minnesota, Dakota, Nebraska and Kansas. To those who have never been in the West and have not had an opportunity to see the opening of new settlements, let them imagine a sketch which will give them a very good idea as to the manner in which such settlements are commenced. They construct their buildings of boards, in the most primitive style. Sometimes they construct them also of sod, or of rough, sun-dried brick, or of clay mixed with straw. In Manitoba, where there is more timber, we presume the brethren have followed, to some extent, the manner of the natives and built their houses of small logs, closing the crevices with clay. They build their houses very substantially, where they have the means and the material. Those who have always lived in large, pleasant and convenient houses may here form some idea of the difference which exists in the comforts and conveniences of life between those who commence new settlements in the West and those who live in the old settled portions of the country (*Funk's Family Almanac*, 1876).

RUSSIAN SETTLEMENT IN THE WEST.

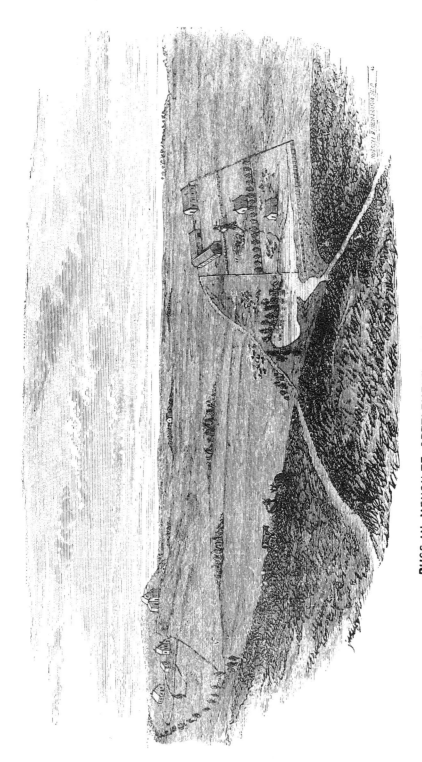

RUSS AN MENON TE SETTLEMENT N JEFFERSON COUNTY.

Russian Settlements in Nebraska.

NEBRASKA is a very large State. It is 412 miles in length and 208 miles wide. There are no mountains in the State. The whole surface consists of rolling uplands and rich valleys. The past twenty years have demonstrated that in no part of the United States can a better country be found for the raising of stock and the growing of wheat, oats, rye, barley, corn and vegetables. In 1880 the population of the State was 452,402 and increasing rapidly. The larger portion of these people dwell in the eastern half of the State, where the 1,500,000 acres of the Burlington and Missouri River Railroad lands are situated.

The Mennonite church near Beatrice consists principally of members who immigrated from Prussia in 1877. Their present Bishop is Gerhard Penner; ministers, John Heinrich Zimmerman, Peter Reinier; deacon, L. E. Zimmerman. Their membership is about two hundred.

The congregation in Jefferson County consists of several divisions, with a membership of about two hundred and fifty. Their Bishop is Abraham Friesen, Fairbury P. O.

The congregation in Hamilton County also consists of several divisions and has a membership of about two hundred and fifty. Their principal Bishop is Isaac Peters. The last two congregations are Russians.

(173)

Periodicals.

THE periodicals published under the auspices of the old Mennonite Church, are: First, *The Herald of Truth*, established in 1864, in the city of Chicago, Illinois, by John F. Funk. The office of publication was removed to Elkhart, Indiana, in 1867, since which time it has been published there. It has also been printed in the German language, under the name of *Herold der Wahrheit*. Both are now published by the Mennonite Publishing Company and have a combined circulation of over 6,000 copies. They have now nearly completed their twenty fourth year.

The same company also publishes a children's paper in the English language, under the name *Words of Cheer*, and a German children's paper, under the title *Der Christliche Jugendfreund*. They also publish a weekly newspaper in the German language, circulating chiefly among the Russian Mennonites, under the name of *Mennonitische Rundschau*.

A large number of the Church books, as *Martyrs' Mirror* in the German language; the complete works of Menno Simons, in the English and German languages; the different hymn books of the Church, Confessions of Faith, tracts, etc., have been published and circulated, and within the last four years the *Martyrs' Mirror* has been translated from the Holland language into English

and published in an illustrated, full bound volume of
1,093 pages.

The Watchful Pilgrim, a semi-monthly journal, in the
interest of the Mennonites, by Abraham Blosser, Editor,
Dale Enterprise, Virginia.

Der Christliche Bundesbote, a weekly paper, published
in the interest of the General Conference of Mennonites
of North America, the object of which is to bring the
several divisions of Mennonite communities more closely
together for the purpose of working more successfully in
the cause of home and foreign mission work, and for the
kingdom of God in general.

Address : *Christliche Bundesbote*, Berne, Adams County,
Indiana.

The Mennonite, a religious monthly journal, devoted to
the interest of the Mennonite Church and the cause of
Christ at large, published by the Eastern Mennonite Con
ference.

Address : N. B. Grubb, 2136 Franklin Street, Philadelphia.

Der Kinderbote.—The *Kinderbote* is a monthly publication for Children and Sunday-schools.   It is published
at Berne, Adams Co., Indiana, by the Publication Board
of the General Conference.   The contents are especially
adapted for children.   It is half German and half English.

European Journals.

Das Gemeinde-Blatt, by Pastor Ulrich Hege, assisted
by several ministers; a monthly journal of eight pages,
published in the interest of the Mennonites, at Reihen,
Amt Sinsheim, Baden.

Mennonitische Blätter, issued monthly by H. Van der Smissen, minister of the Mennonite church at Hamburg, Altona. This journal is now in its thirty-fourth year, and will hereafter be published semi-monthly, instead of monthly, as heretofore. This is the church where Gerhard Roosen and Jacob Denner preached nearly two hundred years ago.

Der Zionspilger, published semi-monthly, in the interest of the old evangelical non-resistant Taufgesinnten-Ge meine (Mennoniten) at Emmenthal, Switzerland, by Samuel Bühler, Langnau, Canton Bern, Switzerland.

December 27th, 1887.

Conferences.

When and where the first Conference in America was held is not positively known. We have records that a conference was held and the Confession of Faith approved and received by the elders and ministers of the congregations of the people called Mennonites in the year 1727, and subscribed their names, as follows:

Skippack, Jacob Godschalk, Henry Kolb, Claes Jansen, Michael Ziegler.

Germantown, John Gorgas, John Conerads, Clas Rittinghausen.

Conestoga, Hans Burgholzer, Christian Herr, Benedict Hirschi, Martin Bear, Johannes Bowman.

Great Swamp, Velte Clemmer.

Manatant, Daniel Langenecker, Jacob Beghtly.

In the Lancaster County Conference there are about seventy-five ministers, representing not less than fifty churches.

The Franconia Conference meets semi-annually, in May and October, in the Franconia meeting-house, in Franconia Township, Montgomery County, Pa. This Conference has been meeting in Franconia long before the Revolutionary War, even as early as 1760; how long before that date we have no record.

The Virginia Conference represents about twelve or fifteen churches. They hold their meetings in three districts alternately, the Upper District in Augusta County, the Middle District in Rockingham County and the Lower District in Rockingham County. This Conference is composed of about thirty-two ministers and deacons; they hold their meetings semi-annually.

The Ohio Conference is composed of about fifteen churches.

Then there are the Indiana, the Illinois, the Missouri, the Iowa and the Kansas Conferences, all in one communion, besides the Amish Mennonite churches, numbering about twelve or fifteen.

Places of worship in several counties of Pennsylvania, as far as I could get them : In Lebanon County, 4, Bishop, Isaac Gingrich; Dauphin County, 4; Adams County, 2, Bishop, David Schenk; Juniata County, 5, Bishop, Isaac Graybill; Franklin County, 5, Bishop, John Hunsicker; Berks County, 4; Cumberland County, 7; York County, 10; Snyder County, 2; Perry County, 2; Washington County, Maryland, 4, Bishop, Michael Horst; Branch County, Michigan, 1, Harvey Friesner.

For the names of ministers and places of worship in Lancaster, Montgomery and Bucks Counties, see the Meeting Calendar of all the Mennonite churches in Eastern Pennsylvania for the year 1887 (Old School), New Holland, Pa., Clarion Printing Office.

Mennonite Immigration to Pennsylvania.

BY DR. J. G. DE HOOP SCHEFFER, OF AMSTERDAM.*

THE extensive tract of land, bounded on the east by the Delaware, on the north by the present New York, on the west by the Ohio River, and on the south by Maryland, has such an agreeable climate, such an unusually fertile soil, and its watercourses are so well adapted for trade, that it is not surprising that there, as early as 1638 —five and twenty years after our forefathers built the first house in New Amsterdam (New York)—a European colony was established. The first settlers were Swedes, but some Hollanders soon joined them. Surrounded on all sides by savage natives, continually threatened and often harassed, they contented themselves with the cultivation of but a small portion of the land. After, however, King Charles II had, in settlement of a debt, given the whole province to William Penn,† there came a great

---

* The article here translated from the Dutch, and annotated, appeared in the *Doopsgezinde Bijdragen* for 1869, under the title of " Vriendschaps-betrekingen tusschen de Doopsgezinden hier te lande en die in Pennsyl-vanie."

† The English Government owed Admiral Penn, father of William Penn, £16,000 sterling for advances made and services rendered; in settlement of the above debt the section of country lying North of Maryland was given to William Penn, and was afterwards called Pennsylvania.—AUTHOR.

change. There, before long, at his invitation and through his assistance, his oppressed fellow-believers, followers like himself of George Fox, found a place of refuge. They settled on the Delaware, and, united by the common sufferings endured for their convictions, they founded a city, to which they gave the suggestive name of the City of Brotherly Love (Philadelphia). The province itself received the name of Pennsylvania from the man who brought its settlers over from a land of persecution to his own estate, and has borne it to the present time, although its boundaries have been extended on the north to Lake Erie, and on the west beyond the Allegheny Mountains to the present Ohio.

In accordance with the fundamental law established April 25th, 1682, complete freedom of conscience was assured to all religious communities, and William Penn and his associates saw a stream of those who had been persecuted and oppressed for their belief pour into the colony, among whom were many Mennonites from Switzerland and the Palatinate.

In Switzerland, for nearly half a century religious intolerance had been most bitter.   Many who had remained there were then persuaded to abandon their beloved native country and betake themselves to the distant land of freedom, and others, who had earlier emigrated to Alsace and the Palatinate and there endured the dreadful horrors of the war in 1690, joined them, hoping in a province described to them as a paradise, to find the needed comforts of life.   The traveling expenses of these exhausted wanderers on their way through our Fatherland were furnished with a liberal hand from the " funds for foreign needs" which our forefathers had collected to aid the Swiss, Palatines and Litthauers. These emigrants settled for the most part at Philadelphia, and to the northward along the Delaware. One of the oldest communi ties, if not the oldest of all, was that at Schiebach, or Germantown. The elder of their two preachers, Wilhelm Rittinghausen, died in 1708, and in his place two new preachers were chosen (presumably Nicholaus Rittenhouse and Dirk Keyser). The same year eleven young people were added to the Church through baptism, and two new deacons accepted its obligations. Moreover, the emigration of other brethren from the Palatinate, with Peter Kolb* at their head, who were enabled to make the journey by the aid of the Netherlanders, gave a favorable prospect of considerable growth. Financially, however, the circumstances of the community left much to be desired. In a letter written to Amsterdam, dated September 3d, 1708, from which these particulars are derived, and which was signed by Jacob Gaetschalck, Herman Kars dorp, Martin Kolb, Isaac Van Sinteren and Conradt Jan sen, they presented " a loving and friendly request" for " some catechisms for the children and little testaments for the young."† Beside, psalm books and Bibles were

---

* But Peter Kolb never came to America; he died in 1727 and is buried at Manheim, aged 56 years 8 months. He was a Mennonite minister.—AUTHOR.

† It is certainly worthy of attention that the first request these people sent back to their brethren in Europe was for Bibles and Testaments. Jacob Gaetschalck was a preacher at Skippack, but lived in Germantown. Martin Kolb, a grandson of Peter Schuhmacher who died in Germantown in 1707, was born in the village of Wolfsheim, in the Palatinate, in 1680, and came with his brothers, Johannes and Jacob, to Pennsylvania, in the spring of 1707. He married May 19th, 1709, Magdalena, daughter of Isaac Van Sintern, who also united in this letter. Jacob Kolb married Sarah Van Sin-

so scarce, that the whole membership had but one copy, and even the meeting-house needed a Bible.

They urged their request by saying "that the community is still weak, and it would cost much money to get them printed, while the members who came here from Germany have spent everything and must begin anew, and all work in order to pay for the conveniences of life of which they stand in need." What the printing would cost can to some extent be seen from the demands of a bookseller in New York, who beside, only printed in English, for the publication of the Confession of Faith in that language. He asked so much for it that the community could not by any possibility raise the money, for which reason the whole plan had to be abandoned.*

The proposition was first considered because of conversation with some people there whose antecedents were entirely unknown, but "who called themselves Mennonites," descendants, perhaps, of the Dutch or English colonists, who in the first years of the settlement established themselves on the territory of Pennsylvania. That

---

tern, May 2d, 1710, a sister to Magdalena. Isaac Van Sintern was born September 4th, 1662, and was a great-grandson of Jan de Voss, a burgomaster at Handschooten, in Flanders, about 1550. He married in Amsterdam Cornelia Claasen, of Hamburg, and came to Pennsylvania with four daughters after 1687. He died August 23d, 1737, and is buried at Skippack.

* It appears from a letter in the Mennonite Archives at Amsterdam that William Rittenhouse endeavored to have the Confession of Faith translated into English and printed by Bradford, and that he died in 1708, aged 64 years (see *Jones' Notes to Thomas on Printing*, Barton's *Life of David Rittenhouse*. PENN MAGAZINE, Vol. II, p. 120). The Mennonites had their Confession of Faith printed in English in Amsterdam in 1712, and a reprint by Andrew Bradford in 1727, with an appendix, is the first book printed in Pennsylvania for the Germans.

the young community was composed of other people besides Palatines has been shown by the letter just mentioned, bearing the Netherlandish signature of Karsdorp, a name much honored among our forefathers, and which has become discredited through late occurrences at Dortrecht.

It is no wonder that a half year later the "Committee on Foreign Needs" cherished few hopes concerning the colony. They felt, however, for nine or ten families who had come to Rotterdam—according to information from there, under date of April 8th, 1709, from the neighborhood of Worms and Frankenthal, in order to emigrate, and whom they earnestly sought to dissuade from making the journey. They were, said the letter from Rotterdam, "altogether very poor men, who intended to seek a better place of abode in Pennsylvania. Much has been expended upon them hitherto freely, and these people bring with them scarcely anything that is necessary in the way of raiment and provisions, much less the money that must be spent for fare from here to England, and from there on the great journey, before they can settle in that foreign land." Naturally, the Rotterdamers asked that money be furnished for the journey and support of the emigrants. But the Committee, who considered the matter useless and entirely unadvisable, refused to dispose in this way of the funds entrusted to them. It was the first refusal of the kind, and little did the Committee think that for twenty-four years they must keep repeating it before such requests should entirely cease. It would, in fact, have been otherwise if they had begun with the rule which they finally adopted in 1732, or, if the determination they expressed in letter after letter had been followed by like action, and they had not let them selves be persuaded away from it continually—some times from perplexity, but oftener from pity. The Pala tines understood the situation well. If they could only reach Holland without troubling themselves about the letters, if they were only urgent and persevering, the Committee would end by helping them on their way to Pennsylvania. The emigrants of April, 1709, accom plished their object, though, as it appears, through the assistance of others. At all events, I think they are the ones referred to by Jacob Telner, a Netherlander Menno nite dwelling at London, who wrote, August 6th, to Am sterdam and Haarlem : " Eight families went to Pennsyl vania; the English Friends, who are called Quakers, helped them liberally."*

His letter speaks of others who also wanted to follow their example, and urges more forcibly than ever the people at Rotterdam to give assistance. " The truth is," he writes, " that many thousands of persons, old and young, and men and women, have arrived here in the hope and expectation of going to Pennsylvania, but the poor men are misled in their venture. If they could transport themselves by their own means, they might go where they pleased, but because of inability they cannot do it, and must go where they are ordered. Now, as

---

* But not only did the leaders of the early Society of Friends take great interest in the Mennonites, but the Yearly Meeting of 1709 contributed fifty pounds (a very large sum at that time) for the Mennonites of the Palatinate who had fled from the persecution of the Calvinists in Switzerland. This required the agreement of the representatives of above four hundred churches, and shows in a strong light the sympathy which existed among the early Friends for the Mennonites" (Barclay's *Religious Societies of the Common wealth*, p. 251).

there are among all this multitude six families of our brethren and fellow-believers, I mean German Mennonites, who ought to go to Pennsylvania, the brethren in Holland should extend to them the hand of love and charity, for they are both poor and needy. I trust and believe, however, that they are honest and God fearing. It would be a great comfort and consolation to the poor sheep if the rich brothers and sisters, from their superfluities, would satisfy their wants and let some crumbs fall from their tables to these poor Lazaruses. Dear brethren, I feel a tender compassion for the poor sheep, for they are of our flesh, as says the Prophet Isaiah, chap. 58 : 7, 8."

It was not long before pity for our fellow-believers was excited still more forcibly.

Fiercer than ever became the persecutions of the Men nonites in Switzerland. The prisons at Bern were filled with the unfortunates, and the inhuman treatment to which they were subjected caused many to pine away and die. The rest feared from day to day that the minority in the Council which demanded their trial would soon become a majority. Through the intercession, however, of the States General, whose aid the Netherland Mennonites sought, not without success, some results were effected. The Council of Bern finally determined to send the prisoners, well watched and guarded, in order to transport them from there in an English ship to Pennsylvania.

On the 18th of March, 1710, the exiles departed from Bern; on the 28th, with their vessel, they reached Manheim, and on the 6th of April Nimeguen, and when they touched Netherland soil their sufferings came to an end at last; they were free, and their useless guards could return to Switzerland.   Laurens Hendricks, the preacher of our community at Nimeguen, wrote in his letter of April 9th (1710): " It happened that very harsh decrees were issued by the rulers of Bern to search for our friends in all corners of the land, and put them in the prisons at Bern, by which means within the last two years about sixty persons were thrown into dungeons, where some underwent much misery in the great cold last winter, while their feet were fast in the iron shackles.

" The Council at Bern were still very much at variance as to what punishment should be inflicted on them, and so they have the longer lain in prison; for some would have them put to death, but others could not consent to such cruelty, so finally they determined in the Council to send them as prisoners to Pennsylvania.   Therefore they put them on a vessel, well watched by a guard of soldiers, to send them on the Rhine to Holland; but on coming to Manheim, a city of the Palatinate, they put out all the old, the sick and the women, but, with twenty-three men, floated further down the Rhine, and, on the 6th of April, came here to Nimeguen.   When they heard that their fellow-believers lived here, one of them came to me, guarded by two soldiers.   The soldiers then went away and left the man with me.   After I, with the other preachers, had talked with him, we went together to the ship, and there found our other brethren.   We then spoke to the officers of the guard, and arranged with them that these men should receive some refreshment, since they had been on the water for twenty days in great misery, and we brought them into the city.   Then we said to our imprisoned brethren: *The soldiers shall not get you out of*

here again easily, for if they use force we will complain
to our magistrates. This, however, did not happen. They
went about in freedom, and we remained with them and
witnessed all the manifestations of love and friendship
with the greatest joy. We spent the time together de-
lightfully, and after they were entirely refreshed, they the
next day departed, though they moved with difficulty,
because stiffened from their long imprisonment. I went
with them for an hour and a half beyond the city, and
there we, with weeping eyes and swelling hearts, embraced each other and with a kiss of peace separated.
They returned to the Palatinate to seek their wives and
children, who are scattered everywhere in Switzerland, in
Alsace and in the Palatinate, and they know not where
they are to be found. They were very patient and cheer-
ful under oppression, though all their worldly goods were
taken away. Among them were a preacher and two
deacons. They were naturally very rugged people, who
could endure hardships. They wore long and unshaven
beards, disordered clothing, great shoes, which were
heavily hammered with iron and large nails; they were
very zealous to serve God with prayer and reading and
in other ways, and very innocent in all their doings, as
lambs and doves. They asked me in what way the community was governed. I explained it to them, and it
pleased them very much. But we could hardly talk with
them, because, as they lived in the mountains of Switzerland, far from cities and towns, and had little intercourse
with other men, their speech is rude and uncouth, and
they have difficulty in understanding anyone who does
not just speak their way. Two of them have gone to
Deventer, to see whether they can get a livelihood in this
country."

Most of them went to the Palatinate to seek their kinsmen and friends, and before long a deputation from them
came back here.   On the first of May we find three of
their preachers, Hans Burchi or Burghalter,* Melchior
Zaller and Benedict Brechtbühl,† with Hans Rub and
Peter Donens, in Amsterdam, where they gave a further
account of their affairs with the Bern Magistracy, and
apparently consulted with the committee as to whether
they should establish themselves near the Palatinate
brethren on the lands in the neighborhood of Campen
and Groningen, which was to be gradually purchased by
the Committee on behalf of the fugitives.   The majority
preferred a residence in the Palatinate, but they soon
found great difficulty in accomplishing it.   The Palatinate community was generally poor, so that the brethren,
with the best disposition, could be of little service in
insuring the means of gaining a livelihood.   There was a
scarcity of lands and farm-houses, and there was much to
be desired in the way of religious liberty, since they were
subject entirely to the humors of the Elector ; or, worse
still, his officers.   For nearly seven years, often supported
by the Netherland brethren, they waited and persevered,
always hoping for better times.   Then, their numbers
being continually increased by new fugitives and exiles
from Switzerland, they finally determined upon other
measures, and at a meeting of their elders at Manheim,
in February, 1717, decided to call upon the Netherlanders for help in carrying out the great plan of remov-

---

* Hans Burghalter came to America and was a preacher at Conestoga,
Lancaster County, in 1727.

† According to Rupp, Bernhard B. Brechtbühl translated the *Wandelnde
Seele* into the German from the Dutch.

ing to Pennsylvania, which they had long contemplated, and which had then come to maturity. Strange as it may appear at first glance, the very land to which the Swiss tyrants had once wanted to banish them had then become the greatest attraction. Still there was reason enough for it; reason, perhaps, in the information which their brethren sent from there to the Palatinate, but, before all, in the pressing invitation or instruction of the English King, George I., through his agent (Muntmeester), Ochse, at the court "Since it has been observed," so reads the beginning of this remarkable paper, "that the Christians, called Baptists or Mennonites, have been denied freedom of conscience in various places in Germany and Switzerland, and endure much opposition from their enemies, so that with difficulty they support themselves, scattered here and there, and have been hindered in the exercise of their religion." The king offers to them for a habitation the country west of the Allegheny Mountains, then considered a part of Pennsylvania, but not yet belonging to it. Each family should have fifty acres of land in fee simple, and for the first ten years the use, without charge, of as much more as they should want, subject only to the stipulation that after this time the yearly rent for a hundred acres should be two shillings, i.e., about a *guilder*, less six *kreutzers*. There is land enough for a hundred thousand families. They shall have permission to live there, not as foreigners, but on their engagement, without oath, to be true and obedient to the king, be bound as lawful subjects, and possess their land with the same right as if they had been born such, and, without interference, exercise their religion in meetings, just as do the "Reformed and Lutherans."

After calling attention to the fact that in Eastern Penn
sylvania the land was too dear (£20 to £100 for a hun
dred acres), the climate in Carolina was too hot, New
York and Virginia were already too full for them to
settle there with good chances of success, an attractive
description of the country followed in these words·
" This land is in a good and temperate climate, not too
hot or too cold; it lies between the 39th and 43d
parallels of north latitude, and extends westward about
two hundred German miles. It is separated from Virginia and Pennsylvania by high mountains; the air is
very pure, since it lies high ; it is very well watered,
having streams, brooks and springs, and the soil has the
reputation of being better than any that can be found in
Pennsylvania and Virginia. Walnut, chestnut, oak and
mulberry trees grow naturally in great profusion, as well
as many fruit-bearing trees, and the wild white and
purple grapes in the woods are larger and better than in
any other place in America. The soil is favorable for
wheat, barley, rye, Indian corn, hemp, flax and also silk,
besides producing many other useful things much more
abundantly than in Germany. A field can be easily
planted for from ten to twenty successive years without
manure. It is also very suitable for such fruits as apples,
pears, cherries, prunes, quinces, and especially peaches,
which grow unusually well, and bear fruit in three years
from the planting of the stone. All garden crops do
very well, and vineyards can be made, smee the wild
grapes are good, and would be still better if they were
dressed and pruned. Many horses, cattle and sheep can
be raised and kept, since an excellent grass grows
exuberantly. Numbers of hogs can be fattened on the

wild fruits in the bushes.   This land is also full of cattle
(Ründvieh), called buffaloes and elks, none of which are
seen in Pennsylvania, Virginia or Carolina.   Twenty or
thirty of these buffaloes are found together.   There are
also bears, which hurt nobody.   They feed upon leaves
and wild fruits, on which they get very fat, and their flesh
is excellent.   Deer exist in great numbers, beside Indian
cocks and hens (turkeys?), which weigh from twenty to
thirty pounds each; wild pigeons more than in any
other place in the world; partridges, pheasants, wild
swans, geese, all kinds of ducks, and many other small
fowls and animals ; so that if the settlers can only supply
themselves for the first year with bread, some cows for
milk and butter, and vegetables, such as potatoes, peas,
beans, etc., they can find flesh enough to eat from the
many wild animals and birds, and can live better than
the richest nobleman.   The only difficulty is that they
will be about thirty miles from the sea ; but this, by
good management, can be made of little consequence."

Apparently this description sounded like enchantment
in the ears of the poor Swiss and Palatinates, who had
never known anything but the thin soil of their native
country, and who frequently met with a refusal if they
sought to secure a farm of one or two acres.   And how
was that land of promise to be reached?   Easily enough.
They had only before the first of March to present themselves to one or another of the well-known merchants at
Frankfort, pay £3, or twenty-seven guilders each (children under ten years of age at half rates), that is, £2
for transportation, and £1 for seventy pounds of biscuit,
a measure and a half of peas, a measure of oatmeal and
the necessary beer, and immediately they would be sent

in ships to Rotterdam, thence to be carried over to Virginia. First, however, in Holland, one-half of the fare must be paid and additional provision, etc., secured, viz.: twenty-four pounds of dried beef, fifteen pounds of cheese, and eight and a quarter pounds of butter. Indeed, they were advised to provide themselves still more liberally with edibles, and with garden seeds and agricultural implements, linen, shirts, beds, table goods, powder and lead, furniture, earthenware, stoves, and especially money to buy " seeds, salt, horses, swine and fowls," to be taken along with them. All of these things would indeed cost a large sum, but what did that signify in comparison with the luxury which was promised them ? Should not the Netherland brethren quickly and gladly furnish this last assistance ? So thought the Palatinate brethren. It is not to be wondered at, however, that the " Committee on Foreign Needs " judged differently. They knew how much exaggeration there was in the picture painted by the English agent. They thought they were not authorized to consent to a request for assistance in the payment of traveling expenses, since the money was intrusted to them to be expended alone for the *persecuted*, and the brethren in the Palatinate were then tolerated; they feared the emigrants would call for more money, and in a word, they opposed the plan most positively and explained that if it was persisted in no help need be expected. Their objection, however, accomplished nothing. In reply to their views, the Committee received information, March 20th, that more than a hundred persons had started, and three weeks later they heard from Rotterdam that those already coming numbered three hundred, among whom were four needy families, who required six

13

hundred francs for their passage; and thirty others were getting ready to leave Neuwied.   Though the Committee had declared positively, in their letters, that they would have nothing to do with the whole affair, they nevertheless immediately passed a secret resolution, that, " As far as concerns our Committee, the Friends are to be helped as much as possible; " and apparently they took care that there should be furnished from private means, what as officials they could not give out of the fund.   Among the preachers who were at the head of these colonists we find principally Hans Burghalter and Benedict Brechtbühl.

The desire for emigration seemed to be entirely appeased in the Palatinate until 1726, when it broke out again with renewed force.   The chief causes were higher burdens imposed upon them by the Elector, the fear of the outburst of war, and perhaps also, pressing letters of invitation written by the friends settled in Pennsylvania. Moreover, the Committee were guilty of a great imprudence.   Though they so repeatedly assured the emigrants that they could not and would not help them, and promised liberal assistance to the needy Palatines who abandoned the journey; still, through pity for a certain Hubert Brouwer, of Neuwied, they gave him and his family three hundred francs passage-money.   Either this became known in the Palatinate, or the stream could no longer be stayed.   Though some of their elders, together with the Committee, tried to dissuade them, and painted horrible pictures of the possibility that, in the war between England and Spain, they might, " by Spanish ships be taken to the West Indies, where men are sold as slaves," the Palatines believed not a word of it.   On April 12th,

1727, there were one hundred and fifty ready to depart, and on the 16th of May, the Committee were compelled to write to the Palatinate that they " ought to be informed of the coming of those already on the way, so that they can best provide for them ; " and they further inquired " how many would arrive without means, so that the Society might consider whether it would be possible for them to arrange for the many and great expenses of the passage."

Some did not need help, and could supply from their own means what was required ; but on the 20th the Committee learned that forty-five more needy ones had started from the Palatinate. These with eight others cost the Society 3271f. 15st. Before the end of July twenty-one more came to Rotterdam, and so it continued. No wonder that the Committee, concerned about such an outpouring, requested the community in Pennsylvania " to announce emphatically to all the people from the pulpit that they must no more advise their needy friends and acquaintances to come out of the Palatinate, and should encourage them with the promise that, if they only remained across the sea, they would be liberally provided for in everything." If, however, they added, the Pennsylvanians wanted to pay for the passage of the poor Palatines, it would then, of course, be their own affair. This the Pennsylvanians were not ready nor in a condition to do. The Committee also sent forbidding letter after letter to the Palatinate, but every year they had to be repeated, and sometimes, as, for instance, May 6th, 1733, they drew frightful pictures : " We learn from New York that a ship from Rotterdam going to Pennsylvania with one hundred and fifty Palatines wandered twenty-four weeks at sea. When they finally arrived at port nearly all the people were dead. The rest, through the want of *vivres*, were forced to subsist upon rats and vermin, and are all sick and weak. The danger of such an occurrence is always so great that the most heedless do not run the risk except through extreme want." Nevertheless, the stream of emigrants did not cease. When finally over three thousand of different sects came to Rotterdam, the Committee, June 15th, 1732, adopted the strong resolution that under no pretence would they furnish means to needy Palatines, except to pay their fares back to their fatherland. By rigidly maintaining this rule, and thus ending where they undoubtedly should have commenced, the Committee put a complete stop to emigration. On the 17th of March they reported that they had already accomplished their object, and from that time they were not again troubled with requests for passage-money to North America.* In the meanwhile their adherence to this resolution caused some coolness between the communities in the Netherlands and in Pennsylvania. Still their intercourse was not entirely terminated. A special circumstance gave an impulse which turned the Pennsylvanians again toward our brotherhood in 1742. Their colony had increased wonderfully; they enjoyed prosperity, rest, and what the remembrance of

---

* This is, of course, correct as far as the Committee at Amsterdam is concerned, but neither emigration nor Mennonite aid ended at this time. The Schwenkfelders, some of whom came over only the next year, speak in warm and grateful terms of the aid rendered them by the Mennonites. Their MS. Journal, now in possession of Abraham H. Cassel, says : " Mr. Henry Van der Smissen gave us on the ship 16 loaves of bread, 2 Dutch cheese, 2 tubs of butter, 4 casks of beer, two roasts of meat, much flour and biscuit, and 2 bottles of French brandy, and otherwise took good care of us."

foreign sufferings made more precious than all, complete religious freedom ; but they talked with some solicitude about their ability to maintain one of their points of belief —absolute non-participation in war, even defensive. They had at first been so few in numbers that they were un- noticed by the government, but now it was otherwise. Could they, when a general arming of the people was ordered to repel a hostile invasion of the neighboring French colonists or an incursion of the Indians, refuse to go, and have their conscientious scruples respected? They were in doubt about it, and little indications seemed to warrant their uncertainty. The local magis- tracy and the deputed authorities looked favorably upon their request for complete freedom from military service, but explained that they were without the power to grant the privilege which they thought existed in the King of England alone.   In consequence of this explanation the Pennsylvania Mennonites resolved to write, as they did under date of May 8th, 1742, to Amsterdam and Haarlem, and ask that the communities there would bring their powerful influence to bear upon the English Court in their behalf, as had been done previously through the intervention of the States-General when alleviation was obtained in the case of the Swiss and Litthauer brethren. This letter seems to have miscarried.   It cannot be found in the archives of the Amsterdam community, and their minutes contain no reference to it, so that its contents would have remained entirely unknown if the Pennsyl- vanians had not written again October 19th, 1745, com- plaining of the silence upon this side, and repeating in a few words what was said in it.   Though it is probable that the letter of 1742 was not received, it may be that our forefathers laid it aside unanswered, thinking it unadvisable to make the intervention requested before the North American brethren had substantial difficulty about the military service; and it must be remarked that in the reply, written from here to the second letter, there is not a word said upon this subject, and allusions only are made to things which, in comparison, the Pennsylvanians surely thought were of much less importance.

In the second part of their letter of October, 1745, which is in German, the Pennsylvanians write: "As the flames of war appear to mount higher, no man can tell whether the cross and persecution of the defenceless Christians will not soon come, and it is therefore of importance to prepare ourselves for such circumstances with patience and resignation, and to use all available means that can encourage steadfastness and strengthen faith. Our whole community have manifested an unanimous desire for a German translation of the Bloody Theatre of Tieleman Jans Van Braght, especially since in this community there is a very great number of newcomers, for whom we consider it to be of the greatest importance that they should become acquainted with the trustworthy witnesses who have walked in the way of truth, and sacrificed their lives for it."

They further say that for years they had hoped to undertake the work, and the recent establishment of a German printing office had revived the wish, but "the bad paper always used here for printing" discouraged them. The greatest difficulty, however, was to find a suitable translator, upon whose skill they could entirely rely, without the fear that occasionally the meaning would be perverted. Up to that time no one had appeared among them to whom they could give the work with perfect confidence, and they therefore requested the brethren in Holland to look around for such a translator, have a thousand copies printed, and send them bound, with or without clasps and locks, or in loose sheets, to Pennsylvania, not, however, until they had sent over a complete account of the cost. The letter is dated at Schiebach, and bears the signatures of Jacob Godschalk, Martin Kolb, Michael Ziegler,* Heinrich Funk, Gilles Kassel and Dielman Kolb. Not until the 10th of February, 1748, did the "Committee on Foreign Needs," in whose hands the letter was placed, find time to send an answer. Its tenor was entirely unfavorable. They thought the translation "wholly and entirely impracticable, as well because it would be difficult to find a translator as because of the immense expense which would be incurred, and which they could very easily avoid." As "this book could certainly be found in the community, and there were some of the brethren who understood the Dutch language," it was suggested "to get them to translate into the German some of the chief histories wherein mention is made of the confessions of the martyrs, and which would serve for the purpose, and have them copied by the young people." By so doing they would secure "the double advantage that through the copying they would give more thought to it, and receive a stronger impression."

The North American brethren, at least, got the benefit of the information contained in this well-meant counsel,

* Michael Ziegler, as early as 1722, lived near the present Skippackville, in Montgomery County, Pa , and was, for at least thirty years, one of the elders of the Skippack Church. He died at an advanced age about 1763, and left £9 to the poor of that congregation.

sent two and a-half years late. In the meantime they
had themselves zealously taken hold of the work, and
before the reception of the letter from Holland aecom-
plished their purpose. That same year, 1748, the complete translation of the " Martyrs' Mirror," of Tielman
Jans van Braght, saw the light at Ephrata. It was afterwards printed, with the pictures from the original added,
at Piermasens, in the Bavarian Palatinate, in 1780, and
this second edition is still frequently found among our
fellow-members in Germany, Switzerland and the Mountains of the Vosges.

Though the completion of this very costly under
taking gives a favorable idea of the energy and financial
strength of the North American community, they had to
struggle with adversity, and were compelled, ten years
later, to call for the charity of their Netherland brethren.
Nineteen families of them had settled in Virginia, " but
because of the cruel and barbarous Indians, who had
already killed and carried away as prisoners so many of
our people," they fled back to Pennsylvania. All of one
family were murdered, and the rest had lost all their
possessions. Even in Pennsylvania two hundred families,
through recent incursions of the savages in May and
June, lost everything, and their dead numbered fifty. In
this dreadful deprivation they asked for help, and they
sent two of their number, Johannes Schneyder and Martin Funk, to Holland, giving them a letter dated September 7th, 1758, signed by Michael Kaufman, Jacob Borner,
Samuel Bohm and Daniel Stauffer. The two envoys,
who had themselves sorely suffered from the devasta-
tions of the war, acquitted themselves well of their mission on the 18th of the following December, when they

secured an interview with the Committee at Amsterdam. They made the impression of being "plain and honest people," gave all the explanations that were wanted, and received an answer to the letter they brought, in which was inclosed a bill of exchange upon Philadelphia for £50 sterling, equal to £78 11s. 5d. Pennsylvania currency, or 550f. The newly-chosen Secretary of the Committee, J. S. Centen, adds: "We then paid their expenses here, and supplied them with victuals and travelling money, and they departed December 17th, 1758, in the Hague packet-boat."

After this event all intercourse between the North American Mennonites and those in the Netherlands ceased, except that the publisher of the well-known "Name List of the Mennonite Preachers" endeavored until the end of the last century to obtain the necessary information from North America for his purpose; but it is apparent, upon looking at the remarkable names of places, that very much is wanting. They wrote to him, however, that he might mention as distinct communities Schiebach (Skippack), Germantown, Mateschen, Indian Kreek, Blen (Plain), Soltford (Salford), Rakkill (Rock-hill), Schwanin (Swamp), Deeproom (Deeprun), Berkosen (Perkasie), Anfrieds (Franconia), Grotenswamp (Great Swamp), Sackheim (Saucon), Lower Milford, with two meeting-houses, Hosensak, Lehay (Lehigh), Term, Schuylkill, and forty in the neighborhood of Kanestogis (Conestoga). In 1786 the community in Virginia is also specially mentioned. For some years this statement remained unchanged. The list of 1793 says that the number of the Mennonite communities of North America, distinct from the Baptists, was two hundred, and some estimate them at over three hundred, of which twenty-

three were in the Pennsylvania districts of Lancaster and
Konestogis (Conestoga). This communication was kept
unchanged in the Name List of 1810, but in the next,
that of 1815, it was at last omitted, because, according to
the compiler, Dr. A. N. Van Gelder, " for many years, at
least since 1801, we have been entirely without knowledge
or information."

In 1856 R. Baird, in his well-known work, " Religions
in America," says that Pennsylvania is still the principal
home of the Mennonites in the United States and that
they have four hundred communities, with two hundred
or two hundred and fifty preachers, and thirty thousand
members, who are for the most part in easy circumstances.
Perhaps these figures are correct, so far as concerns
Pennsylvania ; but according to the " Conference Minutes
of the entire Mennonite community in North America,
held at West Point, Lee County, Iowa, the 28th and 29th
of May, 1860," the number of the Mennonites in all the
States of the Union amounted to 128,000.   After having
for many years almost entirely neglected mutual relations,
and separated into many small societies, they finally
came to the conclusion that a firm covenant of brotherhood is one means to collect the scattered, to unite the
divided and to strengthen the weak.   The delegates of
the communities come together annually, as they did the
present year from May 31st to June 3d, at Wadsworth,
Ohio.   On the 20th of May, 1861, they repeated in their
own way what our fathers did fifty years earlier; they
founded a seminary for the service of the Church, with
which, since that time, Dr. Van der Smissen, formerly
minister at Frederickstadt, has been connected as professor and director.   May it be to them as great a blessing as ours has been to us.

Christopher Dock.

BY SAMUEL W. PENNYPACKER.

THE student of American literature, should he search through histories, bibliographies and catalogues of libraries for traces of Christopher Dock or his works, would follow a vain quest. The attrition of the great sea of human affairs during the course of a century and a half has left of the pious schoolmaster, as the early Germans of Pennsylvania were wont to call him, only a name, and of his reputation nothing. Watson, the annalist, says that in 1740 Christopher Dock taught school in the old Mennonite log-church in Germantown; the catalogue of the American Antiquarian Society contains the title of his "Schul-Ordnung" under the wrong year; and these meagre statements are the only references to him I have ever been able to find in any English book. There may be men still living who have heard from their grandfathers of his kindly temper and his gentle sway, but memory is uncertain and they are rapidly disappearing. Between the leaves of old Bibles and in out-of-the-way places, in country garrets, perhaps, are still preserved some of the Schrifften and birds and flowers, which he used to write and paint as rewards for his dutiful scholars, but the hand that made them has long been forgotten. The good which he did has been interred with his bones,

(203)

and all that he did was good.   The details of his life that
can now be ascertained are very few, but such as they
are it is a fitting task to gather them together.   The eye
will sometimes leave the canvas on which are depicted
the gaudy robes of a Catherine Cornaro, or the fierce
passions of a Rizpah, and gratefully turn to a quiet rural
scene, where broad fields stretch out and herds- feed in
the shade of oaks, and all is suggestive of peace, strength
and happiness.   It may well be doubted whether the
story of the Crusades has attracted more readers than
the *Imitation of Christ* by Thomas a Kempis ; the *Life of
John Woolman* has found its way into the highest walks
of literature, while that of Anthony Wayne is yet to be
written ; and the time may come when the American historian, wearied with the study of the wars with King
Philip to the north of us, and the wars with Powhattan to
the south of us, will turn his lens upon Pennsylvania,
where the principles of the Reformation produced their
ultimate fruits, and where the religious sects who were in
the advance of thought, driven out of conservative and
halting Europe, lived together at peace with the natives
and in unity among themselves, without wars.   The
sweetness and purity which filled the soul of the Mennonite, the Dunker, the Schwenkfelder, the Pietist and the
Quaker, was nowhere better exemplified than in Christopher Dock.   It is told that once two men were talking
together of him, and one said that he had never been
known to show the slightest anger.   The other replied
that, perhaps, his temper had not been tested, and pres-
ently, when Dock came along, he reviled him fiercely,
bitterly and profanely.   The only reply made by Dock
was : " Friend, may the Lord have mercy upon thee."

He was a Mennonite, who came from Germany to Pennsylvania about 1714. There is a tradition that he had
been previously drafted into the army, but had been dis-
charged because of his convictions and refusal to bear
arms. In 1718, or perhaps four years earlier, he opened
a school for the Mennonites on the Skippack. It was an
occupation to which he felt he was Divinely called, and he
continued it without regard to compensation, which was
necessarily very limited, for ten years. At the expiration
of this period he went to farming. On the 28th of 9th
month, 1735, he bought from the Penns one hundred
acres of land in Salford Township, now Montgomery
County, for £15 10s., and, doubtless, this was the tract
upon which he lived. For ten years he was a husband
man ; but for four summers he taught school in Germantown, in sessions of three months each year, and it would
seem to have occurred during this period. While away
from the school he was continually impressed with a consciousness of duties unfulfilled, and in 1738 he gave up
his farm and returned to his old pursuit. He then opened
two schools, one in Skippack and one in Salford, which
he taught three days each alternately, and for the rest of
his life he devoted himself to this labor unceasingly.

In 1750 Christopher Saur, the Germantown publisher,
conceived the idea that it would be well to get a written
description of Dock's method of keeping school, with a
view to printing it, in order, as he said, that other school-
teachers whose gift was not so great, might be instructed; that those who cared only for the money they
received might be ashamed; and that parents might
know how a well arranged school was conducted, and
how themselves to treat children. To get the description

was a matter requiring diplomacy, because of the decided
feeling on the part of Dock that it would not be sinless
to do anything for his own praise, credit or elevation.
Saur, therefore, wrote to Dielman Kolb, a prominent
Mennonite minister in Salford, and a warm friend of
Dock, urging his request and presenting a series of questions which he asked to have answered. Through the
influence of Kolb the reluctant teacher was induced to
undertake a reply, and the treatise was completed on the
8th of August, 1750. He only consented, however, upon
the condition that it should not be printed during his
lifetime. For nineteen years afterwards the manuscript
lay unused. In the meantime the elder Saur had died,
and the business had passed into the hands of his son,
Christopher Saur, the second. Finally, in 1769, some
" friends of the common good," getting wearied with the
long delay, succeeded in overcoming the scruples of
Dock and secured his consent to having it printed. It
met with further vicissitudes. Having read the manuscript Saur mislaid it, and after a careful search concluded that it must have been sold along with some waste
paper. He offered a reward for its return through his
newspaper. People began to report that he had found
something in it he did not like and had put it away purposely. The satisfied author sent a messenger to him to
say " that I should not trouble myself about the loss of
the writing. It had never been his opinion that it ought
to be printed in his lifetime, and so he was very well
pleased that it had been lost." At length, after it had
been lost for more than a year, it was found in a place
through which he and his people had thoroughly
searched. It was at once published in a large octavo

pamphlet of fifty-four pages. The full title is: "Eine einfaeltige und gruendliche abgefasste Schul-Ordnung, darinnen deutlich vorgestellt wird, auf welche weisse die Kinder nicht nur in denen in Schulen gewoehnlichen Lehren bestens angebracht, sondern auch in der Lehre der Gottseligkeit wohl unterrichtet werden moegen. Aus Liebe zu dem menschlichen Geschlecht aufgesetzt durch den wohlerfarnen und lang geuebten Schulmeister Christoph Dock; und durch einige Freunde des gemeinen Bestens dem Druck uebergeben, Germantown, gedruckt und zu finden bey Christoph Saur, 1770."

The importance of this essay consists in the fact that it is the earliest written and published in America upon the subject of school-teaching, and that it is the only picture we have of the colonial country school.*   It is remarkable that at a time when the use of force was considered essential in the training of children, views so correct upon the subject of discipline should have been entertained.   The only copy of the original edition I have ever seen is in the Cassel collection at Harleysville, recently secured by the Historical Society of Pennsylvania, and a ten years' search for one upon my own part has so far resulted in failure.   A second edition was printed by Saur the same year, of which there is a copy in the library of the German Society of Philadelphia.   In 1861 the Mennonites of Ohio published an edition, reprinted from a copy of the second edition, at the office of the *Gospel Visitor*, at Columbia, in that State.   This publication also met with an accident.   A careless printer, who was setting type by candlelight, knocked over his candle

* I know of no publication on the subject written earlier, and the bibliography of the American Antiquarian Society shows none.

and burned up one of the leaves of the original. The work was stopped because the committee having the matter in charge could find no other copy. Finally, in despair, they wrote to A. H. Cassel, of Harleysville, Pennsylvania, who, without hesitation, took the needed leaf from his copy and sent it to them by mail. *Mirabile dictu!* It was scrupulously cared for and speedily returned. It is difficult to determine which is the more admirable, the confiding simplicity of a book-lover who willingly ran such a risk of making his own copy imperfect, or the Roman integrity which, being once in the possession of the only leaf necessary to complete a mutilated copy, firmly resisted temptation.

Volume I, No. 33, of the *Geistliches Magazien*, an exceedingly rare periodical, published by Saur about 1764, is taken up with a " Copia einer Schrift welche der Schulmeister, Christoph Dock, an seine noch lebende Schueler zur Lehr und Vermahnung aus liebe geschrieben hat." It is signed at the end by Dock, and the following note is added: " N. B. The printer has considered it necessary to put the author's name to this piece first, because it is specially addressed to his scholars, though it suits all men without exception, and it is well for them to know who addresses them ; and, secondly, the beloved author has led, and still in his great age leads such a good life that it is important and cannot be hurtful to him that his name should be known. May God grant that all who read it may find something in it of practical benefit to themselves."

No. 40, of the same magazine, consists of " Hundert noethige Sitten-Regeln fuer Kinder." It may be claimed for these Rules of Conduct that they are the first original

American publication upon the subject of etiquette. It is not only a very curious and entertaining paper, but it is exceedingly valuable as an illustration of the customs and modes of life of those to whom it was addressed, and of what was considered " manners " among them. From it a picture of the children, silent until they were addressed, seated upon stools around a table, in the centre of which was a large, common dish wherein each child dipped with his spoon, and of the homely meal, begun and closed with prayer, may be distinctly drawn.

In No. 41, of the magazine, there is a continuation, or second part, containing " Hundert christliche Lebens Regeln fuer Kinder." There is nothing said in either of these papers concerning the author, but if the internal evidence were not in itself sufficient, the descendants of Saur have preserved the knowledge that they were written by Dock.

In No. 15, Vol. II, of the magazine, are " Zwey erbauliche Lieder, welche der Gottselige Christoph Dock, Schulmeister an der Schipbach, seinen lieben Schuelern, und allen andern die sie lesen, zur Betrachtung hinterlassen hat."

He wrote a number of hymns, some of which are still used among the Mennonites in their church services. These hymns, so far as they are known to me, are as follows, the first line of each only being given :

1. Kommt, liebe Kinder, kommt herbey.
2. Ach kommet her ihr Menschen Kinder.
3. Mein Lebensfaden lauft zu Ende.
4. Ach Kinder wollt ihr lieben.
5. Fromm seyn ist ein Schatz der Jugend.
6. An Gottes gnad und milden Seegen.
7. Allein auf Gott setz dein vertrauen.

14

During the later years of his life Dock made his home with Heinrich Kassel, a Mennonite farmer on the Skippack. One evening in the Fall of 1771 he did not re turn from his labors at the usual time. A search was made and he was found in the school-house on his knees —dead. After the dismissal of the scholars for the day he had remained to pray, and the messenger of death had overtaken him at his devotions—a fitting end to a life which had been entirely given to pious contemplation and useful works.

He left two daughters, Margaret, wife of Henry Strykers, of Salford; and Catharine, wife of Peter Jansen, of Skippack.

Der Blutige Schauplatz oder Martyrer Spiegel.

"Among all the things which men have or strive for through their whole lives," said Alphonse the wise, King of Arragon, "there is nothing better than old wood to burn, old friends for company and old books to read. All the rest are only bagatelles." The wise king was something of a book worm, and mentioned last, by way of climax, the treasures that lay next his heart. Doubtless he was thinking all the while how the wood turns to ashes, that sooner or later "marriage and death and division" carry off our friends, and that the pleasure derived from old books alone is pure and permanent. What can exceed the delight of a connoisseur, familiar with authors, imprints, papers and bindings, and educated to an appreciation of the difference between leaves cut and uncut, upon discovering a perfect copy of an extremely rare book? In the present age of the world we measure the value of pretty much everything by the amount of money it will bring. In Europe a copy of the first edition of the Decameron has been sold for £2,260 sterling, and one of the Gutenberg Bible, on vellum, for £3,400. In this country we have not yet reached to that height of enthusiasm or depth of purse, but in the late sale of the library of Mr. George Brinley a copy of the first book printed in New York, by William Bradford, brought $1,600. Up to the

present time the noblest specimen of American colonial
biography has remained utterly unknown to the most
learned of our bibliophilus.

Men, communities and nations have their origin, de-
velopment and fruition; so have books.   In Holland, in
the year 1562, there appeared a duodecimo of about two
hundred and fifty leaves in the Dutch language, called *Het
offer des Heeren*.   This was the germ or starting point.
Of later years a copy of the same was secured by a publishing house in Philadelphia and sold for $120.   It con-
tained biographical sketches of a number of the early
martyrs of the Doopsgezinde or Mennonites, a sect which
was the antetype of the Quakers, and these sketches were
accompanied by hymns describing in rhyme not only their
piety and sufferings, but even the manner and dates of
their death.

To publish such a book was then punishable by fire,
and the title page therefore gives no indications as to
where it was printed or who was the printer.   Meeting
together in secret places and in the middle of the night,
the linen weavers of Antwerp and the hardy peasants of
Friesland cherished their religious zeal and their veneration for Menno Simons by singing and reading about
their martyrs.   Next to the Bible this book was most in
demand among them; so sketches were gathered and
added to it, when later editions were printed in the years
1567, 1570, 1576, 1578, 1580, 1589, 1595 and 1599; but
many copies were, along with their owners, burned by the
executioners, and the book is now very scarce.   It was
followed by a large quarto of eight hundred and sixty
three pages, written by Hans de Ries and Jacques Outer
man, and printed at Hoorn in 1617 by Zacharias Cor-

nelisz. The next edition was a handsome black-letter folio of ten hundred and fifty-six pages, printed at Harlem by Hans Passchier von Wesbush, in 1631, and in 1660, Tielman Jans Van Braght, a Mennonite theologian at Dortrecht, who was born in 1625 and died in 1664, published " Het Bloedigh Toneel der Doops Gesinde en Wereloose Christenen," a folio of thirteen hundred and twenty-nine pages. It was reproduced in 1685 in two magnificent folio volumes, handsomely illustrated with a frontispiece, and a hundred and four copper plates engraved by the celebrated Jan Luyken.

This book in its immense proportions is thus seen to have been a gradual culmination of the research and literary labors of many authors. It is the great historical work of the Mennonites, and the most durable monument of that sect. It traces the history of those Christians who, from the time of the Apostles, were opposed to the baptism of infants and to warfare, including the Lyonists, Petrobusians and Waldenses ; details the persecutions of the Mennonites by the Spaniards in the Netherlands during the time of the Spanish Inquisition, and the Calvinists in Switzerland, together with the individual sufferings of many hundreds who were burned, drowned, beheaded or otherwise maltreated.

Many copies of the book were brought to America, but they were in Dutch. No German translation existed. On the 19th of October, 1745, Jacob Godshalk, of Germantown, Dielman Kolb, of Salford, Michael Ziegler, Yilles Kassel and Martin Kolb, of Skippack, and Henry Funk, of Indian Creek, the author of two religious works, sent a letter to Amsterdam asking assistance to have the book translated into the German language. No reply was received until February 10th, 1748, when no aid was promised. Without waiting longer the Americans had, in the mean time, found a way to accomplish their purpose. An agreement was then made with the brotherhood at Ephrata, Lancaster County, to have their great martyr-book, which was in the Dutch language, translated and printed in German. The printing of the martyr-book was then taken in hand, for which important work fifteen brethren were elected, and it took them three years to complete the work. The price per copy was fixed at twenty shillings. It was printed in large folio, using sixteen quires of paper, and making an edition of thirteen hundred copies. Heinrich Funk and Dielman Kolb were appointed a committee by the Mennonites to make the arrangements with the community at Ephrata and to supervise the translation.* This book had, finally, in the revolutionary war, a singular fate. There being great need of all war material and also paper, and it having been discovered that in Ephrata was a large quantity of printed paper, an arrest was soon laid upon it. Many objections were raised, and among others it was alleged that since the English army was so near this circumstance might have a bad effect. They were determined, however, to give up nothing and that all must be taken by force; so two wagons and six soldiers came and carried off the martyr-books. This caused great offense throughout the land. Thus by an irony of fate the story of the defenseless Christians was made to envelope the powder and ball that were fired into the faces of the British soldiers at Brandywine and Germantown.

---

* The translator was Peter Miller.—AUTHOR.

Among the additions made at Ephrata were twelve stanzas, upon page 939, concerning the martyrdom of Hans Haslibacher, taken from the "Ausbundt" or hymn-book of the Swiss Mennonites. Some of the families in Pennsylvania and other parts of the United States, the sufferings of whose ancestors are mentioned in it, are those bearing the names of Kuster, Hendricks, Yocum, Bean, Rhoads, Gotwals, Jacobs, Johnson, Royer, Zimmerman, Shoemaker, Keyser, Landis, Meylin Brubaker, Kolb, Weaver, Snyder, Wanger, Grubb, Bowman, Bachman, Zug, Aker, Garber, Miller, Kassel and Wagner.

The republication, at that early date, of a work so immense, certainly marks an epoch in the literary history of America. The war of 1812 called forth another American edition, which was published in 1814 by Joseph Ehrenfried, at Lancaster. Shem Zook, an Amish Mennonite, had a quarto edition published in Philadelphia in 1849, and John Funk, of Elkhart, Indiana, issued another in 1870. An imperfect English translation, by I. D. Rupp, appeared in 1837, and in 1853 a translation by the Hansard Knollys Society of London was in course of preparation and afterwards published. The Mennonite Publishing Company, of Elkhart, Indiana, published a new edition of this work, which was translated from the Dutch editions of 1660 and 1685, and was issued in the spring of 1887, in a full bound illustrated royal octavo volume of 1,093 pages, and more complete than any previous edition.

Among the literary achievements of the Germans of Pennsylvania it surpasses, though eight years later, the great quarto Bible of Christopher Saur, the first German Bible in America printed at Germantown in 1743 which, for nearly half a century, had no English rival.

Settlement at Skippack.

THE first impulse followed by the first wave of emigration came from Crefeld, a city of the Lower Rhine, within a few miles of the borders of Holland. On the 10th of March, 1682, William Penn conveyed to Jacob Telner, of Crefeld, doing business as a merchant in Amsterdam, Jan Streepers, a merchant of Kaldkirchen, a village in the vicinity, still nearer to Holland, and Dirk Sipman, of Crefeld, each 5,000 acres of land to be laid out in Pennsylvania. Telner had been in America between the years 1678 and 1681, and we may safely infer that his acquaintance with the country had much influence in bringing about the purchase. On the 11th of June, 1683, Penn conveyed to Govert Remke (Johann Remke was a Mennonite preacher in 1752), Lenart Arets and Jacob Isaacs Van Bebber, a baker, all of Crefeld, 1,000 acres of land each, and they, together with Telner, Streepers and Sipman, constituted the original Crefeld purchasers. On the 18th of June, 1683, the little colony was in Rotterdam accompanied by Jacob Telner, Dirk Sipman and Jan Streepers, and Telner conveyed 2,000 acres of land to the brothers Op den Graeff.

Of the six original purchasers, Jacob Telner and Jacob Isaacs Van Bebber are known to have been Mennonites. Sipman selected as his attorneys here at various times Herman Op den Graeff, Hendrick Sellen and Van Beb-

(216)

ber, all of whom were Mennonites. Of the emigrants, Dirk, Herman and Abraham Op den Graeff were Mennonites. * Jacob Telner was baptized in the Mennonite church in Amsterdam March 29th, 1665 ; his only child, Susanna, married Albertus Brandt.

After deducting the land laid out in Germantown and the 2,000 acres sold to the Op den Graeffs, the bulk of his 5,000 acres was taken up on the Skippack, about 2000 acres, situated on the east side of the Skippack, in a tract for many years known as "Telner's Township." †

In 1702 began the settlement on the Skippack. This first outgrowth of Germantown also had its origin at Crefeld, and the history of the Crefeld purchase would not be complete without some reference to it. As we have seen, of the 1,000 acres bought by Govert Remke, 161 acres were laid out at Germantown ; the balance he sold in 1686 to Dirk Sipman. Of Sipman's own purchase of 5,000 acres, 588 acres were laid out at Germantown, and all that remained of the 6,000 acres he sold in 1698 to Matthias Van Bebber, who, getting in addition 500 acres allowance and 415 acres by purchase, had the whole tract of 6,166 acres located by patent February 22d, 1702, on the Skippack. It was in the present Perkiomen Township, Montgomery County, and adjoining Edward Lane and William Harmer, near what is now the village of Evansburg.‡ For the next half century at least it was known as Bebber's Township, or Bebber's Town, and the name being often met with in the Germantown records has been a source of apparently hopeless confu-

---

* See *Pennypacker's Sketches*, p. 28.
† See Exemplification Records, Vol. 8, p. 360.
‡ Exemplification Records, Vol. 1, p. 470.

sion to our local historians. Van Bebber immediately
began to colonize it, the most of the settlers being Mennonites. Among these were Heinrich Pannebecker, Johannes Kuster, Johannes Umstat, Klas Jansen and Jan
Krey, in 1702 ; John Jacobs, in 1704; John Newberry,
Thomas Wiseman, Edward Beer, Gerhard und Herman
In de Hoffen, Dirk and William Renberg, in 1706;
William and Cornelius Dewees, Hermanus Kuster, Christopher Zimmerman, Johannes Scholl and Daniel Desmond, in 1708 ; Jacob, Johannes and Martin Kolb, Mennonite weavers from Wolfsheim in the Palatinate, and
Andrew Strayer, in 1709; Solomon Dubois, from Ulster
County, New York, in 1716; Paul Fried,* in 1727; and
in the last year the unsold balance of the tract passed
into the hands of Pannebecker. Van Bebber gave 100
acres for a Mennonite burying-ground and church, which
was built about 1725, the trustees being Hendrick Sellen,
Hermanus Kuster, Klas Jansen, Martin Kolb, Henry
Kolb, Jacob Kolb and Michael Ziegler.

The first ministers in the Skippack congregation were ·
Jacob Gaedschalk, Henry Kolb, Claes Jansen, Yilles
Cassel, Michael Ziegler, Martin Kolb, Andrew Ziegler,
Isaac Cassel, Matthias Rittenhouse, Heinrich Hunsicker,
John Hunsicker, Henry Bartolet, Elias Landes, Abraham
Wismer.

In the year 1848 the upper Mennonite meeting-house
in Skippack was built.

In 1849 John Van Fossen sold to Isaac Kulp one acre

---

* This is evidently the same Paul Fried who was married to Elizabeth
Stauffer, daughter of Hans Stauffer, who came to America January 20th,
1710. We do not find any other by that name at that time. See sketch of
the Stauffers.—AUTHOR.

of land adjoining Isaac Kulp's other land, and afterwards Isaac Kulp sold one acre and sixty-three perches for the meeting-house and graveyard to Jacob F. Kulp, Daniel Landes and George Reiff, in trust for the Mennonite congregation, the deed bearing date August 21st, 1849. It appears that the land had been selected, bargained for, the house built and the burying-ground laid out in 1848, and title was made the following year. In 1853 the congregation bought eighty perches more from Abraham Landes. The oldest grave in this graveyard is that of Nathaniel, son of Henry and Mary Reiff, died September 9th, 1848, aged 2 years, 11 months and 19 days.

Their first ministers were Elias Landes and Abraham Wismer; deacons, John Kratz and John Landes, Isaac Longaker, in Worcester, and John Gotwals, in Upper Providence; the two last named belong to the Skippack district. George Detwiler was chosen to the ministry in 1849. John B. Tyson was elected a deacon in 1862 and Jacob Mensch was chosen a minister in 1869. John B. Hunsberger, of Worcester, was chosen a minister in 1873 and was ordained a Bishop in 1877. Abraham Kulp was elected a deacon in 1874. Joseph Gander of Upper Providence, was elected a deacon in 1876. Abraham S. Reiff was elected a deacon in Worcester in 1877. Christian Hunsberger was chosen to the ministry in the year 1879. Henry Wismer was chosen to the ministry in 1883. George L. Reiff was elected a deacon in 1881.

The above-mentioned names I have copied from the Church Book containing financial accounts and other records of the Skippack Mennonite church from the year 1738 down to 1887, and is in possession of John B. Tyson, the present deacon, and bears the following title: " Der Menonisten Oder Taufgesinden Gemeinebuch.   Von Die Gemeinde in Bebberstown Anno Domini 1738."

The old or lower Skippack meeting-house was re-built about the year 1835.

The division took place about forty years ago, when the present occupants held possession of the house and property, with Henry Johnson, Sr. (deceased), as their minister.   His son, Henry Johnson, now one of their ministers, writes the following, under date of December 16th, 1887: " We are generally called the ' Johnson Mennonites;' we hold to the non-resistant Confession of Faith.   The number of our membership here is seventy-five or eighty.   The names of the ministers at present are Amos K. Bean and myself."

MENNONITE MEETING HOUSE IN SALFORD, MONTGOMERY COUNTY, PENNA.

The Organization of the Mennonite Church at Salford.

Of the origin and organization of the Mennonite Church in Salford, Montgomery County, Pa., we have not the records we desire, nor are they known to exist; it is therefore impossible to give an exact account of everything pertaining to its organization. We have, however, information that a deed was given for ten acres, dated October 4th and 5th, 1738. It was purchased by Henry Funk, Dielman Kolb, Christian Meyer, Jr., and Abraham Reiff; the two first were ministers and the two last were deacons. All were residents of Franconia, except Dielman Kolb, who resided in Salford. The said ten acres were purchased of Henry Ruth, whose residence was where John Clemmer's now is, from 1718 to 1747, who mentions in his deed to Christian Stauffer, of the latter date, that ten acres had been cut out of his land for the use of the Mennonite Baptist Church; presumably he did not write the deed himself, or, if so, he would have left the word Baptist out.

In what year the first house was built I have not been able to ascertain, but presumably in the same year, because S. W. Pennypacker says, in his *Biographical Sketches*, p. 93, "that Christopher Dock gave up his farm and returned to his old pursuit; he then opened two

schools in 1738, one in Skippack and one in Salford,
which he taught three days each alternately." Therefore it seems as if the house had been built immediately
after the land had been bought. When or in what year
the second house was built we have nothing definite.
The house was built of stone, one story high, and of considerable length, so that a room was partitioned off at the
east end for a school room. The writer of this work was
teaching school in that room in 1839. The present,
or evidently the third house, was built in 1850.

The earliest date on a tombstone in the graveyard is
1741. This was Ann Reiff, wife of Hans Reiff.

Who the first ministers were we have no record.
Martin Kolb and Henry, his brother, the ancestor of
George Brubaker Kulp, member of the Bar at Wilkesbarre, Luzerne County, came to Pennsylvania as early
as 1707, and was one of the earliest Mennonite preachers
in this country, says George B. Kulp in his pamphlet.
He further says, on page 4: "Dielman, or Thielman
(as the name is sometimes spelled), Kolb, another
brother of Henry, came to Pennsylvania somewhat later.
He was at Manheim, where he attended as a preacher to
the Mennonite congregation, "making himself most valuable by receiving and lodging his fellow-believers who fled
from Switzerland," as appears from a letter dated August
27th, 1710. He settled here in Salford about the year
1718 on a tract of one hundred and fifty acres. In 1721
he purchased two hundred and twenty-five acres more,
and afterwards a third tract, making altogether about five
hundred and fifty acres. He married a widow, Snavely,
and had by her one daughter, named Elizabeth, who was
afterwards married to Andrew Ziegler, son of Michael

Ziegler, a Mennonite minister at Skippack. Dielman Kolb died in the beginning of the year 1757. His will was probated April 30th, 1757. The witnesses were Robert Jones, Martin Kolb and Isaac Kolb. There is a clause in his will which reads thus: "I nominate my loving and trusty friends, Henry Funk and Ulriegh Bergher (presumably now Bergey), both of Salford aforesaid, yeomen, trustees of this my last will and testament."

In 1750 Christopher Saur, the Germantown publisher, conceived the idea of having Christopher Dock's method of keeping school with a view of printing it. Saur, therefore, wrote to Dielman Kolb, a prominent Mennonite minister in Salford, and a warm friend of Dock (says S. W. Pennypacker). So it is evident that Dielman Kolb was a minister and undoubtedly officiated at Salford; also more likely on account of him and Dock being intimate friends, and Dock commenced teaching school in Salford in 1738. Andrew Ziegler, born March 14th, 1737, died October 26th, 1811, aged 74 years, 7 months, 12 days. Married to Catharine Lederach, was a grandson of Dielman Kolb and a Bishop in the congregation at Salford, also officiated as Bishop in the Mennonite congregation at Germantown.

Christian Haldeman was also one of the earliest ministers in Salford. He was born May 24th, 1743, old style, and died July 3d, 1833, new style, aged 89 years, 1 month and 12 days. Isaac Alderfer was also a preacher in Salford. He was born October 1st, 1773, and died November 8th, 1842, aged 69 years 1 month and 1 day. John Bergey followed Alderfer in the ministry. He was born August 23d, 1783, and died December 6th, 1865, aged 82 years 3 months and 13 days. Jacob Kulp born

November 2d 1799, died April 18th, 1867, aged 67 years
5 months and 16 day, having been in the ministry a
number of years.

The ministers now living in Salford (September, 1887)
are Isaac Clemens, Henry Bauer and Jacob Moyer.*

---

* For part of the above information I am indebted to James Y. Heckler,
of Harleysville.

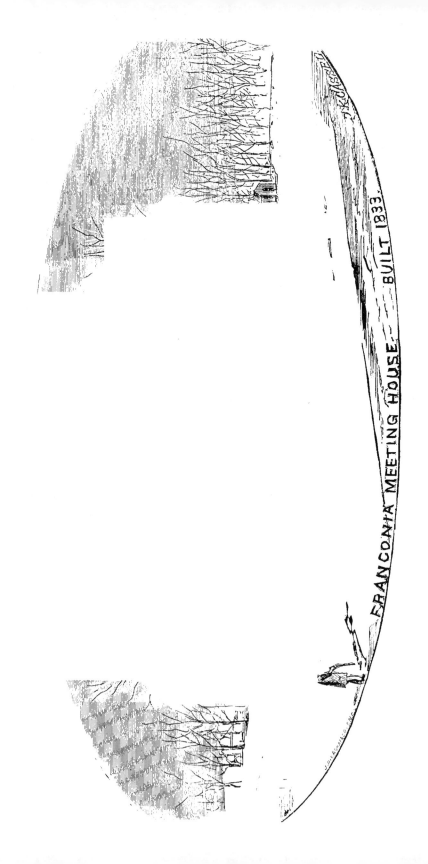

FRANCONIA MEETING HOUSE. BUILT 1833.

Franconia.

HEINRICH FUNK emigrated from Holland or the Palatinate and settled on the Indian Creek, in Franconia Township, now Montgomery County, Pa., in 1719, several miles from his nearest neighbor. Soon after his arrival a number of his brethren also came from Europe, and having considerably increased in numbers, formed a congregation of which he was chosen minister. The first Mennonite meeting-house in Franconia Township was built of stone in the year 1730.* The second house was also of stone, 45 by 75 feet, and was built in 1833, and has a seating capacity of over seven hundred. The present membership numbers about four hundred and fifty.

Josiah Clemmer was chosen to the ministry in the year 1860, and was elected Bishop in 1867, which he is at present; his co-workers in the ministry are Jacob Landis and Michael Moyer. Henry Nice was chosen to the ministry in 1839 and died in 1883, aged 79 years 6 months and 21 days. Jacob Godshall was chosen to the ministry in 1804, was elected Bishop in 1813, and died in 1845, aged 75 years 9 months and 2 days.

Among the first ministers after Heinrich Funk, who

---

* J. D. Souder.

died in 1760, was his son, Christian Funk* who was chosen to the ministry in 1757. He was a faithful worker until 1774, when the war. broke out and his troubles commenced.

Jacob Funk is also mentioned as a minister in 1765 in the records of Franconia, and Christian Meyer a deacon. A Christian Meyer is also mentioned as a minister. In 1770 Henry Rosenberger is mentioned as a confirmed deacon (*bestaetichter Vorsteher*); he was the last confirmed deacon in the Mennonite congregation known. In 1775 Jacob Oberholzer is mentioned as a minister; in 1779 Johannes Birke† is mentioned as a minister in Franconia; in 1760 Isaac Kolb was chosen Bishop. Samuel Bechtel was also a minister about that time.

S. W. Pennypacker says: " Henry Funk, always one of the most able and enterprising of the Mennonite preachers, and long a Bishop, settled on the Indian Creek, in Franconia Township, now Montgomery County, in 1719. He was ever faithful and zealous in his work, and did much to advance the interests of his church. He wrote a book upon baptism, entitled ' Ein Spiegel der Taufe,' published by Saur in 1744, which has passed through at least five editions. A more ambitious effort was the ' Erklaerung einiger hauptpuncten des gesetzes,' published after his death by Armbruster, in 1763. This book was reprinted at Biel, Switzerland, in 1844, and at Lancaster, Pa., in 1862, and is much esteemed. He and Dielman Kolb, of Salford, supervised

---

* Known as Christel Funk.

† Now Bergey,

the translation of Van Braght's ' Martyrer Spiegel ' (*Martyrs' Mirror*), from the Dutch to the German, and certified to its correctness. Beside these labors, which were all without pecuniary compensation, he was a miller by trade and acquired a considerable estate. He died about 1760."

The Souderton meeting-house was built in 1879 of brick, 40 by 50 feet, and is under the supervision of the Franconia congregation.

Kulpsville.

Mennonite Church at Towamencin, Montgomery County, Pa.*

In what year the first house of worship may have been erected is given by the following records: In 1764, August 27th, a deed was given from Herman Godshalk to Christian Weaver, William Godshalk, Goshen Shroger,† Peter Hendricks, Nicholaus Yeles and Garret Godshalk, for eighty-two perches of land, not recorded; and my informant, John C. Boorse, states that the first house was built the same year.

October 13th, 1807, a deed from Garret Godshalk to the elders and members of the Mennonists for the same ground was given and recorded in Book No. 24, page 331, etc.; part of this ground is a burying-ground.

June 16th, 1798, a deed was given from John Boorse, Sr., to Abraham Godwals and John Boorse, Jr., for 24 perches of land.

Also on June 29th, 1799, a deed was given from Catharine Godshalk and Janiken Godshalk to Joseph Hendricks and William Godshalk, trustees, for 60 perches of land.

Again, on August 5th, 1837, a deed was given from George Snyder to Joseph Hendricks, John Boorse, Sr.,

---

* The old spelling is retained in the above article so as not to destroy the original.

† Goshen Shroger. We find Gerhardt Schrager in the list of those who paid quit-rents prior to 1734.

Daniel Boorse, Abraham Godshalk, Peter Metz and David Allebach, Jr., trustees, for 114.48 perches of land, recorded in Book No. 56, page 525, etc.

Again, March 23d, 1844, a deed was given from Abraham Godshalk to John Boorse, Abraham Godshalk, Daniel Boorse, Peter Metz, David Allebach and Henry Boorse, for 46 perches of land, recorded in Book No. 64, page 99, etc.

Again, on March 28th, 1862, a deed was given from George Snyder to Peter Metz, Henry C. Boorse, David G. Allebach, Abraham M. Nise, Christian Sauder and Jonas K. Moyer, for 102 perches of land; recorded in Book No. 125, page 503, etc.

Again, on December 2d, 1876, a deed was given from Elias Cassel to Peter Metz and others for 40 perches of land; recorded in Book No. 235, page 76, etc.

Again, on August 16th, 1879, a deed was given from Jacob B. Moyer to Peter Metz and others, for one acre of land ; recorded in Book No. 250, page 284, etc.

It seems evident that an organization existed in that vicinity long before the first house was erected, for the following reasons : First, we find gravestones in the graveyard bearing the dates of 1733 and 1741; many of the inscriptions are in German, and many among the oldest have become illegible. Consequently a graveyard was there prior to 1733. Secondly, records show that the following-named persons lived in that vicinity and paid quit-rents prior to 1734 : Peter Weber, Christian Brenneman, Herman Godshalk, Henrich Frey, Yellis Yellis, Christian Weber, Jacob Frey, Peter Tison, Gerhardt Schrager (presumably afterwards Schrack) and Abraham Lüken.

About the year 1805 the first meeting-house was

destroyed by fire, when the second house was built on or near the same spot whére the first house stood. The third or present meeting-house was erected in the year 1862, considerably larger than the second. David Allebach, Sr., has been their deacon (or Vorsteher) for many years. He is now well advanced in years. Their present minister is Christian Allebach, son of John Allebach, preacher at Rockhill, Bucks County, Pa.

We now come to the most historic spot in the grave-yard. Here repose the remains of General Francis Nash, Colonel Boyd, Major White and Lieutenant Smith of the Continental Army, either slain or mortally wounded in the attack at Germantown. On the morning of October 4th, 1777, Washington retreated with his army and established his camp nearly a mile northwest of Kulpsville, in the vicinity of the above-mentioned meeting-house, near the Lower Salford line. The officers wounded in the battle were brought to a farmhouse on the Forty-foot road, about a mile southwest of the meeting-house. Washington ordered that General Nash should be interred at 10 o'clock in the above-named burying-place. Over the body of General Francis Nash has been placed a white marble monument about twelve feet high, erected in 1844 by the citizens of Germantown and Norristown. He was a resident of Virginia, being also a descendant of the Mennonite Church. The city of Nashville, Tennessee, is named after him.

This congregation was generally attended by ministers from neighboring congregations in turn. Jacob Kulp, of Hatfield, Montgomery County, Pa., had charge of it as Bishop in serving communion and baptism.*

---

* As far as the title to the above is concerned I am indebted to John C. Boorse, Esq., of Kulpsville, Montgomery County, Pa.

Lansdale, Montgomery County, Pa.

THE Mennonite meeting-house above Lansdale, or commonly called Plain, in Hatfield Township, Montgomery County, Pa., is evidently a very old place. My informant says a deed cannot be found, therefore dates cannot be given, but it is evident that a congregation was organized and a meeting-house built before the Revolutionary War, because David Ruth and Jacob Oberholzer, ministers in the first house, are mentioned in the Christian Funk controversy in the year 1774, of the Plain congre gation. The second meeting-house was built in 1815. The following ministers served during the time of the second house: John Krupp, Jacob Kulp and Joseph Cassel. The third was built in 1867; ministers of which were Jacob C. Loux and Henry Godshalk.

Bishop Jacob Kulp, of Hatfield, Montgomery County, Pa., was born in 1799; was ordained a minister in 1838; four years afterwards he was elected a Bishop, in which capacity he served faithfully until he died, in 1875, in his seventy-sixth year. His father was Dilman Kolb, who was married to Barbara Cassel, daughter of Hupert Cassel, in 1779. Johannes Wireman is mentioned as a deacon in the year 1804.

Bartolet's Mennonite Meeting-house

IN

Frederick Township, Montgomery County, Pa.

BARTOLET's old burying-ground existed about a hundred years or more prior to the building of the meeting-house; the oldest stone with an inscription is 1766. It had been in existence many years prior to 1766. Of those who sleep here, the stones give us the family names of Bertolet, Bertolette (two distinct families), Bliem, De Nice, Dotterer, Frey, Godshalk, Grubb, Hummel, Hunsberger, Nyce, Shoemaker, Smoll, Weidman, Zoller, Schmidt, Schlick. Many of the first or oldest graves have no inscription; among them are the Esterlines, Hahn, Grode, Smith, etc. A colored family of former times, also a number of slaves, are buried here. Their names are not known. Here also sleep the Lutheran, Reformed, Mennonite, Dunkard, Moravian, Methodist, Friend and Amish. In 1829 Daniel Bartolet and Jonathan Nyce had this graveyard enclosed with a stone wall, mostly at their own expense.

Bartolet's Mennonite meeting-house was built in 1846 on the ground purchased of Daniel and Catharine Bertolet. The deed is dated April 1st, 1847; the consideration money was twenty-five dollars. The ground comprises half an acre, and adjoins the old burying-ground above

described.   It was dedicated on Whitsuntide, 1847.
Pastor Henry S. Bassler of the Reformed Church
preached on this occasion; also John Oberholzer and
Abraham Hunsicker.   In the Fall of 1847 the following-
named persons joined the congregation: Samuel Bertolet
and Elizabeth his wife, Abraham Hunsberger and Catha
rine his wife, John Stauffer and Ann his wife, and Elizabeth Hunsberger.

The deed was given to Abraham Hunsberger, Henry
Bertolet and John Hunsberger, in trust and for the use
of a meeting-house for the Society of Mennonites, and for
the use of the inhabitants who are burying in the burying-ground adjoining said tract known as Bartolet's burying-ground, that all of them can at all times get their
ministers whereto said persons may belong, and shall
have a right in the house to hold their funeral services.
Further it says: In trust and for the society or congregation of Mennonites, and the free use or right of all the
inhabitants in the neighborhood to take the meeting-
house in use when there is a funeral at said graveyard, to
have the house for holding their funeral services undisturbed at all times, and their successors.

On April 3d, 1874, there was purchased of Michael S.
and Elizabeth Wagner $39\frac{95}{100}$ perches adjoining the old
burying-ground, for the use of a free burying-ground at
a cost of fifty dollars, which was all paid by Miss Esther
Bertolette, of Pottstown, Pa., with the understanding that
it should be free without distinction.

In the Summer of 1848 the first Sabbath-school in this
section of the county was opened in this house

GEORGE S. NYCE, OF FREDERICK.

April 12th, 1886.

Gottshall's, or Schwenksville.

By William S. Gottshall.

THIS congregation, sometimes called Schwenksville, received its name from its present Bishop, Moses Gottshall. The origin of this congregation and its present location was brought about in the following manner. Previous to 1818 there was preaching by different ministers of the Mennonite Church in a school-house which stood in the graveyard at (now) Keely's Church, there being no church there at that time. On one cold Sunday morning, when Heinrich Hunsicker came to preach, the chimney was stuffed with wet flax and tow, so that no fire could be made. The Mennonites, not wishing to make any disturbance, immediately left and made arrangements to build a meeting-house of their own. Gottshall Gottshall offered them land about a mile and a half south west from where Andrew Ziegler also offered them some land; when a vote was taken the majority were for Ziegler's, where, in 1818, a piece of ground, containing one acre and seven perches, was bought for the consideration of one dollar, in order to make legal title. The trustees, who had previously been elected, were Henry Ziegler, William Gottshall, Samuel Pannebacker, Jr., John Holdeman, John Bingaman, John Keelor, Jr., and John Herstein. A stone meeting-house was erected thereon the

(234)

same year. Services were held every four weeks by different ministers of the Mennonite Church, and for several years the deacon, William Gottshall, had to go to the Conference to procure ministers to preach at stated times, until the year 1847, when Moses Gottshall was chosen as their minister, and three years later he was ordained a Bishop. The congregation was under the jurisdiction of the Skippack District. In 1851 the present brick meeting-house was erected, and in 1859 thirty-three perches of land on the southwest side were exchanged for thirty-three perches on the northeast side with John Steiner. In 1884 an addition was made to the grave-yard.

Moses Godshall was the first minister and Bishop. Other ministers were S. H. Longaker, N. B. Grubb and William S. Gottshall.*

---

* After the above was written, William S. Godshall was ordained a Bishop, on the 25th day of November, 1886.—AUTHOR.

Herstein's.

THIS little place is located in Limerick Township, Montgomery County, about four miles west from Schwenksville. Tradition has it that Johannes Herrstein, a Mennonite, then living in that locality, took great interest in the Mennonite Church; accordingly he prepared himself with money and went over to Europe and made arrangements to have Jacob Denner's sermons printed and bound for the use of his Mennonite brethren in America. The books were printed at " Frankenthal am Rhein," in the year 1792, as the title page states, at the expense of " Johannes Herrstein und Johannes Schmutz." It is said he brought to America about five hundred copies, which were sold in Montgomery, Bucks and Lancaster Counties.

In 1821 the Mennonites bought seventy-four perches of land from Jacob Shoemaker, for the consideration of one dollar, for the purpose of erecting a school and meeting-house, and also a burying-place; many of the oldest Mennonites in that vicinity lie buried there. A congregation has been organized there with a membership of about forty, but no regular minister was ever stationed there. William Godshall was ordained. deacon, but afterwards united with the Mennonites at Schwenksville, and services were held only occasionally during the summer. The ministers who preached there from time to time were Heinrich Hunsicker, Jacob Godshall, Christian Halteman, John Minnich, Gebhard, High, Latshaw, Rittenhouse and Moses Godshall. The Mennonites have a permanent right here, which is kept up only for funerals and occasional services during the summer.

Rockhill, or Gehman's.

I HAVE found the first deed given by Samuel Bechtel and wife to George Derstine and Abraham Gehman, trustees, dated June 2d, 1773, for one-fourth of an acre of ground in Rockhill Township, Bucks County, for *three pounds*, for the purpose of erecting a meeting-house and a burying-place. The first house was built in 1773, and was used as a meeting-house by the Mennonites for sixty-five years. It was built of logs and plank, with light weather-boarding. In 1838 it was taken down and a large stone house was built, 40 by 52½ feet, one story, with slate roof, and seating capacity for three hundred people. The building committee appointed by the congregation were Jacob Derstine, Samuel Horning and John Moyer. Since that time three or four additions of land have been made, so that the whole tract now contains upwards of three acres of ground. In 1875 Brother Samuel Landis died. His will provided that $1,500 should go to this congregation as a fund and be invested, the interest thereof should be used to pay for the building of a house for a sexton, to have care of the meeting-house, and after that is paid for, the trustees can use it as they see proper. In 1883 Samuel K. Detweiler offered a small tract of land as a present to the congregation, providing they would build a house thereon, and some of the brethren offered to donate cash sufficient to pay for it, providing the house would be built now. So the offer was accepted and at once a house was built, at a cost of about $1,500, including out-buildings and all.

As regards ministers, the above-named Samuel Bechtel was a minister. When and where he was ordained I could not learn ; he was ordained before the house was built.* He died January 15th, 1802, age not given on his tombstone. Samuel Gehman, Bechtel's grandson, and grandfather of Abel Horning, was ordained to the ministry in 1798, and was a faithful watchman on the walls of Zion for forty-seven years, and died September 24th, 1845, aged 78 years 4 months and 15 days. He was assisted by George Derstine, who served in the ministry about twenty-five years, and died in 1837, aged 66 years 5 months and 8 days. After him Jacob Detweiler was ordained in 1840. He served about thirty-nine years, and died July 13th, 1879, aged 84 years 5 months and 4 days. Abraham Fretz was ordained to the ministry in 1843. He served faithfully through trials and afflictions about thirty-two years, and died, April 23d, 1875, aged 81 years 11 months and 4 days. John Allebach was chosen as deacon; after serving two years he was ordained to the ministry, in which capacity he has served about forty years. He is now in his eighty-first year, and is still attending the meetings regularly. Abel Horning was ordained to the ministry in 1862 and has already served about twenty-four years; he is now in

---

* He may have been ordained in Franconia, because Franconia meeting-house was called Bechtel's, and a Bechtel is also mentioned in the Funk controversy in 1777.—AUTHOR,

his sixty-first year. Samuel D. Detweiler was ordained to the ministry in 1876; is now forty-five years old.

The deacons were as follows: First, Michael Derstine,* John Detweiler, John Allebach, Samuel Souder, John F. Detweiler, and at present (August, 1886), Joseph B. Allebach.

---

* Michael Derstine is mentioned as a minister in 1765, in the Franconia Record.

Perkasie, or Hilltown.

THE first Mennonite meeting-house in Perkasie was built of log in 1753, about the size of one of our old school-houses, on a small lot taken out of Henry Funk's farm, with a graveyard 44 feet square. Whether it was bought or donated is not known, as there is no deed. The above-named house stood seventy years, and was torn down and a new one built in 1823, on a lot adjoining the above-mentioned lot, about 75 feet from where the old log house stood. This house stood sixty-nine years. In the year 1882 this second house was torn down and a new one built on the same spot where the old or second house stood. The membership now is about three hundred. A partition deed was made in the year 1735 to John Penn, Thomas Penn, Richard Penn and Magdalena Freame, daughter of William Penn, of the Manor of Perkasie, and a tract adjoining the Pro prietory's Manor, making in all ten thousand acres. About the year 1742 Germans from the Province of Philadelphia commenced to buy these lands.

Amongst the first Mennonite settlers who settled in the vicinity when the first meeting-house was built was Henry Funk and Christian Lederach, in 1747; John Funk, in 1748; Andrew Godshall, in 1752; Valentine Kratz, in 1748, and Hoopert Cassel, in 1758. Among the rest who settled about the same time, or soon after, were Moyers, High, Hunsberger, Kulp, Rickert, etc.

About the first ministers (I am informed) was a Wismer and a Moyer, followed by Jacob Hunsicker and Jacob Hunsberger

The ministers now living (March, 1886) are Isaac Overholt,* Abraham F. Moyer, Henry B. Moyer and Henry Rosenberger.

---

* Since the above was written the above-named Isaac Overholzer departed this life on the 6th of November, 1887, aged 72 years 9 months and 18 days. He was born in Bedminister Township, Bucks County, Pa., on the 9th of February, 1815, moved to Hilltown Township and was ordained to the ministry about 1847, and a short time after to the office of Bishop, in what is now called the Blooming Glen Meeting (Perkasie), and served the Church in the ministerial office about forty years.—AUTHOR.

16

Deep Run Meeting-house.

THE Mennonite congregation of Bedminster Township is one of the oldest of that denomination in Bucks County, Pa. The meeting-house stands in the southeast corner of the Township, on the north side of a branch of Deep Run, on a knoll facing the east. The land was given by William Allen, together with a farm of fifty acres adjoining, and the deed bears date the 24th of March, 1746. It was executed in trust to Abraham Swartz, Hans Friedt, Samuel Kolbe and Marcus Overholtzer, the Bishops and deacons of the Church at that time. About the same time Mr. Allen presented them with a silver cup, still used by the congregation for sacramental purposes. The above-named Abraham Swartz emigrated from Germany to Pennsylvania.* He was a Bishop, and during the time of his ministry he lost his eyesight and became perfectly blind, but he still continued to preach. He would get some one to read a portion of Scripture, from which he would select his text for the occasion. His faithfulness in the fulfilment of his ministerial duties under this difficulty is indeed commendable. The first house of worship erected was built of logs, probably in the year the land was given,

---

* The probability is that he was ordained before he came to this country, as already in 1746 he is mentioned as the first Bishop on the list to whom the deed for the ground for the meeting-house was given.—AUTHOR.

which was used by the congregation until the year 1766, when it was replaced by a stone house, 35 by 58 feet. The old log house stood about fifty yards from the present one; it was used many years as a school-house, and

ENLARGED MEETING-HOUSE.
(Second House.)

taken down in 1842. The stone house was rebuilt or repaired in 1794, at which time the accommodations for worship were also increased by taking down a division wall, which separated a portion of the building previously used as a dwelling from the audience room. This whole building was torn down in 1872 and a modern structure erected in its place.

The next preacher was Jacob Gross, who also came

from Germany, and was a noted and greatly esteemed preacher. He was a Bishop, and took a prominent part in the efforts which were made to settle the difficulties existing between the Church in Franconia and Christel Funk and his adherents. He is frequently mentioned in this connection by Funk, in his little book, as late as the years 1806 and 1807. Next in order followed Abraham Wismer, Abraham Overholt and Daniel Landis; the latter was a mason by trade and a good preacher; he was still living in the early part of the present century. Then followed Christian Gross and Abraham Kulp, who were ordained at the same time. The next were Abraham Myers, Isaac Moyer, Samuel Godshall and John Gross.

Mr. Samuel Nash says: " The deacons since my recollection were my grandfather, Henry Moyer, who died in 1832, in the eighty-fourth year of his age; my grandfather, Joseph Nash, who died in 1830, in the seventy-ninth year of his age; Abraham Fretz, Abraham Wismer, Samuel Shelly, Jacob Overholzer and Abraham Moyer."

Shelly was ordained in Milford and afterward removed to Bedminster.

The following is a copy of a letter written by the above-named Bishop, Jacob Gross, to his congregation a short time previous to his death ·

" My last sincere words to the Church, whom I must now leave, among whom I, as an unworthy servant, preached the word, especially the churches at Deep Run, Perkasie and New Britain. Brethren and sisters and others: I embrace you in the arms of love, precious, blood-bought souls; I regret that I must leave you under the circumstances of which the Lord spake; and because iniquity shall abound, the love of many shall wax cold, but he that shall endure to the end shall be saved, Matt. 24: 12. O love! O indispensable love to God and His Word, how little room findest thou in the human heart towards Thee and Thy Word, towards friend and foe! O love of the world! O lust of the eye, and lust of the flesh! O pride of life, how high hast thou risen up! But farewell! This is my last admoni tion to you, written with my dying hand, therefore, re pent; come diligently to the public meeting and hear the Word of God; love your teachers and ministers, so shall both they and you be strengthened, and if not, the candlestick shall be taken away altogether. No more. Any brother who is able to read so that he may be understood by all, may read this before the Church, as it is of interest to all of them.

JACOB GROSS.

December 7th, 1810."

Abraham Godshall, father of Samuel Godshall, already mentioned in this article, has also been a prominent minister for many years. He was the author of a small work of about one hundred pages, entitled "A Descrip- tion of the New Creature, from its birth until grown up unto a perfect man, unto the measure of the stature of the *fullness* of CHRIST, with its *necessity*, ORIGIN, GROWTH, and final *glorious* and *happy* state, *through* JESUS CHRIST." This book was originally written in the German language and printed at Doylestown, in 1838, by Joseph Young; a German copy is in possession of the author of this work.

Afterwards it was translated by its author into Eng- lish. It bears date 1838, and was printed by William

Large, at Doylestown. He was a farmer by occupation, as he himself states in the preface of the book, but was, at a pretty early age, called to the ministry of the Gospel, and though not possessing the advantages even of a common school education, he was a zealous and effective laborer in the vineyard of the Lord, possessing a good command of language, an extensive knowledge of Scripture, and maintained sound and well-defined theological views. He also left, as a rich legacy to his children, numerous productions, both poetical and in prose, which have never been published.

By a clause in the Allen deed, it was provided that if at any time the Society should be without organization and not hold regular services for a period of five years, the land granted was to revert to the heirs of the donor, but if a minister would again be ordained, according to the creed of the Mennonites and officiated at the church, the title to the real estate was to reinvest in the Society. We believe continued services have been maintained there since the first house was built, in 1746.

On the pulpit is a German Bible, printed at Germantown, Pa., by Christopher Saur, in 1743, with heavy back and brass clasps, and beside it are two hymn books also in German, which bear the imprint of 1803.

Doylestown.

ABOUT a mile west of Doylestown is an old-fashioned stone Mennonite meeting-house, built many years ago, and among the ministers who have officiated there we find the names: Kephart, Jacob Kolb, Abraham Godshall, John Gross, Isaac Godshall, Jacob Hiestand and Isaac Rickert, and Samuel Gross, the present minister.

This is the old church edifice standing in middle Bucks County. In the graveyard connected with this church lies buried David Evans, the first and only Universalist minister in Bucks County. He had gathered a small congregation of that denomination in New Britain Township, to which he preached until his death, in 1824, in his eighty-sixth year.

Lexington.

In 1752 a lot of about one acre was bought of James McCalister, in the northwest corner of New Britain Township, Bucks County, Pennsylvania, on which a log meeting-house was erected. The lot was afterwards enlarged to between three and four acres. The first deed was made in trust to one Roar and Christian Swartz, of New Britain, and Henry Shooter and John Rosenberger, of Hatfield. When the log house was too small for the growing congregation, it was torn down and a stone one erected in its place. This was again enlarged in 1808, and in 1868 it was torn down again and a new house erected, 45 by 60 feet, built of stone. Services were held in the German language until 1887, when the congregation decided to hold English services in connection with the German. New Britain was one of the first townships of Bucks County in which the Mennonites settled.

The Lexington congregation is one of the oldest in the County. Pastor John Geil, son of Jacob Geil, who emigrated from Alsace, near the Rhine, at the age of eight years, and settled in Plumstead Township, Bucks County, was one of the ablest ministers of this congregation. He was called to the ministry in 1810 or 1811, and preached until 1852; he died in 1866, in his eighty-eighth year. The congregation is flourishing. Since it has been decided to hold English services there seems to be a greater interest manifested, and quite a number have presented themselves for church membership.

In 1796 David Ruth is mentioned as a minister and Bishop, and in 1784 Marks Fretz as deacon.

Historical Sketches of the Swamp Mennonite Church.

THE Swamp Mennonite Church, in Milford Township, Bucks County, Pa., was one of the earliest organized churches of this persuasion in our county. German Mennonites from the Palatinate were among the first settlers of this section of the county. Among the list of names of early settlers we find the names Clymer⁻or Clemmer, Shelly, Musselman, Brecht, Hiestand, Yoder and many others, whose descendants are still in part living in this section, and almost invariably belong to the Mennonite Church. In what year a church organization was formed cannot now be accurately ascertained. History has it, however, that as early as 1727 Mennonites held their first regular church meetings,* and we may infer from this that the organization of a congregation was effected about that time. The first meeting-house is reported to have been erected in the year 1735, on land now owned by Christian Musselman. If this date is correct (of which I have my doubts) the first Mennonite church building was erected on the land of William Allen, an English landholder, who was not a member of the Mennonite Church.

In the year 1743 Jacob Musselman came over from Germany and purchased a tract of land from William

---

* Velty Clemmer is mentioned as a minister in Great Swamp in the year 1727.

Allen, to which tract the plot whereon this first church building was erected belonged. As this Jacob Mussel-man was either a Mennonite preacher when he emi-grated, or was soon after called to that office, it is more than probable that the first meeting-house was erected on his land, and hence not before the year 1743. This, however, is mere conjecture, as William Allen may, for some cause, have given his Mennonite friends the privilege to build on his land before his disposal of it.

It appears that no burial ground was even connected with this first church building, and that the dead were buried at this early date in the graveyard now belong-ing to the East Swamp Church, about a mile to the east from where the first church building stood.

About the year 1771 another church building was erected on the site where the present East Swamp Church stands, upon a lot of ninety-one perches of land, con-veyed for this purpose by Ulrich Drissel, Abraham Taylor and John Ledrach, by an indenture bearing date June 15th, 1771, to Valentine Clemmer, Peter Saeger, Christian Bieler and Jacob Clemmer, "trustees of the religious society or congregation of Mennonites in the great swamp." Other tracts were added to this original lot by indentures made August 17th, 1818; April 3d, 1848; April 13th, 1850, and February 18th, 1867. After the completion of this new house of worship, services were held in both meeting-houses alternately. After some time the new house of worship was destroyed by fire; in what year this occurred cannot now be ascer-tained. A substantial log house was then erected in its stead, which served the double purpose of school-house and meeting-house at the same time, which, no doubt, had been the case with the former building, as well as with most of the church buildings of that early day— one portion being partitioned off for school purposes in such a manner that the whole could be thrown open for church purposes if needed. In later years no school was held in this building, but it was used as a meeting-house until 1850, when a large and substantial brick church was erected on its site.

By an indenture made the 18th day of January, 1790, Michael Musselman, son of the above named Jacob Musselman, and owner of the land formerly belonging to his father, and who, like his father, was a minister in this congregation, with Margaret his wife, conveyed to Peter Zetty, Christian Hunsberger and Michael Shelly, "now the elders or overseers of the Mennonite congretion," a tract of eighty perches of land "for a church and graveyard." To this lot, the site of the present West Swamp Church, the original meeting-house was removed, and services held therein as before until 1819, when a more commodious stone building was erected, which also served the double purpose of meeting and school-house until 1839, when a separate school-house was built and the church building was used for church purposes only. A new and much larger church was erected in 1873, in order to better accommodate the increased number of worshipers and the demands of the Sunday-school.

Who the first ministers of this congregation were is not now fully known. Tradition informs us, however, that Felty (Valentine) Clemmer, who came to this country in 1717, and who was a minister and Bishop of the Mennonite Church prior to his coming over, min-

istered in this congregation.   Whether he was a resident
minister here, or whether he merely came here to preach
and administer the Sacrament, the writer does not know;
at all events, it seems certain that if he was not *the* first
minister, which, however, it seems probable he was, he
must have been among the first and was the first to have
the oversight of this flock and to administer baptism and
serve communion for them.   The above Jacob Musselman was also one of the most early ministers.   Among
those that followed were his son, Michael, and grandson,
Samuel, who was called to the ministry and died September, 1847, at the advanced age of eighty-seven years.
The other ministers serving this flock from time to time,
partly simultaneously, were Jacob Nold, Christian Bliem,
Christian Zetty, Jacob Hiestand, John H. Oberholzer,
William N. Shelly, Levi O. Shimmel and Andrew B.
Shelly, the present pastor.

John H. Oberholzer was elected to the ministry in
1842. He being a man of more than ordinary intelligence and of a progressive mind, his ideas were in advance of some of his fellow-ministers at the time; his
more liberal views in regard to dress, and his advocating
a more systematic church organization, gave cause to a
schism, not only in this congregation, but throughout
the congregations connected with the " Franconia Con
ference," to which this congregation belonged.   Ober
holzer, with a number of other ministers and deacons
siding with him, were, in October, 1847, declared sus-
pended from Conference. This gave rise to the organization of the so-called " New School Mennonite Conference " by the following: John Hunsicker, Israel
Beidler, John H. Oberholzer, Abraham Hunsicker and

Christian Clemmer, Bishop; William Landis, Joseph Schantz, William Shelly, Moses Gottshall and Henry G. Johnson, ministers; and John Detweiler, William Gottshall, Henry B. Shelly, Daniel Geisinger, Samuel Moyer, Peter Young, John Latshaw, Samuel Kaufman, John Bauman, Jacob Benner, Nathan Pennypacker, David Taylor and Abraham Grater, deacons. This Conference was organized October 28th, 1847. The Swamp Church, of which Oberholzer was the principal minister at the time, adhered to him and connected itself with the new Conference. A small portion of the members, however, who were dissatisfied with Oberholzer, left the church, and in 1847, before Oberholzer's suspension from Conference and the organization of the new Conference, erected a church building and organized a church of their own. This church remained true to the old Conference, and forms the "Old Mennonite Swamp Congregation" of the present day. The persons regularly ministering to this church, up to the present date, were: Jacob Beidler, now deceased, and his son, John A. Beidler, the present pastor, together with Abraham Young.

The old churches constituted one and the same congregation, holding its services alternately in both church buildings for a long while. In the course of time, however, the eastern and western divisions, as they were designated, became more and more separated, until some years ago separate church organizations were formed, and the one was called the East Swamp and the other the West Swamp Mennonite Church. They, together with the Flatland Church in Richland, constituted the Swamp charge of the same ministers, to which the Saucon

Church, near Coopersburg, was later added. The Flatland Church is a comparatively new one, it having been
organized in 1837 by members formerly belonging either
to the Springfield, or the Swamp churches. The membership is still very limited, and services are held there
regularly every two weeks in the afternoon by the pastor
of the Swamp charge.

The Swamp churches were among the first to intro-
duce the Sunday-school work. J. H. Oberholzer, at
an early date of his ministry, had general catechetical
instructions for the young people introduced. These
meetings were attended by the young people generally
for a number of years, and were blessed with a visible
good effect to many of those who attended them. Later,
however, these catechetical meetings were for some cause
discontinued, and for several years no special meetings
for the young were held, until in the Spring of 1857 a
Sunday-school was organized in the West Swamp Church,
with A. B. Shelly as Superintendent. About the same
time, or soon after, a Sunday-school was also established
in the Eastern Church. These were the first Mennonite
Sunday-schools in existence; they have both been maintained up to the present day. At first they were only
held during the Summer months, but for a number of
years they have now been kept open the year round.
They are both in a good and flourishing condition, the
West Swamp school under the superintendency of U. S.
Stauffer, and the East Swamp of A. S. Shelly.

Services have been held in the West Swamp Church
every Sunday since the Spring of 1872. The East
Swamp Church has services every other Sunday. The
West Swamp congregation numbers upwards of two

hundred, the East Swamp about one hundred, and the Flatland Church about twenty-five communicant members. A. B. Shelley, who was called to the ministry in 1864, is at present the principal minister of these churches. Father Oberholzer, now almost eighty years old, also assists in ministering to these flocks.

MILFORD SQUARE, April 9th, 1887.

Springfield and Saucon.

THE present Mennonite meeting-house in Springfield Township, Bucks County, was built about sixty years ago, or about the year 1826, and is the second house; but in what year the first house was built my informant could not tell, but might have been about the year 1775, because on September 10th, 1753, George Schimmel, one of the first Mennonites in Springfield, came to Pennsylvania and settled there; others of the same denomination soon followed, so that it is presumable that the first meeting-house might have been built about the year 1775, probably earlier. Previous to the building of the first meeting-house they worshiped in private houses.

According to accounts extant it appears that Saucon is the oldest place, and an organization was effected and a meeting-house was built previous to that in Springfield, but the two congregations were united at that time. The first members in Saucon were Moyer, Gehman, Funk, Schleifer, etc. The names of the ministers were Jacob Moyer, Samuel Moyer, Michael Landis, Valentine Young and William Landis. The names of the ministers in Springfield were Peter Moyer, Jacob Gehman, Peter Moyer, Jr., Jacob Moyer, Abraham Geissinger; the latter was ordained in 1836.

In 1847 a separation took place. The minister of the New School Mennonites in Saucon was Samuel Moyer.

(256)

In Springfield, John Geissinger was ordained in 1849 and Samuel Moyer in 1851. Their deacons were John Schimmel, Elam Schimmel and Peter Moyer. Jacob Moyer and Abraham Geissinger remained with the Old School Mennonites as their ministers. The deacons in Springfield were: T. Schleifer, Abraham Oberholzer, Daniel Geissinger and Jacob Kolb.

The New School Mennonite congregation at present counts about eighty members. Its present pastor is Jacob S. Moyer; deacon, Peter A. Moyer. The Old School counts about twenty members and holds meetings every two weeks, but has no stated minister. In Saucon there are only a few families of the Old School Mennonites remaining; they hold service only occasionally. Those few generally come over to Springfield meeting.

Deep Run.

A Brief Sketch of the Incorporated Mennonite Church at Deep Run (New School), in Bedminster, Bucks County, Pa.

THE division of 1847, which affected a number of congregations in Eastern Pennsylvania, also affected the time honored and flourishing Deep Run congregation.

Members of more progressive views and siding with the progressive party, of which John H. Oberholzer, pastor of the Swamp congregation at that time, was a leading member, as already shown in the article of the Swamp congregation, then met and framed a constitution as a basis of a new organization, and on May 15th, 1848, applied to the court of Bucks County for a charter of incorporation, which was granted on April 25th, 1849, and recorded in Book No. 10, p. 465, May 4th, 1849.

On June 16th, 1849, the members of the new corporation met at the house of Isaac Fretz, in Tinicum Township, Bucks County, and agreed to build a new meeting-house, and to purchase a lot of ground near the old meeting-house for that purpose. A lot of ground was accordingly bought, and a substantial brick meeting-house was built the same year, and services were held weekly by ministers from other churches of the same organization until 1883, when Allen M. Fretz was or-

(258)

dained as their pastor. The congregation now has a membership of about one hundred and fifty, and also a flourishing Sunday-school, open nine months in the year. This congregation is also connected with the so-called General Conference of Mennonites of North America.

This congregation also takes an active part in the Mission cause, both home and foreign.

Hereford.

As early as 1728 it is known that two brothers by the name of Bechtel, "both Mennonites," were among the settlers of Hereford Township, now part of Washington. These with others settled in Montgomery and Lehigh Counties, and were on very friendly terms with Father Theodore Schneider, the Jesuit Missionary. They cooperated with him in building the first Catholic Church in 1743, and as a compensation to them for their assistance, an acre of land was granted to the Mennonites out of the tract belonging to his society (Father Schneider's). The deed of this tract bears date of 1755, but it is not known how soon after that the low wooden meeting-house was built which still stands; but in 1790 an addition was built to it, which was used as a school-room. To this tract, two additional tracts have been bought, so that it now contains three acres.

It is traditionally reported that all that section of country where the Hereford meeting-house stands formerly belonged to a Mennonite, who was, for some cause, expelled from the congregation. He then threatened to be revenged, and vowed he would plant them a thorn bush. He then sold the land to Theodore Schneider, the Jesuit, and on that very land the Catholic church in Hereford was built. It is also asserted that a small frame house was there prior to the present old house. The congregation obtained from Schneider the lot mentioned above and got the title as above mentioned, dated 1755. The above may be substantiated by the fact that Daniel Longenaker and Jacob Beghtly were the ministers there as early as 1727, and attended a conference and signed their proceedings.

It is claimed that a minister by the name of Bechtel has always been connected with this congregation. The present ministers (August, 1887) are John B. Bechtel, Andrew Mack and John M. Esht.

Boyertown.

THE Boyertown congregation was from the commencement of its organization and is yet a branch of the Hereford congregation. About the year 1730 a number of Mennonites settled in Colebrookdale Township, Berks County, Pennsylvania, in the vicinity of the present Boyertown, about six miles west of Hereford.

In the year 1790 a Mennonite named Heinrich Stauffer gave one acre of ground for a burying-ground and to build a school-house thereon for school purposes, and also for divine worship; later, when the house was no longer needed for a school-house and was too small for a meeting-house, the congregation built a new brick meeting-house in the year 1819, in which service was held once in four weeks until the year 1876, when the house was torn down again for the purpose of building a new one, which was, however, through unforeseen circumstances, delayed until about the year 1882 or '83, when the house was built.

The ministers in Hereford also had charge of the Boyertown congregation. Their names as far as known were George B. Bechtel, Bishop, who died in 1754; afterwards his son Johannes Bechtel, also a Bishop, who died in 1795; then Johannes Boyer, also a Bishop, afterward moved to "Harmonie" in the year 1816; then Abraham Bechtel, who died in 1815, and Heinrich Funk,

(262)

who died in 1826; then Johannes C. Bechtel, Bishop, who died in 1843; then Johannes Gehman, who died in 1884.

The ministers now living (February, 1888,) are Johannes B. Bechtel, Andrew Mack, Bishop, and Johannes Esht.

I also find that the following-named ministers were present at a Conference held in 1727, which was, as far as known, the first Mennonite Conference held in America:

Great Swamp—Velte Clemer.

Manatant—Daniel Langenecker and Jacob Beghtly.
—Author.

Mennonite Congregation in Upper Milford, Lehigh County.

A Short Historical Sketch.

BY SAMUEL STAUFFER.

THE first Mennonite congregation in Upper Milford, Lehigh County, was founded and organized as near as can be ascertained between the years 1735 and 1760. The founders of this congregation were: Ulrich Basler, Heinrich Schleifer, Johannes Schwartz, Conrad Stamm, David Jansen, Benjamin Meyer, Abraham Funk, Heinrich Funk, Johannes Mayer, Samuel Mayer, Conrad Mayer, Michael Mayer, Johannes Gehman, George Weisz, Kilian Weisz, Rudolph Weisz, Jacob Weisz, Jacob Hiestand, Abraham Hiestand, Daniel Greber and others.

At what time the first meeting-house was erected is not definitely known. The land on which the first meeting-house was built, together with the graveyard, included one-half acre, which was cut out of a one hundred and four acre tract of land, which, according to records yet extant, and dated October 3d, 1740, was sold to Heinrich Noll. He afterwards conveyed said tract to Heinrich Schleifer, November 16th, 1745, who afterwards conveyed to Johannes Schantz and Benjamin Mayer in trust for the congregation, the above-mentioned half acre, dated February 10th, 1772. Later the congregation bought three small tracts of ground in addition to the above, so that the whole lot now contains two and one-half acres of ground. It is said that the above-mentioned tract of ground had been used for a burying-ground many years previous.

It is asserted that the first meeting-house was a log house and was used for church and school purposes until 1816, when a new building was erected of stone, which was divided in two parts—one for worship and the other for school purposes. In the year 1843 the house was repaired, the walls built higher, new roof, floor, windows and pews added. Again, in the year 1876, the congregation agreed to build a new and more comfortable house, and built one of brick, at a cost of $7,000.

It is said that the Mennonite congregation in Upper Milford, Lehigh County, is one of the oldest Christian churches in that vicinity. It is not positively known who the first minister of this congregation was. It is traditionally reported that a man by the name of Hulzhauser was the first minister of this congregation. The first one positively known to have been a minister of this congregation was Hannes Gehman, who served for many years. He was born February 12th, 1741; died December 23d, 1806. After his death his son, John Gehman, born March 22d, 1771, was ordained to the ministry of this congregation and served thirty-five years; died July 31st, 1848. About the year 1828 John Schantz was ordained to the ministry. He was born December 19th, 1774; he served about twenty-seven years, and died January 8th, 1855. In the year 1844 his son, Joseph Schantz, was ordained as a minister; he served about thirty-seven years and died June 23d, 1881, in his sixty-seventh year.

In October, 1849, William Gehman was called to the ministry, but on account of differences of opinion he, with a portion of the members, separated themselves from the congregation and formed a congregation of their own, and called themselves Evangelical Mennonites, afterward Mennonite Brethren in Christ.

In the year 1874 a young man by the name of Uriah S. Schelly was ordained as a minister of the Upper Milford congregation. He served several years faithfully and with energy, but on account of his health failing he was compelled to resign as their minister and withdrew from the ministry.

After the death of Joseph Schantz the congregation chose as their pastor Carl H. A. van der Smissen, who was born in the Kingdom of Prussia, Europe, who is at the present time (October, 1886) their minister and Bishop.

Philadelphia (New School).

THE first Mennonite Church of Philadelphia was organized with thirty members on the 27th day of October, 1865, in a public hall which stood where Liberty Council Hall now stands, on Germantown Avenue below Norris Street. In January, 1866, a chapel located on Diamond and Managan Streets, the property of the "Church of God," was bought, and the congregation fully organized, with Pastor Moses H. Godshall, of Schwenksville, as Bishop, and David Taylor (formerly Schneider), deacon.

In the Spring of 1868 a call was given Pastor Samuel Clemmer, then assistant minister in Herford District, who accepted and entered upon his duties on April 5th, 1868. The pastorate of Bro. Clemmer was crowned with success; but in less than two years the Lord saw fit to call him to his eternal home. Pastor A. B. Shelly, of Milford Square, then took charge of the congregation, either preaching himself or providing for their services.

In 1872 Pastor L. O. Schimmel was called from East Swamp Congregation, who accepted and entered upon his duties March 10th, 1872, and continued for one year. Albert E. Funk, having just returned from the Seminary at Wadsworth, Ohio, was then chosen and ordained into the ministry and continued until June, 1882, when he resigned. During the last year of the ministration of Pastor A. E. Funk a new brick church building was erected at a cost of $9,000.   Pastor N. B. Grubb, assistant minister in the Schwenksville District, was next called and entered upon his duties October 1st, 1882.   Under the ministration of Pastor N. B. Grubb the congregation became an independent bishopric and the pastor was accordingly ordained Bishop in May, 1884.   The church is at present (February, 1887) in a prosperous condition.

The address of the present pastor, N. B. Grubb, is 2136 Franklin Street, Philadelphia.

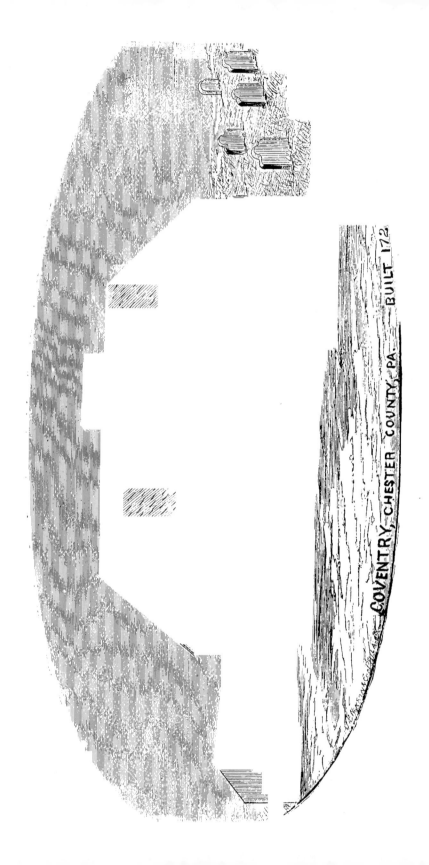

COVENTRY CHESTER COUNTY, PA. BUILT 172

Chester County, Pa.

THE Mennonite Church is one of the early churches of Chester County. Between the years 1725 and 1785 three Mennonite churches had been built on the Schuylkill, as appears from the name-list of the preachers, published at Amsterdam* in the last-named year. These must have been in Chester County, as the Montgomery County churches are included in other districts. Probably the most ancient of these is the one on the Schuylkill Road, in East Coventry Township, about three miles below Pottstown. The date 1728 on the wall shows that the building is now (1887) one hundred and fifty-nine years old. The building is one story high and is very small. It is accessible from the main road by a drive, on each side of which is a graveyard; the one on the south side of the drive was laid out but a few years ago, but the one on the north side contains graves one hundred and sixty years old.

The first Mennonite church in the vicinity of Phœnixville was located on the Ridge, near the residence of the Heckel family, now in Vincent Township. Abraham Haldeman was their minister and Bishop for many years;

---

* The Mennonite preachers in this section in 1785, as given in Amsterdam name-list before referred to, were Martin Bechtel, Johannes Longeneaker and Joseph Showalter.

he afterwards moved to Juniata County, Pa., where he died. Jacob Hunsberger and John Funk are the present ministers. The date of its erection I was not able to ascertain. S. W. Pennypacker, Esq., of Philadelphia, says there was another in the valley where Israel Beidler used to preach. In 1772 was erected the Mennonite meeting-house in Phœnixville. It was located on Main Street, near Nutt's Road, and since has been known successively as Buckwalter's and Morgan's school-house. It was designed by its founders both as a church and school building, and was used as such for many years. Among the original settlers of Phœnixville the Buck-walters were all of this faith. In 1794 they erected a meeting-house at the southwest corner of Main and Church Streets in Phœnixville, which is the oldest place of worship now standing in the township. The first preacher was Matthias Pennypacker, who for five years previous had charge of the congregation at Buck-walter's school-house. Upon his death he was succeeded respectively by John Buckwalter, Daniel Showalter, George Hellerman and Jacob Haldeman, Jesse Beidler, Joseph Haldeman, John Showalter and Israel Beidler.

The ministers at the present time are David Buck walter, Jacob Hunsberger and Jacob Funk; deacons, John Latshaw and Jonathan Kolb.

Cumberland County, Pa.

THE Mennonites commenced to settle in Cumberland County about 1800. Few, if any, lived in this county prior to this date. At first they were few in number; they held meetings in their dwelling-houses. Their first meeting-house was built about 1815, in the eastern section of the county. This house was torn down and a larger one built in 1876, called the Slate Hill Church, with about ninety communicant members.

Another meeting-house was built about three miles east of Carlisle, about the year 1838, with a small membership at the time in that neighborhood.

In the year 1885 a comfortable meeting-house was built in Churchtown, with a membership of about forty.

There is another congregation west of Boiling Springs with a small membership.

Another congregation is organized near Newville with a membership of about forty. Also a small organization seven miles south of Newville.

It is said that the first resident minister in Cumberland County was —— Hauser, the next —— Westhaser, then Henry Rupp, ordained about 1815, then Henry Martin, then George Rupp, a son of Henry, ordained about 1830, David Martin a few years later. Samuel Zimmerman was ordained about the year 1865 and Jacob Mumma in 1877; Samuel Hess in 1883, and Benjamin

(271)

Zimmerman in 1887. All the above-named ministers were members of the Slate Hill Church.

In the church east of Carlisle the first resident minister was John Erb; the next was Christian Herr, who died about the year 1863. His son, Jacob, was ordained soon after, who also preached in the Boiling Springs church. Henry Weaver was ordained in 1865, in Boiling Springs congregation.

The ministers at Newville are —— Burkard, —— Burkholder and Martin Wissler, who afterwards moved to Hanover, York County, in 1884.

SLATE HILL, Cumberland County, Pa.

December 13th, 1887.

Northampton County Mennonites.

A Brief Sketch of the Mennonite Meeting-house and Congregation, situated in Allen Township, Northampton County, Pa., on the Road leading from Bethlehem to Kreidersville.

THE last of the year 1798 had hardly passed into history before the question concerning the advisability and practicability confronted the brethren of the Mennonite congregation around Siegfried's Bridge and vicinity, to select a suitable location, somewhat central, to erect a meeting-house to the honor and glory of God. This location was secured from Thomas Horner, in Allen Township, Northampton County, Pa., consisting of half an acre of ground, for the sum of twenty dollars. The committee appointed to purchase said lot were Jacob Baer, Jacob Heston, John Ziegler and Samuel Landis. At a congregational meeting called by the brethren, the following brethren were elected as a building committee, viz.: John Ziegler and Samuel Funk. The lot was pur chased and the deed made in 1802, and the house was built the same year.

The congregation passed the following resolution as one of their first acts, viz.:

"The object shall be a meeting, or house of worship,

for all such who believe in and love our blessed Lord and Saviour Jesus Christ sincerely, and are willing to be guided and led by the precepts of the Gospel through those who are entrusted with the Divine mystery to proclaim the glad tidings of good news. And as the Apostle Peter did declare: Of a truth I perceive that God is no respector of persons; but among all nations, he that feareth Him and worketh righteousness, is accepted by Him. All those who belong unto Him must walk together in the unity of the Spirit and love. For without love or peace it is impossible to please God. . Without Divine aid it is impossible to build a house of God. Except the Lord build the house, they labor in vain who build it. But if it is erected in meekness and humility unto the Lord, then the Lord will hear in His time."

In the above spirit the brethren of those days went to work, in good faith and will, and secured their object. They had imbibed the good old German custom, from house to school, from school to church, from church to heaven. Consequently they also made provision for the young to be taught in the parochial school, which they incorporated in the deed of the property. Thus school had been taught in this building for a number of years, till the present system of common schools has superseded the old custom.

In reference to its membership there is no record extant, but from what can be gathered there must have been at one time a membership of from sixty to one hundred members. Of its organization there is nothing to be found, save what a few survivors still remember who had been members at this place. The following ministers officiated here from time to time; Valentine Young,

Samuel Musselman, Christian Bliem, John Bechtel, William Gehman, John Oberholzer, Christian Clemmer, David Henning, William Shelly, Henry Diehl, Jonas Musselman and Samuel Moyer, until about twenty years ago, when the number was reduced considerably. Still, there were some of the descendants who loved the old place, and through their influence preaching has been kept up by the following brethren: Samuel Landis, Lewis Taylor and Jonas Y. Schultz, who still have stated services every four weeks.

In August, 1884, steps were taken to raise funds to defray the expense of having the meeting-house and graveyard thoroughly renovated and put in good repair, which was accomplished, and of a truth it may be said that the latter place of worship by far exceeds the former. The graveyard must have been established at an early date. We find the date on tombstones of the year 1805, 1819, also of 1802; we find the names on the tombstones as follows: Bliem, Bechtel, Funk, Gerhard, Hiestand, Baer, Landes, Latshaw, Swartz, Young, Ziegler.*

June 13th, 1887.

---

* Since the above was put in type it has been discovered that several errors occurred on the part of my informant.

I have since learned that a plan or draft exists yet, which shows that a meeting-house was there prior to 1761. It is traditionally reported that their meetings had frequently been disturbed by Indians.

I also find that a deed was given for one acre of land dated March 10th, 1770, for the use of the Mennonites for all times. In 1829, part of the land was sold and the proceeds used to renovate the meeting-house and build a stone wall around the graveyard. The right to sell was granted upon the instance of a petition by Jacob Funk and others, dated February 6th, 1828, and the Act was passed January 29th, 1829, and signed by the Governor, J. A. Schulze,

Bangor.

Minister David Henning of the above place died July 2d, 1881, from injuries received about six weeks before. Deceased had been preaching in Bucks County, and on his way home was thrown against the seat of a car while getting on the train at Bethlehem; he was injured internally and had been confined to his bed most of the time since the accident. Father Henning was respected by the whole community, and his death, which was quiet and peaceful, was in keeping with his life. He was seventy-five years of age and had been engaged in preaching for the past twenty-five years; he was the last of the Mennonites in this vicinity. This section was originally settled by the Mennonites,· which fifty years ago was a large and flourishing congregation and owned the church property which recently passed into the hands of the Lutherans. Death and removals to other parts of the country gradually reduced the number of the Mennonites, until Father Henning was the sole remaining representative.

He was buried July 6th, 1881, in the old cemetery back of the church, which has been used by the Mennonites as a burying-ground for the past century. The funeral services were conducted by a Mennonite minister, William Gehman, of Bucks County, B. F. Apple, Lutheran and James M. Salmon, Presbyterian.*

---

* For the above information I am greatly indebted to W. R. Grubb, proprietor of the *Bangor Observer*.

York County, Pa.

STRICKLER'S and Witmer's.—Ministers, David Witmer and Joseph Forry; deacon, Michael Strickler.

Grallstown, Hershey's, Bare's, Codorus, Gerber's.—ministers, S. L. Roth, Jacob Hershey, Isaac Kauffman · deacon, Andrew Hershey.

Bare's, Hanover, Hanover, Hostetter's and Zimmerman's in Maryland.—Ministers, Samuel Moyer, Martin Whisler and Jacob Hostetter; deacons, Samuel Groff and Samuel Forry.

Meeting-Houses in Juniata County, Pa.

THE first meeting-house was built about the year 1800, of log, and in 1868 a new house was built of brick in its place, about one and a half mile west of Richfield.

The next house was built in 1819, called the Lost Creek meeting-house, and was rebuilt in 1869.

Another meeting-house was built a half mile north of Richfield, in Snyder County, in 1854, called Graybill's.

Another was built in 1867 called Lauver's, and another in 1872 called the Delaware meeting-house.

Thomas Graybill, Solomon Graybill and William Bergey, ministers; these three withdrew from the Old Mennonite Church in 1884.

Lebanon County, Pa.

GINGERICH'S Congregation.—Bishop, Isaac Gingerich; Cyrus Witmoyer, minister, and D. Westenberger, deacon.

Dohner's, Light's and Krall's Congregations.—Minister, Jacob Wenger; deacon, Christian Krall.

Snyder, Juniata and Perry Counties, ·Pa.

JOHN GRAYBILL moved from Lancaster County to Snyder County, one-half mile north of Richfield, about the year 1774. This was the first Mennonite family in this district. His son, John, was the first minister and Bishop, Abraham Witmer was the next Bishop. Michael Funk was a minister in Juniata County; Jacob Brubaker Bishop in Snyder County; Isaac Gilmer was a minister in Juniata County; Christian Aucker minister in Juniata County, and Christian Graybill minister in Snyder County; Henry Aueker minister in Perry County, and Henry Shelly a minister in Juniata County.

Bishop Abraham Haldeman moved from Chester County, Pa., to Juniata in the year 1842. The ministers in Juniata County are Jacob Graybill, Bishop, John Scherk, Samuel Gehman, William Graybill; Samuel Winny assistant Bishop in Snyder County, and William Aueker, a minister in Perry County, Jacob Kurtz minister in Juniata, and John Kurtz minister in Snyder County.

(278)

Dauphin County, Pa.

STRICKLER's and Schopp's.—Ministers, John Strickler and John Erb; deacon, Christian Mumma.

Stauffer's and Halifax.—Ministers, Benjamin Lehman, John Stauffer and John Ebersole; deacon, John Snyder.

Franklin County, Pa.

THE Chambersburg Congregation.—Bishop, John Hunsicker; ministers, Philip H. Parret, Peter Wadel, and Samuel D. Lehman, deacon.

Marion and Williamson Congregations. — Benjamin Lesher, Peter Wadel and Philip H. Parret, ministers, and Michael Hege, deacon.

Row Congregation.—Ministers, Peter Wadel, Philip H. Parret; deacon, Peter Horst.

Strasburg Congregation.—Ministers, John Hunsicker, John Lehman and Samuel D. Lehman; deacon, Samuel L. Horst.

Mennonite General Conference.

By A. B. SHELLY, Pastor of the Swamp Church.

THE Mennonite General Conference was organized May 28th, 1860, at West Point, Lee County, Iowa. During the days previous to the organization of the Conference a joint mission festival was held by the members of the West Point Church and those from Zion's Church in the vicinity. An invitation having been sent to brethren in Eastern Pennsylvania to come and assist in celebrating this festival, in accordance with this invitation the brethren J. H. Oberholzer and Enos Loux, both ministers of the " New School Mennonites," went to Iowa and assisted in the services of the festival. Besides these a number of brethren from Iowa were present.

At the close of the mission festival it was resolved to hold a conference of the brethren present on the following day, with the view of further discussing the subject of missions, a subject until then wholly neglected by the Mennonite churches of our land. Accordingly the brethren assembled on the day following (May 28th), and organized themselves into a Conference by electing J. H. Oberholzer, from Pennsylvania, President, and Christian Schowalter, from Iowa, Secretary. The Conference remained in session two days, the principal points discussed being to devise plans for bringing in closer union the different divisions of the Mennonite Church of our land, and to carry on mission work. A remarkable degree of unanimity prevailed and a number of resolutions pertaining to these subjects were adopted. These resolutions were, by a Conference held at Wadsworth, Ohio, May 20th to 23d, 1861, at which a greater number of congregations were represented, reconsidered, revised and as a basis for the " General Mennonite Conference of America," adopted. At this Conference it was decided, as soon as possible, to establish a Theological Institute for the education of teachers and ministers. Pastor Daniel Heges, from Summerfield, Illinois, was chosen to visit the churches throughout our land and solicit subscriptions towards the erection of said Institute.

The third meeting of the General Conference was held at Summerfield, Illinois, October 19th to 24th, 1863. At this session the plan for the Educational Institute, as it was then termed, was consummated, and the erection of a suitable building was, during the following year, begun at Wadsworth, Medina County, Ohio. This building was dedicated the 13th and 14th of October, 1866, and a school was soon after opened under the principalship of Pastor Christian Schowalter, from Lee County, Iowa. Later, Pastor C. J. van der Smissen was called from Friedrichstadt, Schleswig-Holstein, Germany, as Professor of Theology and Principal of the Institute, which for a number of years flourished, turning out a number of young men who occupied prominent and useful positions in the Church. Later, the number of students diminished, and lacking the necessary support, the Institute was discontinued and the building sold.

Meanwhile the General Conference, which holds its

sessions every three years, established missions among the Arapahoe and Cheyenne Indians at Darlington and Cantonment, Indian Territory. These missions are still carried on, and include two boarding and industrial schools for the young Indians, as well as Sunday-schools and religious services for the older ones. These missions cost the Church $4,000 to $5,000 annually.

Besides the Indian mission work, the Conference carries on the home mission work Besides a number of temporary workers, it now has one permanent Home Missionary elected for three years, whose mission is to visit the different churches belonging to said Conference, as well as such other places and congregations as the Home Mission Board may find proper. The Conference also carries on the publication work. It has a central publishing house at Berne, Indiana, and publishes the *Christliche Bundesbote*, a German weekly Church paper, and the *Kinderbote*, a monthly children's paper, printed partly in German and partly in English.

Since its organization churches have continually been added to this Conference, and it now numbers between thirty and forty different congregations, embracing a membership of nearly five thousand souls. The following is a list of the churches belonging to the General Conference

Pennsylvania.—Bartolett's, Bowmansville, Boyertown, Deep Run, Flatland, Hereford, Saucon, Schwenksville, Springfield, East Swamp, West Swamp, Philadelphia, Upper Milford.

Ohio.—Dalton, Wadsworth.

Indiana.—Berne.

Illinois.—Summerfield.

Missouri.—Bethel, Elkton.

Iowa.—Zion's Franklin, West Point.

Kansas.—Alexanderwohl, Bruderthal, Christian, Em mans, Canton, Gnadenberg, Halstead, Hoffnungsan, New-ton, Zion's.

Dakota.—Salems.

New York.—Clarence, Centre, Niagara.

Canada.—Stevensville.

MILFORD SQUARE, Bucks Co., Pa.
    February 11th, 1888.

The New School Mennonite Conference for the Eastern District of Pennsylvania was organized October 24th, 1847. It meets semi-annually, on first Tuesday in May and November, and is composed of the ministers, deacons and delegates representing the congregations in Bucks, Montgomery, Lehigh, Berks, Lancaster and Philadelphia Counties.—AUTHOR.

Mennonites in Lancaster County.

BANCROFT says : " The news spread that William Penn, the Quaker, had opened an asylum to the good and the oppressed of every nation, and humanity went through Europe gathering the children of misfortune." Out from their hiding-places in the forest depths and the mountain valleys which the sun scarce penetrated the Men nonites came, clad in their homespun dresses, their dialects unintelligible, their feet shod with wood, and set their faces toward that far-off land in which some strange prophecy had told them " the Mennonites would be pros- perous and happy."

About the beginning of the eighteenth century the Holland Mennonites, whom, we have seen, had become rich and powerful, determined to erect an organized sys- tem of charity to assist their brethren in distant and hostile communities. This determination culminated in the formation of " The Committee on Foreign Needs," and the step was made necessary by the utter helpless- ness of the many refugees on the one hand and by the shameful impositions of the Dutch and English trading firms who gave them passage, on the other. It was under the direct supervision of this Committee that the greater part of the Lancaster County Mennonite immi- gration was made. The story of this Committee and its

---

* For the following I am indebted to E. K. Martin, Esq., of Lancaster.

extensive labors in behalf of the early colonization of Pennsylvania is one of the interesting chapters of our memory which yet remains to be written.   It existed and pursued its valuable labors for eighty years, and only ceased when persecution relaxed its rigors and extortion was regulated by law.

The first authentic account we have of the Lancaster County settlement is that Hans Meylin, his son, Martin, and Hans Herr, John Rudolph Bundly, Martin Kendig, Jacob Miller, Martin Oberholtzer, Hans Funk, Michael Oberholtzer, Wendell Bowman and others, with their families, came as far as the Conestoga, in 1709, and there selected a tract of ten thousand acres to the north of Pequea Creek.   The warrant for this was recorded and the land surveyed to them October 23d, 1710.   A very quaint account of them says the sect came from a German Palatinate at the invitation of William Penn.   " The men wore long red caps on their .heads. The women had neither bonnets, hats nor caps, but merely a string passing around the head to keep the hair from the face.   The dress both of female and male was domestic, quite plain, made of coarse material after an old fashion of their own.   Soon after their arrival at Philadelphia they took a westerly course, in pursuit of a location where they could all live in one vicinity.   They selected a rich limestone country, beautifully adorned with sugar maple, hickory and black and white walnut, on the border of a delightful stream abounding in the finest trout.   Here they raised their humble cabins.   The water of the Pequea was clear, cold, transparent, and the grape-vines and clematis intertwining among the lofty branches of the majestic buttonwood formed a pleasant retreat from the noonbeams of a Summer sun."

Rupp, who wrote in 1844, though commonplace and sometimes tiresome, alone, of all the earlier chroniclers of their people, has put us under obligations for the scanty details he has preserved in an historical form of the early colony. " On the 23d of October the land was surveyed and divided among the Meylins, Herr, Kendig and others of the company. Having erected temporary shelters, some set about it and put up dwellings of more durableness. Martin Kendig erected one of hewed walnut logs on his tract, which withstood the storms and rain, the gnawings of the tooth of time, for more than one hundred and ten years, and might, had it not been removed in 1841, and its place taken up by one of more durable material, have withstood the corroding elements for generations to come. They now began to build houses and add new acquisitions of land to their first possessions. To depend upon their Indian neighbors for provision was useless. The Indians depended mainly upon game and fish. Of course, the supplies of provisions were scanty, and what they had they were under the necessity to transport from a distant settlement for some time, till the seeds sown in a fertile soil yielded some thirty, others sixty-fold. Fish and fowl were plenty in the wilds. The season of their arrival was favorable ; around them they saw crowned the tall hazel with rich festoons of luscious grapes. After they had been scarce fairly seated they thought of their old homes, their country and friends. They sighed for those whom they left for a season. They remembered them that were in bonds as bound with them and which suffered adversity, and ere the earth began to yield a return in kindly fruits to their labors consultations were held and

measures devised to send some one over to their ' Vaterland' to bring the residue of some •of their families—
also their kindred and brothers in a land of trouble and
oppression to their new home—into a land where peace
reigned and abundance of the comforts of life could not
fail. They had strong faith in the fruitfulness and
natural advantages of their choice of lands; they knew
these would prove to them and their children the home
of plenty. Their anticipations have never failed.

"A council of the whole society was called, at which
their venerable minister and pastor, Hans Herr, presided,
and after fraternal and free interchange of sentiment,
much consultation and serious reflection, lots, in con-
formity to the custom of the Mennonites, were cast to
decide who should return to Europe for the families left
behind and others. The lot fell upon Hans Herr, who
had left five sons, Christian, Emanuel, John, Abraham,
and one whose name we have not learned. This decision
was agreeable to his own mind, but to his friends and
charge it was unacceptable. To be separated from their
preacher could be borne with reluctance and heaviness
of heart only. They were all too ardently attached to
him to cheerfully acquiesce in this determination. Re-
luctantly they consented to his departure, after much
anxiety manifested on account of this unexpected call of
their pastor from them; their sorrows were alleviated by
a proposal made on the part of Martin Kendig that, if approved, he would take Hans Herr's place. This was
cordially assented to by all. Without unnecessary delay, Martin, the devoted friend of the colony, made ready,
went to Philadelphia, and there embarked for Europe.
After a prosperous voyage of five or six weeks he

reached the home of his friends, where he was received with Apostolic greetings and salutations of joy. Having spent some time in preliminary arrangements, he and a company of Swiss and some Germans bade a lasting adieu to their old homes and dissolved the tender ties of friendship with those whom they left. With this company, consisting of the residue of some of those in America, and of Peter Yordea, Jacob Miller, Hans Tschantz, Henry Funk, John Houser, John Bachman, Jacob Weber, Schlegel, Venerick, Guldin and others, he returned to their new home, where they were all cordially embraced by their fathers and friends. With this accession the settlement was considerably augmented, and now numbered about thirty families. Though they lived in the midst of the Mingo or Conestoga, Pequea and Shawanese Indians they were nevertheless safely seated, and had nothing to fear from the Indians. They mingled with them in fishing and hunting. The Indians were hospitable and respectful to the whites and exceedingly civil. The little colony improved their lands, planted orchards, erected dwellings and a meeting and school-house for the settlement, in which religious instruction on the Sabbath, and during the week knowledge of letters, reading and writing were given to those who assembled to receive information." Other and more numerous groups of colonists followed these pioneers in 1711, 1717, and a large settlement was made in the more northern parts of Lancaster County and within the limits of Lebanon in 1727. Very scanty, indeed, are the details of these early Mennonite movements, but scanty as they are, a little that may be regarded as authentic of the Lancaster County settlers has lately

struggled into life through the labors of Professor Scheffer, of Amsterdam, among the old records of the " Dutch
Committee on Foreign Needs."

"It is no wonder that, half a year later, the Committee
on Foreign Needs cherished few hopes concerning the
colony. [This evidently refers to the Germantown settlement.] They felt, however, for nine or ten families, who
had come to Rotterdam, according to information from
there under date of April 8th, 1709, from the neighborhood of Worms and Frankenthal, in order to emigrate,
and whom they earnestly sought to dissuade from making
the journey. They were, said the letter from Rotterdam,
altogether very poor men, who intended to seek a better
place of abode in Pennsylvania. Much has been expended
upon them hitherto freely, and these people bring with
them scarcely anything that is necessary in the way of
raiment and provisions, and much less the money that
must be spent for fare from here to England and from
there on the great journey, before they can settle in that
foreign land   The emigrants of April, 1709, aecom-
plished their object, though, as it appears, through the
assistance of others ; at all events, I think they are the
ones referred to by Jacob Tellner, a Netherlander Mennonite, dwelling at London, who wrote, August 6th, to
Amsterdam and Haarlem : ' Eight families went to Pennsylvania : the English Friends, who are called Quakers,
helped them liberally.'" Barclay, in his *Religious Societies of the Commonwealth*, says: " But not only did the
leaders of the early Society of Friends take great interest
in the Mennonites, but the Yearly Meeting of 1709 contributed fifty pounds (a very large sum at that time) for
the Mennonites of the Palatinate, who had fled from the

persecution of the Calvinists in Switzerland." This re
quired the agreement of the representatives of above four
hundred churches, and shows in a strong light the sympathy which existed among the early Friends for the
Mennonites.

There can be little doubt that this was the group of
Mennonites who appeared in the autumn of 1709, on the
banks of the Pequea. The dates correspond exactly, as
does also the number and the nationality of them.

The first Lancaster County settlement of Mennonites
seems to have been composed of persons who had fled
from the persecutions of the Swiss Cantons in the previous
century, and remained for some time settled at various
points on the Rhine, particularly in the Palatinate, the
Elector of which at that time seemed kindly disposed.

The group of 1717, however, who settled higher up on
the Conestoga, came fresh from a new Swiss outbreak.
Professor Scheffer says: "Fiercer than ever became the
persecution of the Mennonites in Switzerland: the prisons
of Bern were filled with the unfortunates, and the inhuman
treatment to which they were subjected caused many to
pine away and die. The rest feared from day to day
that the minority in the Council, which demanded their
trial, would soon become a majority. Through the intercession, however, of the States-General, whose aid the
Netherland Mennonites sought, not without success, some
results were effected. The Council of Bern finally determined to send the prisoners, well watched and guarded,
in order to transport them from there in an English ship
to Pennsylvania. On the 18th of March, 1710, the exiles
departed from Bern: on the 28th, with their vessel they
reached Manheim, and on the 6th of April, Nimeguen;

and when they touched Netherland soil their sufferings came to an end at last.   They were free, and their useless guards could return to Switzerland. . . .   Most of them went to the Palatinate to seek their kinsmen and friends, and before long a deputation of them came back here. On the first of May we find three of their preachers, Hans Burchi or Burghalter, Melchior Zaller and Benedict Brechbiehl, with Hans Rub and Peter Donens, in Amsterdam, where they gave a further account of their affairs with the Bern magistracy, and apparently consulted with the Committee as to whether they should establish themselves near the Palatinate brethren or on the land in the neighborhood of Campen and Gronigen, which was to be gradually purchased by the Committee on behalf of the fugitives.   The majority preferred a residence in the Pala tinate, but they soon found great difficulty in aecomplishing it.   The Palatinate community was generally poor, so that the brethren, with the best disposition, could be of little service in insuring the means of gaining a livelihood.   There was a scarcity of land and farmhouses, and there was much to be desired in the way of religious liberty, since they were subject entirely to the humors of the Elector, or, worse still, his officers.   For nearly seven years, often supported by the Netherland brethren, they waited and persevered, always hoping for better times.   Then, their numbers being continually increased, they finally determined upon other measures, and at a meeting of their elders at Manheim, in February, 1717, decided to call upon the Netherlanders for help in carrying out the great plan of removing to Pennsylvania, which they had long contemplated, and which had then come to maturity."   Hans Burghalter, the leader of this movement, is mentioned by Rupp in his list of early Mennonite preachers, and Pennypacker speaks of him as still preaching on the Conestoga in 1727. On the 20th of March, 1717, the Committee on Foreign Needs received information that over one hundred persons had set out, and soon afterwards they learned from Rotterdam that the number had been increased to three hundred souls.

In 1726 another movement began, and emigration started afresh and with renewed force from the Palatinate. Again: "On the 12th of April, 1727, there were one hundred and fifty ready to depart, and on the 16th of May the Committee were compelled to write to the Palatinate that they 'ought to be informed of the coming of those already on the way, so that they could best provide for them,' and 'how many would arrive without means;' but on the 20th the Committee learned that forty-five more needy ones had started from the Palatinate. These, with eight others, cost the society 3271f. 15st. Before the end of July twenty-one more came to Rotterdam, and so it continued. The Committee also sent forbidding letter after letter to the Palatinate, but every year they had to be repeated, and sometimes, as for instance, May 6th, 1733, they drew frightful pictures: 'We learn from New York that a ship from Rotterdam going to Pennsylvania with one hundred and fifty Palatinates wandered twenty-four weeks at sea. When they finally arrived at port nearly all the people were dead. The rest, through want of *vivres*, were forced to subsist on rats and vermin, and all are sick and weak. The danger of such an occurrence is always so great that the most heedless do not run the risk except through extreme want.' Nevertheless, the stream of emigrants did not cease." God bless the

"Committee on Foreign Needs" of Holland; and may the people of Lancaster County learn the value of its friendship to their stricken and persecuted ancestry. After 1733 we lose trace of any distinct Mennonite emigrations to this country, though Mennonites came through the entire remainder of the eighteenth century.

There is an address extant (it being a memorial of the Amish Mennonites to William Penn) which breathes the fervent spirit which animated them, and at the same time illustrates their principles and aims in the land of their adoption. It is dated May 20th, 1718, the month and year in which Penn died, and reads as follows:

To the most worshipful and respectable Proprietor of the Province, William Penn, and his Deputy Governor:

We came to Pennsylvania to seek an asylum from the persecution to which we had been subjected in Europe. We know the character of William Penn, and rejoiced God had made such a man. We had been told that the Indian right to the soil had been extinguished by purchase, to enable the conscientiously scrupulous to settle and enjoy their religious opinions without restraint. It was with primitive notions like the Patriarchs of antiquity we removed to the land of promise, but to our grief and surprise and mortification the government neither respected the conscience of the proprietary nor the faith of the Amish. We were invited to settle in this land by William Penn.

" Listen to us; if you do not, who will? We are required to obey laws in whose making we cannot participate (the Amish differing from the other Mennonites at that time in not voting). We are governed by the laws of God, you by the laws of man. Those of human authority cannot control us in opposition to His will declared in the Holy Scripture. We do not attend elections. We enter not your Courts of Justice. We hold no offices, neither civil or military. We did not object to the payment of our land, because it was purchased by William Penn, and *you* are entitled to remuneration, but we hold it to be a grievance that, entertaining nearly the same opinions as the respectable Society of Friends, we should like them be subjected to military and civil jurisdiction, especially when it is recollected that the head and proprietor, whom we now have the honor through you to address, is himself a member of that Society. The Society of Friends at least ought to have escaped such treatment. We are not a *little people*, for our neighbors, the Mennonites and the Tunkers, are also liable to be insulted by the tyranny of authority.

" We came to Pennsylvania to enjoy freedom of mind and body, expecting no other imposition than that de clared by God. As we have been taught to hurt not our neighbors, so do we expect that our neighbors will do us no injury. As we cannot contract debts, we re-quire no law for their recovery.

" If we should be so unfortunate as to have indigent neighbors we shall provide for their wants. The same inclination that tends to the preservation of our children prompts to the care of every member of our flock. Con-science, the voice of God, deters us from the commission of crime. As we commit no crime, hard is it for us to suffer for those of others. We ought not to be com-pelled to pay for the maintenance of convicts.

" We ask you for permission to pass our lives in inno-cence and tranquillity. Let us pursue our avocations un-molested. We respect your rights, respect our customs. We ask nothing of you but what the Word of God can justify."

Here is a little of the lofty spirit of the first emigration; it is the spirit of the Swiss mountains. It brought the answer. The deputy governor sent orders to the judicial officers to mitigate the civil duties imposed upon the peace sects in the valley of the Conestoga, and they have been mitigated ever since.

Their religious views were at an early date and since misrepresented, and no small degree of prejudice excited against them. To allay such unfounded prejudices they had " The Christian Confession of Faith, etc., containing the chief doctrine held by them, translated into English, and published at Philadelphia in 1728." In the preface to that publication they say " that the Confession of Faith of the harmless and defenceless Christians, called Mennonites, is as yet little known. Therefore it hath been thought fit and needful to translate, at the desire of some of our fellow-believers in Pennsylvania, our Confession of Faith into English." This Confession, which is given in another portion of this work, is approved and received by the elders and ministers of the congregations called Mennonites. " We do (say they) acknowledge and hereby make known that we own the Confession. In testimony whereof, and that we believe the same to be good, we have subscribed our names, A.D. 1727:

" Skippack: Jacob Gaedtschlack, Henry Kolb, Claes Jansen, Michael Ziegler.

" Germantown : John Gorgas, John Conerads, Clas Rittinghausen.

" Conestoga : Hans Burgholtzer, Christian Herr, Benedict Hirshi, Martin Baer, Johannes Bowman.

" Great Swamp: Velte Clemer.

" Manatant: Daniel Langenecker, Jacob Beghtly."

Eby Family.

THE ancestor who first came to America, and from whom the greater part of the family has sprung, was named Theodorus; he was a Mennonite in faith. According to the colonial records he arrived in 1715. Five years later, in 1720, Peter Eby arrived. So far as can be judged from the oldest known members, they must originally have been an active, quick-tempered, brown-eyed, dark-haired family.

The name of only one of the sons of Theodorus is now certainly known, which was Christian. He married a Mayer, and settled in Elizabeth Township, about three miles north of Litiz. He died in 1756 and left ten children. His oldest son, Christian Eby, married Catharine Bricker. He was an elder in the Mennonite Church, and wore a long beard which in his later years had turned white. Regular stated Mennonite meetings were held at his house, until a building for that special purpose was erected in the neighborhood. He died in 1807, leaving eleven children. The third son, Peter, moved to Pequea Valley, and afterwards became a Mennonite Bishop.

The tenth son, Benjamin, moved to Canada, was made a minister in the Mennonite Church, and succeeded his brother Peter as Bishop of the Mennonites in Canada. Christian, the third from Theodorus, left nine children.

The sixth son, Benjamin, served as minister among the Mennonites for many years, up to the time of his death.

Peter* Eby, married to Margaret Hess, moved to Salisbury Township, near the Gap, in 1791, and followed farming when his time was not taken up by his duties as a minister of the Gospel or Bishop in the Mennonite Church. He was ordained a minister in 1800, and was the second in his denomination in that neighborhood. Up to 1814 he preached in private houses; then a school-house was erected, and afterwards a meeting-house for that special purpose.

This member of. the family deserves more than a passing notice. His fame as a preacher was widely known, and served to fill the houses to their utmost capacity wherever he was known to officiate. His preaching was altogether extemporaneous, and its effect upon an audience great. And yet he was not a sensational preacher. It frequently happened that strangers hearing him for the first time, although otherwise informed, would not be convinced that he was not a person regularly educated and trained for the ministry. He died April 6th, 1843, in his seventy-eighth year, leaving nine children.

---

* Peter the second.

Herr Family.

HANS, OR JOHN, HERR came to this country in 1710, from Switzerland, with his four sons; the fifth son, Christian, had come to this country before the rest of the family.

Christian Herr was a minister of the Mennonite Church, and was the first of the family in this country; he came in 1709.

John Herr, son of Emanuel, who came over in 1710, was a minister in the Mennonite Church.

D. K. Herr, grandson of Martin, and son of Henry, was married to Susan Musser, and was a Mennonite minister.

Amos Herr, a son of Christian, was also a Mennonite minister.

Benjamin, a brother of Amos, was a Mennonite minister and Bishop.

John Herr, the founder of the New Mennonite Church, or Herrenleute, was born in Lancaster County, Pennsylvania, September 18th, 1781. His father, Francis, was the son of Emanuel Herr, one of the five sons of Hans Herr, who came over in 1710.

Hershey Family.

ANDREW HERSHEY was born in Switzerland in the year 1702, and moved with his father to the Palatinate. In the year 1719 he and his brother, Benjamin, sailed for America and settled in Lancaster County. His brother Christian also came to America, settling in Lancaster in 1739. Each of the three brothers was chosen a minister in the Mennonite Church. Andrew died in the year 1792, aged ninety years.

A Brief Sketch of the First Mennonite Settlers in Pennsylvania.

By a Non-Mennonite.

From the year 1537 until the present century the Mennonites were subjected to the most terrible persecutions. On this account they saw the necessity of fleeing from one country to another, consequently they were scattered; many of them went to Russia, Prussia, Poland, Holland and Denmark, and by invitation of the noble and liberal minded William Penn, the founder of the State of Pennsylvania, many families sought and found better homes beyond the great sea. This happened in the year 1683. Later, in 1693, a second party followed, and also settled themselves at Germantown, where they erected for themselves a school and meeting-house in 1708. In the year 1709 a third party followed, consisting mostly of persecuted Swiss families, who settled themselves in Pequea Valley, Chester, now Lancaster, County. Among these, we find the names of Herr, Meylin, Kendig, Miller, Oberholzer, Funk, Bauman and others. They settled themselves right in the midst of the Mingo or Conestoga, Pequea and Shawanese Indians, where they were subjected to many trials and hardships in establishing their new homes. Notwithstanding all that they felt themselves more secure among those wild domestics than in the midst of those raw hordes of antichrists of Europe.

In the years 1711, 1717 and 1727 other emigrants came from Europe, so that in the year 1735 they already counted over five hundred families in Lancaster County. For some time they held their meetings in school-houses which were built very plain, as was the custom among those people. As they were not possessed of large amounts of money to spend for large or costly churches, but were more inclined to spend for their home comfort, they did not pay so much attention to beautifying outwardly. Their plain, clean way or habit in their houses, more particularly in their apparel, has pleased the writer very much. But it seems to me as if the beloved rising generations were very indifferent in keeping up the old customs of our devout forefathers, and are, I am sorry to say, following the fashions of this world.

The Mennonites have spread themselves over almost the whole of North America and Canada, so that already twenty-five years ago (1847) their number was estimated at one hundred and twenty thousand souls. In Pennsylvania, Virginia, Maryland, Ohio, Indiana, Illinois, Iowa and other States they are found in the most fertile valleys, and are richly blessed with this world's goods.

On one occasion, when conversing with an old brother, I remarked that he had selected a beautiful home for himself, he answered, " Our beloved Saviour said, ' Blessed are the meek, for they shall inherit the earth.' " There is no doubt those old forefathers, noble, living children of God, who had the grace of God to leave their all for the sake of the Lord, there is yet a blessing from those dear forefathers which will not permit the light to be extinguished.   Oh! that their mantle may fall on all of us, and the Spirit of the Lord may awaken all mortal bodies to be living spirits, to re-awake and resurrect all congregations that are called by His name.   This is the wish from the bottom of the heart of your humble brother.

The Swiss Mennonites in Ohio.

MANY of the Mennonite congregations were organized from 1820 to 1830 by Swiss Mennonites who came direct from Switzerland. Six such congregations are in exist ence at the present time; the oldest is called the "Sonnenberg" congregation, in Wayne County, Ohio. The next, also in the same county, is the "Chippeway" congregation. About one hundred and fifty miles further west in Ohio, in the counties of Putnam and Allen, is the great Swiss and Alsace community, known as the Putnam congregation. Next is the congregation at Berne, Indiana; and lastly, two congregations in Missouri, viz · the Bethel congregation, at Tipton; and the Elkton congregation, in Hickory County. The two last named have been organized since 1860, principally by Swiss Mennonites who came from the older congregations eastward. During the session of the Conference in Berne, Indiana, November, 1884, representatives were present from all these congregations. A number of visiting brethren also came together in Berne, which created a renewal of friendship and acquaintanceship by mutual communications, and reminding each other of their trials and hardships in olden times.

The Mennonites in Switzerland had to endure persecution as late as the seventeenth century and in the begin

ning of the eighteenth century, and as they were driven
from their homes they emigrated to the territory of
Basel, which belonged to the Archbishop of the city of
Basel. There they were tolerated under certain restric
tions: they were compelled to live on the mountains,
and were only allowed to occupy the poorest land, and
they could not buy it, they were only allowed to rent it;
neither were they tolerated in towns, nor to rent or lease
any land near a town. After a time all kinds of slander-
ous reports were raised by their enemies and brought
before the Prince Bishop of Basel; consequently he
issued an edict that all Baptists (as the Mennonites were
then called) should leave the country by a certain time,
under penalty, which created much sorrow and grief
They did not know what to do, and they wept and
prayed. In this time of affliction a prominent official
took pity on these poor people and interceded for them
before the prince. He told the prince how these people
tilled the land on the hillsides, which could not be culti-
vated with the plow, and they paid their rents, also the
tenth of their products to the government. Consequently the edict was recalled by the prince, on the condition that they should remain on the mountains. On
receiving information that the edict was recalled they
rejoiced and thanked God, and encouraged each other to
lead an humble and virtuous life, and the congregation
resolved to make a present to the prince of a piece of
linen cloth of their own manufacture, also the same to
each of his successors, as a token of fidelity to the
government. David Baumgartner, who died in 1853, in
Adams County, Indiana, in his eighty-eighth year,
remembered and related in conversation, in the last

year of his life, that his father helped to take a piece of their cloth to the prince, which was accepted with thanks.

To escape similar persecutions many Mennonites left Switzerland and emigrated to other countries, viz.: the Palatinate, Alsace and later to America, so that from the years 1709 to 1735 over five hundred families emigrated to Pennsylvania from Switzerland and the Palatinate and settled in Lancaster County, Pennsylvania, among the Indians. In other parts of America we also find large congregations of Mennonites, of Swiss origin, which can be shown by reliable writers.

About fifty or sixty years ago a prominent Swiss writer, Heinrich Zschokke, traveled through the Jura Mountains, in the Bishoprick of Basel, and gave a description of its inhabitants. In regard to the Mennonites, he says: " More than one hundred families of the Baptists (as the Mennonites were then called) live here in the valleys and on the mountains, and through their skill make the poorest soil productive. They are a sturdy race, healthy, true-hearted, peaceable and good natured, beloved by their neighbors; Protestants and Catholics would trust them rather than their own people. These people were driven out of the country by the government of Bern (the Calvinists) because they refused to swear an oath and to take up the sword in war. This shows that the Prince Bishop of Basel was even more tolerant than the Protestant Calvinists."

He further says: " I was among the Baptists (now called Mennonites) as content as if I were among the first Christians in olden times; they were merry, but God-fearing, hospitable and industrious; among them

20

are no drunkards, no gamblers, no rowdies, no liars. They assist each other when in need, and on Sunday they meet at a neighbor's house to hold Divine service, sometimes in the open air, sometimes in a barn."

The emigrants to Pennsylvania in 1815 and 1818 were Benedict Schrag and family, from Canton Basel, and a young man named Hans Burkholter. Schrag afterwards settled in Wayne County, Ohio, and wrote a long letter to Switzerland, which created a desire among others to come to America, among whom were Peter Lehman, Isaac Sommer (grandfather of the present editor of the *Bundes Bote*, J. A. Sommer), Ulrich Lehman and David Kilchhofer. They started on their journey in 1819. In the year 1821 came Hans Lehman (deacon), Abraham Lehman, Hans and Christian Lehman, Abraham and David Zircher, Jacob Bichsel, Jacob Moser and Peter Hofstetter; in 1822 and 1824 sixteen families arrived, and in 1825, 1828 and 1835 a number of other families arrived, some from Alsace. The Chippeway congregation was organized in 1825, and the Putnam congregation in 1835, and the congregation at Berne, Indiana, was organized about the year 1838.

At present a trip or journey to Switzerland and back to America again, by steamer and railroad, would be only a pleasure trip; but what was it about sixty or more years ago, when our forefathers first came over and settled in Ohio? When they had made up their minds to go to America the first thing for them to do was to get a wagon and a horse; they had to see to get enough money for that. The next was to get a chest for their wearing apparel, and a chest for their victuals, and beds; that was about all they would or could take on the wagon with the family. Then they commenced their journey, with a

"Good-bye, ye Alps, ye shepherds and ye brethren, God be with you," then, with tears in their eyes, gave their last look over their mountainous home. They then proceeded on their journey, the father alongside of the wagon, also the rest who were old enough to walk at times. In this manner they traveled through France, by way of Paris, to Havre (the seaport where they took the sailing ship). So far they had already traveled a distance of about five hundred miles. There they sold their horse; their baggage and wagon were put on board the ship for America. A journey across the ocean generally took from seven to eight weeks. The first four families landed in New York; then their baggage and wagon were taken out of the ship, the wagon put together again and loaded, a horse was bought and they proceeded on their journey to the Far West—as it then was—the wilderness of Ohio, a distance of about five hundred miles. Some of them who had not the means to go any further remained with their brethren in the Shenandoah Valley of Virginia, others in Lancaster, Pennsylvania, where they were properly entertained, and provisions and money were given them to enable them to finish their journey. Thus after a tedious journey of five or six months they arrived in the wilderness of Ohio, where those who had a little money bought land from the pioneers that was already improved to some extent; others who were without means went right in the wilderness and bought government land that was yet cheap.

In the first place they selected a suitable spot to build a house. Then they commenced to clear the timber away; then they cut the logs to a suitable length, and after they had logs enough ready they all joined together one day to put the house up, what they called "logging;" generally by sundown the house was up, and after a merry day's work the owner could look upon it with satisfaction. Next it wanted a roof. They then had to split the shingles and put them on the house and put heavy poles across to keep them down, as they had no nails. Then they had to cut out a door and windows, and build a fire-place and chimney, as iron stoves were not then known in the West. The nearest mills were from twenty to thirty miles away and the roads very bad; it would take a man two to three days to go and come, and time was precious, so they had to find other means to crack their corn to prepare it for food, but they soon overcame that difficulty. The women made gardens, prepared the ground and raised vegetables; they got pigs, which would fatten without any expense, and bought cows as soon as they could, which would support themselves in the woods. The greatest difficulty was to get clothing; that which they brought from Switzerland was soon worn out, and for their produce they had no market nearer than one hundred miles. Wheat was worth twenty-five cents per bushel and muslin fifty cents a yard, and other articles in proportion. Money was at that time very scarce. In the whole settlement there was not money enough to pay postage on a letter to Switzerland, but they were ambitious, and one day one of them traveled fifteen miles to a settlement of Amish brethren to borrow twenty-five cents to pay postage to Switzerland. Under such circumstances they could not think of buying new clothing, but made every effort to help themselves. They planted flax, and as soon as they could got sheep, raised wool, the women spun it into yarn, the men wove it into cloth, and then dyed it yellow or black with bark from trees.

A Sketch of the Mennonite Settlement in Canada.*

By Dr. A. Eby.

ABOUT the year 1683 the first Mennonite emigrants arrived and settled themselves in the vicinity of Philadel phia, and called the place Germantown. They came from Crefeld on the Rhine. In the year 1709 a number of Swiss Mennonites emigrated to Pennsylvania and settled in Chester, now Lancaster, County, and others soon followed. As they lived in peace and enjoyed liberty of conscience, they understood well how to value these blessings, which they enjoyed under the English Crown. So that in the commencement of the opposition to the English Government on the part of their fellow-citizens they could not sanction such movements, and they were in danger of losing the liberty which they enjoyed heretofore, and consequently the privilege to serve God according to the dictates of their own con-science. As they believed it to be contrary to the doc trine of Christ to take up the sword against their neigh-bors, neither could they sanction the doings or actions of their fellow-citizens. At this point they were in a very awkward predicament. The English looked upon them as rebels, because they refused to defend the

---

* This article was published in German in 1871, and translated into English by D. K. Cassel in 1887.

English Government with arms; on the other hand, they were looked upon by the Americans as sympathizing with the English, because they would not take an active part in throwing off the English yoke.

In the commencement of the war many American soldiers advocated, and asked that the Mennonites and other defenceless Christians should be deprived of their citizenship. In order to escape that, they sent a petition to the Continental Congress on the 7th of November, 1775, in which the doctrine and principles of these defenceless people were explained. This petition was, after due consideration, accepted by Congress, and their privileges and doctrines were ratified by the new government,* but, at the same time, there were many of the Mennonites who were opposed to recognize and live under a government that was established by revolution.

Under such circumstances many of these defenceless people, not feeling exactly satisfied in their minds, became desirous of living under the English Government again. They heard of a country lying northwest of Pennsylvania, then not much known, which was yet under the government of George the Third, to whom they were more or less inclined, perhaps for the reason that he was a German, as they were themselves. Therefore many came to the conclusion to emigrate to Canada.

In the year 1799 seven families emigrated and settled in Niagara District, in Upper Canada; other families soon followed, so that the settlement soon prospered and spread in the Townships of Louth and Clinton, in Lin-

---

* A short and sincere declaration was then sent to the Continental Congress as an acknowledgment, which I have already mentioned in the article, " Mennonite Meeting at Germantown."

coln County, where the first settlement was established. They spread themselves over the neighboring counties of Haldimand, Welland and Wentworth, in which several congregations are in existence at the present time. The first Mennonite settlers in this district came from Bucks County, in Pennsylvania.

As early as 1801 Samuel Moyer wrote in the name of the new settlers to the congregations in Bucks County, asking them to advise, help and assist them in ordaining a minister, as they had none yet. But none of the ministers in Bucks County felt inclined to undertake so long and dangerous a journey,' as it then was, to comply with their request. After the matter had been carefully considered in a conference of the ministers in Bucks County, it was resolved to advise their brethren in Canada, through prayer and intercession for God's divine guidance, to select by ballot, and from among those balloted for by lot, a minister and a deacon. The letter containing this advice was written in Bedminster Township, Bucks County, dated September 4th, 1801, and signed by Jacob Gross, Abraham Wismer, Abraham Oberholzer, John Funk, Rudolph Landis and Samuel Moyer.

Whether the above advice to the young congregation in Canada was accepted and carried into effect is not clearly known, as all the witnesses are dead, and no written records of their proceedings in the matter known to exist; but it is a well-known fact that Valentine Kratz was the first Mennonite minister in Canada, and was ordained in 1801. It would have required at least three or four weeks to bring the letter containing the above advice to its proper destination, which would then have been the beginning of October before the congregation in Canada would have received it, so that the time would have been too short to write to any other congregation in Pennsylvania and await an answer, and ordain a minister before the end of the year; it is quite evident, then, that the congregation followed the advice of the brethren from Bedminster, Bucks County, and selected Valentine Kratz as their minister, without any other minister being present to install him.   This advice of the Bucks County conference is sufficient to show that a minister can be selected and installed, in case of a similar emergency, without the presence of another minister.   It is quite certain that Valentine Kratz was chosen as a shepherd of the little flock that was gathered in the wilderness of Canada in 1801, in the house of Dillman Moyer, but it is not certain whether he was chosen by lot, or whether he was the only person voted for.   It is said that he actually had but one vote.   He would have been entitled to have been one of the number when the lot was cast if there had been more candidates; but as that is not known, it is therefore not possible to decide whether he was chosen by lot or whether he was the only person voted for.   In the same year, but whether at the same time is not known, John Fretz was selected a deacon in the same congregation.

In the next year, 1802, Jacob Moyer was chosen a minister, and five years later he was ordained a Bishop. Why this congregation, yet so young and small, in so short a time elected a second minister is not clear, but probably for the reason that Kratz, although a very devout and well-meaning Christian, was not a fluent speaker, while Moyer was a fluent and earnest speaker, and a very energetic man in his actions.   The two were working together until 1824, when Kratz departed this life in his sixty-fifth year. About this time Jacob Moyer, the second, was called to the ministry by the same congregation by lot. He served until the year 1831, when he departed this life in the thirty-ninth year of his age. About three months after the death of Jacob Moyer the second, Daniel Hoch was chosen by lot as his successor in the ministry. In the year 1833 Bishop Jacob Moyer made a visit to Pennsylvania, where he was taken sick while visiting his friends in Bucks County, and died in the sixty-sixth year of his age (and is buried in the Mennonite burying-ground in Perkasi, Bucks County). In the Fall of the same year Jacob Gross was chosen as his successor in the ministry, and in the following year he was ordained a Bishop; on these two occasions Bishop Benjamin Eby, of Berlin, Waterloo County, officiated. Several years after Jacob Gross had been ordained a Bishop, the congregation so increased that it was thought necessary to have more ministers ; not only had the membership increased, but the settlements also, so that it was necessary to hold meetings in different places.

About the time the dissension took place, in 1848, there were at least three meeting-houses. To supply the increased demands and to accommodate the membership, Dillman Moyer and Abraham Moyer were called to the ministry ; these were the sons of Jacob Moyer, deceased. This was about the year 1850, and in 1872 they were both yet living.

In the same year in which the settlement in the Niagara district took place (1799), Samuel Betzner and Joseph Scherch, two energetic young men, with their families, left their homes in Franklin County, Pennsylvania, and undertook the journey, which at that time required weeks, a distance of over five hundred English miles, mostly through the wilderness, in search of that country in which the King of England was still honored. It is not necessary for this subject to describe the many hardships they had to endure; the mountains they had to climb, the rivers they had to cross, and the swamps they had to wade through were many hindrances in their way, but they trusted in God and did not fear the hardships which were before them. After a long and tedious journey they arrived safely on the Canadian shore of the great Niagara. Here they left their families, while they went further inland to examine the country. They heard of a beautiful and fertile country (presumably through hunters or Indians), which was watered by a magnificent stream, and they resolved to see this district, which was reported to be in a northwesterly direction from Ancaster, at that time a place of importance, before they would settle themselves anywhere. They easily found their way through the woods by following the path of the Indians until they came to the Township of Waterloo, at that time said to be the property of a certain Robert Beasley; but afterwards it was found that the whole township was heavily mortgaged. But as this mortgage created a great drawback in the settlement of Waterloo, I will take it up again in the future.

When Betzner and Scherch first came to Waterloo there were no settlers there, except a few hunters or traders, and surveyors perhaps never saw it. They soon resolved to settle in the vicinity of Preston, so called after the name of one of the traders who had been there to locate a home for themselves for the future. After they saw the country and satisfied themselves, they went back again to their families until the Spring of 1800, when they with their families moved up to Preston, in Waterloo County, and thus they were the first settlers in the richest and now most populous district of Canada. Their number was increased in the same year by two families of Brethren, or Dunkards, who came from Lancaster County, Pennsylvania.

In the year 1801 their number was further increased by the arrival of seven families, of whom the majority were Mennonites. Among other arrivals in the year 1802 were Joseph Bechtel and family. He was afterward chosen to the ministry and was the first Mennonite minister in Waterlo. He served alone until 1811, when the well-known and renowned Benjamin Eby was called to the ministry and afterward elected the first Bishop in Waterloo, in which capacity he served many years. He was born in Lancaster County, Pennsylvania, about the year 1784, where he received only an ordinary common school education; he afterward married a Miss Brubacher, and in 1807 he came with his wife to Canada and settled in the eastern part of the present town of Berlin; his wife was a sister of John Brubacher, deacon, at Berlin. Here he lived highly honored and respected until his death in 1853. He wrote several small works, among others a spelling and reading book; also a condensed history of the Mennonites.

In the beginning of this article I remarked that the anxiety to live again under the English Crown was what brought the first Mennonites to Canada. This was not the case with all the first settlers in Waterloo. Where true Christian love is manifested there is always a readiness to offer a brother a helping hand, otherwise there would have been few of the Schneiders, Erbs, Schantzs, Brubachers, Baumans, Webers, Martins and the Ebys, who, at the present time, form such an important portion of the Mennonite population, to come to the province. All the first settlers bought their land, for which they paid the greater portion of their worldly goods, from the above-named Richard Beasley. But he did not tell them that the whole Township of Waterloo was heavily mortgaged, and that he could not give them a good and clear title. They themselves were so absolutely honest, and so little were they acquainted with the trickery and charlatanry of this world, that they could hardly think that any man could be so extremely dishonest that he would undertake to sell that which belonged to two others in common, and besides that, yet covered by mortgage. As they did not doubt the honesty of Beasley, they did not think it worth the trouble to examine into the matter to determine whether the title was clear or not. He undoubtedly had intended to sell as much land as possible before it would be found out that it was mortgaged, then these poor people could see how they could settle with the mortgage holders; but God, in His Providence, watched over them and frustrated the intentions of Beasley.

In the winter of 1802–3 Samuel Bricker, then quite a young man, made a business tour to Toronto, then called York. The previous summer he had come from Cumberland County, Pennsylvania, to Waterloo, and was about to occupy an important position in the new settlement. He stayed over night in a hotel in Toronto, where a stranger, whose name we have not, took notice of him and asked where he came from. He told the stranger he came from Waterloo, whereupon the stranger expressed his joy to have met with him, as he had heard that a number of honest ·people had bought land there which was mortgaged. Young Bricker at first could not and would not believe such unpleasant news, but the stranger directed him to the Register's Office, which was at that time in the same town. Here he found the next day the stranger's message only too true. With a heavy heart he went home and told his brethren and friends what he had learned. At first no one would believe him, but as he insisted upon his information being correct, they agreed to send two out of their midst to York to investigate the matter. When Beasley learned that his fraud was detected he had at first refused to do anything to make satisfaction, but when he learned that no more settlers could be induced to buy land from him, then he offered to sell to a company as much land as would be required to pay the mortgage. Samuel Bricker and Joseph Scherch were then sent to Pennsylvania to make an effort to raise the required amount of money. They first went to Cumberland County, the former home of Bricker, but met with no success, and Scherch, being quite discouraged, went home again; but Bricker, not being so easily discouraged, went to Lancaster County, where he met John Eby, brother of Bishop Benjamin Eby, of Berlin, Canada, and to him he explained the circumstances. Brother John Eby took the matter to heart and sympathized with his brethren in Canada in their troubles. Through the night he considered the matter, and the next morning he went out on horseback and invited all his neighbors to meet at his house, to consult and determine what to do in the case. In consequence of this conference an association was formed for the purpose of buying enough land to clear the township of the mortgage. Accordingly they bought 60,000 acres of land in Waterloo from Beasley, which was sufficient to cover all incumbrances. But Beasley tried another dodge to defraud them. He wrote a deed for the land they had bought from him, which he offered, but as they had been defrauded once they would not trust him a second time. They engaged a competent lawyer to examine the deed offered by Beasley and to close the purchase, who found the deed prepared by Beasley worthless. He then made an affort to bring the matter in proper shape for them and succeeded. He not only saved their money, but also prevented much trouble and worriment, which would have been entailed upon them had they accepted the worthless deed. Their deed was dated June 20th, 1805. They could now take possession of their land without any danger of being molested by anyone; but all trials and privations of this life in a new settlement were not yet at an end. The greater portion of the township was now the property of the brethren of Lancaster County, Pennsylvania, and many emigrated from Lancaster to Canada for a number of years, except through the war of 1812 to 1815.

In 1803, the same year in which Beasley's fraud was detected, a number of families emigrated to Canada and settled in Markham, about twenty miles north of Toronto. What induced them to settle there, I have not learned, but I presume they turned their attention to Markham when they learned that it was not safe to buy land in Waterloo. One thing is certain, in 1803 no new

emigrants came to Waterloo.   From this it is to be supposed that those who were about to emigrate to Waterloo,
which was without doubt the case, when they learned about
the trouble and difficulty there, concluded to go to Markham.   Among the first settlers in that district was Henry
Weitman.   He was afterwards called to the ministry, and
was the first Mennonite preacher in the congregation at
Markham.   Several years later, as he was assisting in cut-
ting out a street, he lost his life by a tree falling on him.
We see from this that the Mennonite ministers in Canada
not only had to contend with ordinary difficulties as ministers in thinly settled districts, but were also in danger of
losing their lives while they had to work for the support of
their families, and to engage in the same labor as their
neighbors; as they served the congregation without any
remuneration, therefore they were directed to support
themselves and families the same as their neighbors.   On
account of their voluntary service they were for many
years the only German preachers in Canada, and on many
occasions were called on to serve at funerals of their
neighbors of other denominations.   Heinrich Weitman's
successor in the ministry was his son, Adam, while at
the same time Andrew, another son, served as deacon.
After Adam followed his son, Jacob, in the ministry in
Markham.   This congregation also extended over the
neighboring townships, and had several preachers and
Bishops.

A short time after the formation of the association
which bought the greater portion of Waterloo, another
association was formed in Pennsylvania with the intention
of buying another tract of land in Woolwich, located
north of Waterloo.   This purchase was effected in 1807,

consisting of 45,000 acres.   This led to a further emigration from Pennsylvania, among whom the families of
Martin were largely represented.   The year 1806 is
memorable in the early history of the Mennonites in
Waterloo, through the destructive forest fires that occurred in the spring of that year.   The forests were full of
dry leaves, so that the fire would run over a large portion
in a very short space of time, and destroyed everything
within its reach.   The first and greatest of these fires took
its start in the vicinity of (now) Blair, and by a southwesterly wind it soon extended beyond the Grand River,
and spread itself out over a vast portion of clear land
and destroyed houses, barns, pasture and fences, also
cattle and sheep in its course.   Among other sufferers is
to be mentioned Abraham Bechtel.   Not only was his
barn burned but also his house, in which was stored a
large quantity of provisions, for the purpose of support-
ing some of his friends who were coming from Pennsylvania.   So scarce were provisions at that time in Waterloo,
that Bechtel, after his stock was destroyed by fire, was
compelled to go fifty miles to obtain enough to support
his family and friends until harvest time.

The second fire occurred a few miles east of where
Preston now is, on the farm of Martin Baer, who, with
much labor, saved his house, while everything else was
burned for him.   Minister John Baer, Martin's son, then
a little boy of two years, has a vivid recollection of this
great fire.   He well remembers how his father filled every
vessel with water and carried it on the house top to protect the house against the fire.   The third fire occurred
in the district where the city of Berlin now stands, but as
the whole district was yet covered with timber, it was not
of so much importance for our subject.

The above mentioned Martin Baer emigrated from York County, Pennsylvania, to Canada in the year 1801, and settled on the farm now occupied by his son, John Baer, the preacher. He was called to the ministry several years after Bishop Benjamin Eby, and was the third preacher in the congregation in Waterloo.

From this time on the congregation in Waterloo increased, not only in numbers, but they were also blessed with this world's goods. Early steps were taken to educate the rising generation of the colony. A school was opened in 1802 in the vicinity of Samuel Betzner's. Their meetings for divine service were generally held in private houses, or in school-houses where they existed.

The first meeting-house was built in 1811, on the land of Bishop Benjamin Eby. In 1838 it was rebuilt, as the congregation increased and the old house was too small. This meeting-house is at present known by the name of Christian Eby's, or Berliner. The second meeting-house in Waterloo was built in the vicinity of Preston by John Erb, at his expense, after the war of 1812. He was a miller by trade, and was not compelled to leave his home or family, like the rest of his neighbors, to do public service on the frontiers; therefore determining to do something for the general welfare of the community, he concluded to build this house of worship. He built it free for the use of all denominations without distinction, but he had the bitter experience in later years, on several occasions, of being locked out of the house which he built and paid for, by other denominations.

What the spiritual condition of the Church was at that time cannot be stated at present, because there are no letters or journals at hand from which the feelings or de-

sires of the brethren can be learned; but to judge by
what can be remembered from the early settlers of
Waterloo, we might say that only a small portion actually
tasted or enjoyed the water of life, while many who had
the appearance of piety had their hearts filled with the
things of this world, and many could much better tell
the stories of their dear Pennsylvania fatherland than
the narratives of the Gospel of Jesus.   I wish that this
remark might not be correct and that I might be taught
better things in the future, but until then honesty re
quires that which I have learned as the truth, even perhaps a few who I otherwise would love, might have their
feelings hurt.

The war of 1812 was a time of trial and affliction for
the Mennonites in Canada, as they believed they were
entirely exempt from all military service in Canada. They
considered it a great wrong, so soon after their arrival, to
be compelled to' leave their homes and families to do
public service in the army, while their neighbors, who
did not understand the doctrine of Christ the same as
they did, could not see why the Mennonites should not
be compelled to fight their enemies with the sword, even
if they personally were their friends.   The government
compelled them to go into the ranks, but could not com-
pel them to fight.   After the government had learned
this they were employed as teamsters, but they had to
furnish their own teams.   This prepared for them a heavy
loss in property.   Not only did they lose the time which
they should have had to work on their farms, but in the
battle on the Thames, where several of the brethren were
employed as teamsters, the English were compelled to
retreat; to escape the enemy, the soldiers took the breth-

ren's horses from their wagons and fled, and the brethren's wagons fell into the hands of the enemy. They
thus lost not only their wagons, but also many of their
horses. After the war they had to go to Pennsylvania to
get new wagons, and their trials and afflictions can better
be imagined than described. While the men were absent on duty the women and children had to attend to
the farm work, or would have been in danger of starva-
tion should the father for any reason not return. Hardly
had they enjoyed a little rest and peace before another
affliction was upon them. The summer of 1816 was so
cold that the crops almost entirely failed. It is said that
there was frost almost every week through the whole
summer. Potatoes, the chief article of food among the
new settlers, failed almost entirely. Food was so scarce
that many people were compelled to live on soup made of
bran. The following year was likewise cold, but the
crops were better. It is said that in 1817 some people
worked in the harvest field wearing their overcoats. It
is to be wondered that they did not leave the cold Canada
with disgust and select a home in a milder climate, but it
appears that the Lord had brought them here for the
all-wise purpose of carrying out His providential plans.
Have they fulfilled their mission? Have they endeavored
to so spread the doctrine of peace so that the spirit of
war may not be the ruling power?

After this their condition and the Church prospered
and increased, not only in numbers through the rising
generation, but also by emigration from Germany as well
as from Pennsylvania. New meeting-houses were erected
in different localities, and ministers ordained to take
charge of the congregations in Waterloo and surrounding

townships.   Among these ministers I will mention
Scherch and Baer.   Both were born and raised under
laborious burdens and trials of life in a new settlement.
Bro. Scherch was born in 1801 and is the oldest person
born in Waterloo yet living (1871).   May the Lord spare
him yet through many years.   Bro. Baer, previously mentioned, was born in the year 1804.   Notwithstanding the
many hardships he had to undergo in his early life, he is
yet quite strong and robust bodily, but what is far better,
strong in his religious belief and a true teacher of Christ's
doctrine, and warning the sinners in their manifold ways.
He frequently made long journeys to localities where
there were but few members, for the purpose of preaching
the Gospel to them.   He has all his lifetime been a diligent student of the Scripture.

As the membership of the congregation increased the
more it became necessary to increase the number of ministers and Bishops.   During the last few years three
Bishops were ordained, one in each of the townships of
Waterloo, Dumfries and Woolwich.   Everything seemed
to prosper until the year 1848, when a dark cloud threatened the Lincoln Congregation.   This storm increased
and extended itself until it ended in a separation, not
only in Lincoln County alone, but also in Waterloo and
Markham.   This split, or separation, has not been healed
to this day.

The following is from Col. W. W. H. Davis' *History of
Bucks County, Pennsylvania:*

THE FIRST MENNONITE SETTLERS IN CANADA.

It is generally considered that the first Mennonites
emigrated to Canada about the beginning of the year

1800. We find, however, that Plumstead and the neighboring townships of Hilltown, Bedminster and Tinicum have sent a considerable number of emigrants to Canada within the last century, principally Mennonites. The immigration commenced in 1786, when John Kulp, Dillman Kulp, Jacob Kulp, Stoffel Kulp, Franklin Albright and Frederick Hahn left Bucks County, Pa., and sought new homes in the country beyond the great lakes. Those who had families were accompanied by their wives and children. These pioneers must have returned favorable accounts of the country, for in a few years they were joined by many of their old friends and neighbors, mostly from Bucks County. In 1799 they were followed by Jacob Moyer, Amos Albright, Valentine Kratz, Dillman Moyer, John Hunsberger, George Althouse, Abraham Hunsberger and Moses Fretz; in 1800 by John Fretz, Lawrence Hipple, Abraham Grubb, Michael Rittenhouse, Manassah Fretz, Daniel High, Jr., Samuel Moyer, David Moyer, Jacob High, Jacob Hausser, John Wismer, Jacob Frey, Isaac Kulp, Philip High, Abraham High and Christian Hunsberger. In 1802, Isaac Wismer and Stoffel Angeny went to Canada from Plumstead—the latter returned, but the former stayed; a few years afterwards Jacob Gross also moved to Canada. A number of the Nash family emigrated to Canada, among whom was the widow of Abraham Nash, who died near Danborough, in 1823. Her three sons, Joseph, Abraham and Jacob, and four daughters accompanied her. Bucks County families generally settled in what is now Lincoln County, near Lake Ontario, about twenty miles from Niagara Falls.

Visit Among the Mennonites.

It must be conceded that the disciples of Menno Simons have more closely adhered to his teachings in this respect than most others. We visited a large number of their congregations, and it was a source of satisfaction to notice how large a part of those we met with were clothed in plain apparel, often strikingly resembling that worn by consistent Friends. The similarity was increased by their habit of not wearing a beard, so that many of the men had far more the appearance of a Quaker minister than some who come among us under that profession.

We found that there are several branches of the Mennonite family, differing from each other mainly in the degree of strictness with which they observe the principle of nonconformity to the world, to which I suppose they all adhere. We made frequent inquiries in regard to the point of difference between the various Mennonite non-resistant bodies, but were unable to find that there were any differences in doctrine. All, so far as we can learn, would adopt the Confession of Faith issued by the Convention of their ministers at Dortrecht, in 1632, as representing their present belief. Next in point are the Amish Mennonites, who are so named from Jacob Amen, of Switzerland, a zealous reformer in their earlier days.

In Germany the discontent of the peasants under the oppression of their feudal lords led to political distur-

(326)

bances, in which Thomas Müntzer, a Lutheran minister, who zealously propagated Anabaptist views, became involved. He attempted to establish by force an ideal Christian commonwealth, with absolute equality and a community of goods. The defeat of the insurgents and the execution of Müntzer, in 1525, proved only a tempo rary check to the movement. A second and more deter mined attempt to establish a theocracy was made at Münster in Westphalia (1532–1535). The town was besieged in 1534 by Count Waldeck, its expelled bishop.

The supreme authority within its walls was in the hands of Johann Bockhold, a tailor of Leyden, better known as John of Leyden. Giving himself out as the successor of David, he claimed royal honors and absolute power in the new " Zion." He justified the most arbitrary and extravagant measures by the authority of visions from Heaven. With this pretended sanction he legalized polygamy, and himself took four wives, one of whom he beheaded with his own hands in the marketplace, in a fit of frenzy. As a natural consequence of such license, Münster was for twelve months a scene of unbridled profligacy. After an obstinate resistance it was taken by the besiegers, and John and some of his more prominent followers were put to death. It would be gross injustice to confound these people with other Baptists, or with the non-resistant Mennonites, who differ from them in many points.

The customs and character of the Mennonites will be further illustrated by a reference to some of the scenes and incidents that were witnessed during our visit. The first of the meetings which we attended was at Deep Run, north of Doylestown, in Bucks County, on third

month 7th, where several hundred assembled.   We found
a large, plain, one-story building, seated with plain, movable benches, and provided with a narrow platform on
one side, elevated one step from the floor, on which was
a single bench for the ministers.   A retiring-room was
partitioned off at one end; and this was furnished with
shelves to receive the bonnets of the sisters, who leave
them there and enter the main room with their heads
covered only with simple clear-starched caps, very similar
to those worn by our plain women Friends.   It was an
interesting spectacle.   Bench after bench was filled with
nice-looking, plainly-dressed women, sitting in a reverent
manner, a number of them having their infant children
with them.   Many of the men also were plainly dressed,
and looked like old-fashioned Friends.   We were favored
with a comfortable meeting and warm feelings of affec-
tionate interest were excited, under the influence of which
we could greet them as beloved brethren.   At Blooming
Glen meeting-house, in the same county, being somewhat early, we walked into the graveyard and noticed
that the graves were arranged in rows, which were not
parallel to the walls of the inclosure, but extended diag-
onally across; we found the object was that the bodies
might be placed in an east and west direction, with the
feet pointing to the sunrise.—From *The Friend*, a religious and literary journal.

A Visit Among Russian Mennonites.

WHEN Stephen Grellet, a minister in the Society of Friends, was paying a religious visit in Russia in the year 1819, he met with some settlements of Mennonites in the southern part of that country. His journal speaks of his visit to them as follows :

" Accompanied by dear Contenius we left Ekaterinoslaw early in the morning of the 23d of fifth month, for the colonies of the Mennonites, on the Dnieper; we came sixty-five versts to the chief village of the fifteen that form this part of their settlement. They are an interesting people; much simplicity of manner and genuine piety appear prevalent amongst them. I felt my mind so drawn towards them in the love of Christ, that I apprehended it my duty to endeavor to have a religious meeting among them. Their Bishop, who resides in this village, was sent for by Contenius to consult on the place and most proper time to hold the meeting; the dear man, who is very plain in his manners and way of living, was at the time in the field behind the plough, for neither he nor any of the clergymen receive any salary. They maintain themselves and families by their honest industry. They are faithful also in the maintenance of their testimony against oaths, public diversions and strong drink. The Empire exempts them from military requisitions. The Bishop concluded that there was no better or more

(329)

suitable place than their meeting-house, which is large
and in the centre of the other villages ; the time was fixed
for the next day, and he undertook to have notice spread.
At the time appointed they came from all the other villages ; the house was crowded with the people and their
ministers ; much solidity was evinced.   The people gathered at once into such stillness and retiredness of spirit,
that it seemed as if we were amidst our own friends in
their religious meetings.   I was enlarged among them in
the Gospel of Christ. Contenius interpreted from the
French into the German ; dear Allen had an excellent
communication to them which I first rendered into
French, and then Contenius into German ; we also had
access together to the place·of prayer, our spirits were
contrite before the Lord ; the dear children, who also
felt the Lord's power over them, were in tears.

"We went thence about thirty-five versts to Kortitz
Island, in the Dnieper, where we stopped awhile with
Peter Hildebrand, one of their pious ministers ; we had
with him and his wife a refreshing season before the Lord.
Then they accompanied us, in small boats, about eight
versts down the river to one of their villages below Alex
androwsk, where we had that evening a large and satisfactory meeting.   We felt much concerned for parents in
that place ; their young people are exposed by being so
near a city of resorts and temptations.   Before we took
our departure, the next morning, we had a tendering opportunity in the family, where also several others met us.
Peter Hildebrand's heart was full on parting with us. We
left with them, as we had done in the other villages, some
of our books in German.

"We then traveled sixty-five versts, over what is called

a steppe, where not even a shrub grows, only coarse grass. That night we came to a village of German Lutherans, where are kept beautiful flocks of Merino sheep for the use of thirty villages. We had some religious service, but we did not find much piety among them. Thence we went over the river called Molotschna, which divides the settlement of the German colonies from a settlement of the Mennonites, composed of twenty villages. We stopped at their first village, where they have a large cloth manufactory; their land is in high cultivation; formerly not a tree or shrub was to be seen on these vast steppes; now they have fine orchards of various kinds of good fruit. Traveling over these steppes we saw, as we thought, at a distance large groves of beautiful trees, and to our astonishment the scenery continually changed; at first it appeared as if the trees were in motion; on com ing nearer, we found that they were flocks of cattle feed ing. At other times we thought we saw large sheets of water, like lakes; but all this was an optical delusion, caused by the state of the air.

" The Mennonites here are preserved in much Christian simplicity, in their worship, manner of living and conversation. They have also a testimony against making the Gospel chargeable, and against wars and oaths. I felt it my religious duty to have a meeting amongst them. It was agreed to be held in the evening of the next day, and the Bishop readily offered to have notice of it sent to the villages around—ten in number.

" In the forenoon we had a meeting with the children of several villages, collected on the occasion; their sobriety and religious sensibility gave pleasing proofs that their parents have not attempted in vain to instruct them,

by example and precept, in a Christian life. We also
visited with much satisfaction several of their families.
The meeting in the afternoon was largely attended. The
Lord owned us by His Divine presence, and gave us an
evidence that He has here a people whom He graciously
owns as members of His Church. We afterwards went
a few versts further, and lodged at an aged couple's;
Christians, indeed, they appeared to be; we were much
refreshed with them in our bodies and spirits.

"Next morning we had another meeting with about
five hundred of their young people. I have rarely met
more general religious sensibility than among these. I
had not spoken many sentences when a great brokenness
and many tears gave evidence of their religious feelings.
In the afternoon we had a meeting with the people at
large; a very satisfactory season. Dear Contenius is a
faithful helper to us; he is so feeling in his manner of
interpreting. After visiting many of these people in their
families we went to another village, where we had a very
large meeting. Many of these dear people came to it
from fifteen different villages round, their meeting-house
being large. It may be said to have been a holy solemnity; the Lord's baptizing power was felt to be over us.

"We then went to Altona, their most distant village,
which stands pretty near the colonies at the Duhobortzi.
We put up at the house of a Mennonite, a young man
who is a minister among them. The order of his family
and children is most gratifying; piety seems to prevail
over them all; the simplicity and neatness of the house
are beautiful. Much quietness and simplicity is also apparent in the religious meetings of this people. They are
very regular and punctual to the hour at which their

meetings for worship are held. When gathered they all kneel. They continue so in total silence, in secret meditation or prayer about half an hour. After resuming their seats, their minister is engaged either in preaching or in prayer, both extempore. Before they separate they kneel down again, and continue for some time in silent prayer. The Emperor grants them every privilege and liberty of a civil and religious nature. They choose their own magistrates, and are not under the authority of the police of the Empire. This is exercised by themselves. They are exempt from military requisitions, and have no taxes, except those requisite amongst themselves for their own government, and they are placed under the superintendence of those persons who preside over the colonies in the Crimea generally. Contenius is the chief person on whom that care now devolves."

For the above account of Stephen Grellet's visit among the Russian Mennonites in 1819 we are indebted to the kindness of Friend Joseph Walton, of Moorestown, New Jersey, editor of *The Friend.—Herald of Truth.*

Mrs. Catharine Gabel.

Mrs. Catharine Gabel celebrated the one hundredth anniversary of her birth on December 19th, 1884, and the little village of Gabelsville, Berks County, about five miles from Pottstown, where she lived for seventy-five years, donned its holiday attire and did honor to the occasion. Many neighbors long living in the vicinity walked or drove to the house of the centenarian, while the incoming train brought scores of relatives, who gathered to do honor to their aged ancestor.

Under the same roof were assembled five generations of the Gabel family, and it is questionable if among the vast assemblage there was one who more thoroughly enjoyed the occasion than the venerable hostess. Mrs. Gabel is the daughter of John High (Hoch), and was born December 19th, 1784, on the farm in North Coventry, Chester County, now occupied and owned by Samuel Stauffer, and situated about two miles and a half from Pottstown. She was the eighth of a family of eleven children, and lived with her parents until 1803, having married, in 1802, John Gabel, a farmer and miller. In 1803 she removed with her husband to her present home, and has all these years lived on the same property. Her husband died in 1823, and a vow made by her a few years after his death, when hearing of a second marriage made by a friend which proved unhappy, that she

(334)

would remain a widow the rest of her life, she has faithfully kept. She bore her husband eleven children, of whom eight still live, as follows: Mrs. Elizabeth Gabel, wife of Henry Gabel, aged 80 years, and living in Pottsgrove Township; Mrs. Magdalena East, aged 78 years, of New Berlinville, Berks County; Henry Gabel, aged 76 years, and one of this county's most valued and influential citizens, living on South Hanover Street, this borough; Mrs. Susan Landes, aged 72 years, living with her mother at Gabelsville; Mrs. Mary Gabel, widow of David Gabel, aged 68 years, and living on the old homestead; Jacob H. Gabel, aged 64 years, a bachelor, living with his brother Henry in the borough; Miss Barbara Gabel, aged 62 years, living with her mother.

Notwithstanding Mrs. Gabel's great age her general health is good, and although her memory fails her occasionally in recalling events of recent occurrence, she talks by the hour of events in the early part of this century. Her eyesight, until recently very good, is now becoming dimmed. Mrs. Gabel is a tall, muscular woman, and up to within a few years always inclined to sparseness of flesh.

Of her father's family several other members attained good old ages, the mother dying at the age of 90 years and a sister at 91 years. The premises upon which Mrs. Gabel lives came into the possession of the Gabel family in the latter portion of the eighteenth century, her father-in-law, Henry Gabel, in conjunction with a half brother, Jacob Latshaw, having purchased a large tract of land from Thomas Potts. A few years after the joint purchase a division was made of the property, Mr. Gabel retaining that portion upon which was located the family

mansion of Thomas Potts, where many of the descendants of the Potts family were born, and known in their
family records as " Popodickon," after a famous Indian
king named " Popodick," who is buried under a magnificent chestnut tree.   Mr. Gabel subsequently divided
his portion between his two sons, Jacob and John, the
former the husband of Catharine, and to whom was
assigned the portion upon which the old mansion was
located, and which Mrs. Gabel occupied from 1803 up to
1857, when she removed to the house which she has
occupied ever since.—*Philadelphia Press.*

Mrs. Gabel died May 24th, 1886, at the great age of
101 years, 5 months and 5 days, and is buried at the old
Mennonite Church at Boyertown, where she had been a
member for many years.

Jacob Funk,

Mennonite Minister at Germantown from 1774 to 1816.

HEINRICH FUNK came to America and settled at the Indian Creek, now Franconia Township, Montgomery County, Pennsylvania, in the year 1719. When the Franconia Mennonite congregation was organized he was chosen their minister, in which capacity he served for many years and became very prominent. He died in 1760. He made his will June 13th, 1759, which was witnessed by Jacob Funk, Jacob Oberholzer and Benedict Geman, and his two sons, John Funk and Christian Funk, were appointed as his executors. His wife Anne died July 8th, 1758. She was a daughter of Christian Meyer.

His daughter Esther being lame and helpless he set aside £400 good current money for her maintenance. In this case he appointed as directors the elders in the Congregation of Christ, named the Mennonites, namely Christian Meyer and Michael Dirstein. Henry Funk had ten children, four sons and six daughters, viz.: John, Christian, Abraham and Henry, Esther, Barbara, Anne, Mary, Fronica and Elizabeth. His second son Christian was born in 1731, married in 1751, and was called to the ministry in 1757 in the Mennonite congregation in Franconia. He died in 1811 in his eightieth year, and is buried in Delp's graveyard in Franconia.

On May 16th, 1734, a patent was granted by the Honorable the Proprietors of Pennsylvania to Jacob Funk, Sr., who emigrated to Pennsylvania shortly before. He was a nephew of the above-named Heinrich Funk. This patent is recorded in the Roll's Office at Philadelphia in Patent Book A, Vol. 6, page 311, etc., for one hundred and forty acres, and six per cent. allowed for roads, etc., situate in the Township of Franconia, County of Philadelphia. Jacob Funk, Sr., made his last will in writing, bearing date May 15th, 1756, and bequeathed to his son, Jacob Funk, Jr., all that tract of land mentioned above under said patent. He says: "I appoint my loving friend and cousin, Christian Funk, and my wife, Barbara Funk, as my executors." The will was probated June 14th, 1756, and is registered in Book K, page 407, at Philadelphia, and a deed was given by the executors to Jacob Funk, Jr., dated April 20th, 1759. The above-named will of Jacob Funk, Sr., is witnessed by Christian Meyer, Samuel Meyer and Henry Funk. He had four children, viz.: two sons, Jacob Funk, Jr., and Samuel Funk, and two daughters, Barbara Funk and Maria Funk.

Jacob Funk, Jr., was chosen a minister in the Mennonite congregation at Franconia in 1765.* His name also appears on the name list of American ministers in 1770, in the Mennonite Archives at Amsterdam, Holland, as a minister at Indian Creek. On May 7th, 1774, Jacob Funk, Jr., and Anna his wife, of Franconia Township, Philadelphia (now Montgomery County), conveyed to

* See MSS. Congregational Records.

Andrew Hans their right and title in a tract of land situate in Franconia Township, Philadelphia County (now Montgomery), recorded in Book No. 9, page 290, at Norristown. On March 4th, 1774, Jacob Funk, Jr., bought of Jacob Keyser a tract of land containing 125 acres, and shortly afterwards an additional tract of 35 acres, making in all 160 acres, situated in Cheltenham Township, now Montgomery County. I also find that Jacob Funk, of Cheltenham Township, and Anna his (second) wife, late widow of Sebastian Benner, released Abraham Benner and Christian Benner, said releases bearing date September 30th, 1774, recorded in Book No. 3, page 485, at Norristown.

According to the records of the Germantown Mennonite congregation, Jacob Funk, preacher, and Anna his wife connected themselves with the Mennonite Church at Germantown in 1774, where he served as a minister for forty-two years. He made his last will and testament in writing dated September 15th, 1802, which was proven April 16th, 1816, and is registered No. 43, Book 4, page 221, at Norristown, and was witnessed by Michael Leppert, John Minnich and Jacob Knorr. He had six children, two sons, John and Samuel, and two daughters, Barbara and Mary, by his first wife, and two daughters, Anna and Elizabeth, by his second wife. Jacob Funk was born on the 13th of the third month, 1730, and died on the 14th of the third month, 1816, aged eighty-six years and one day, and lies buried near the door of the church in the Mennonite graveyard at Germantown. His children were: John Funk, married to Catharine Knorr, first wife, Margaret Fitzgerald, second wife; Samuel Funk, married to Esther Kolb; Barbara Funk, married to Christian Souder; Mary Funk, married to David Kelter; Anna Funk, married to Matthias Kolb; Elizabeth Funk, married to Daniel Kolb.

John Funk, the oldest son of Jacob Funk, Jr., occupied the old homestead in Cheltenham after the death of his father Jacob. He was a deacon in the Germantown Mennonite congregation for many years. The old farm had been in the Funk name and occupied by them about one hundred and ten years. On this farm General Murray, who lost his life in the battle of Germantown in 1777, lies buried in a vault which still exists. Mention is made of it in Jacob Funk's will in regard to a division line in dividing his farm between his two sons, John and Samuel. John Funk had five children, viz.: Hannah Funk, married Abraham Springer; John Funk, married Catharine Slingluff; Elizabeth Funk, married Joseph Lenhard; Susanna Funk, married Samuel Harmer; Catharine Funk, married Mark Brannan.

Samuel Funk married Esther Kolb, April 29th, 1788. They had eleven children, viz.: Jacob, died single; Isaac, died single; Samuel, died single; Anna, married Jesse Gilbert, and died in her eighty-ninth year; Abraham, died single; David, married Mary Heiser; Maria, died single; Martin, died single in his eighty-first year; Daniel, died single; Nellie, married John G. Wolf, and died in her eightieth year; Wilhelmina died single.

Christopher Funk settled himself in Germantown. He bought fifty acres of land adjoining the Friends' meeting-house and Main Street in Germantown, on May 10th, 1726, recorded in the Germantown Book. He had one son and five daughters, viz.: Henry Funk; Elizabeth Funk, married to George Kaschke; Sophia Funk, married to Anthony Gilbert; Barbara Funk, married to John Keyser; Sarah Funk; Susanna Funk.

After the death of Christopher Funk his son Henry took the old homestead in Germantown, and was to pay certain amounts to his sisters, in order to make equal shares. Auditors were appointed by the Court, March 20th, 1749,* and on May 20th, 1750, he sold it again to John Keyser, his brother-in-law. It is presumable that Christopher Funk was a brother to Heinrich Funk, of Indian Creek, by comparing dates and the similarity of family names.

Abraham Funk, a son of Heinrich Funk and brother of Christian Funk, of Indian Creek, moved to Springfield Township, Bucks County, Pa., and built the mill in Springtown known as Funk's Mill from that day to the present. Abraham Funk had a son named John Funk, who then moved from Springtown to near Dublin, Bucks County, Pa., about the year 1800, and died there when about forty-eight years of age. He then had a son named Jacob Funk, who also lived in Hilltown Township, Bucks County, Pa., the greater part of his life, and died at Line Lexington in 1875, and was the father of minister John F. Funk, of Elkhart, Indiana, who was called to the ministry in the Mennonite church in the spring of 1865. He is also the President of the Mennonite Publishing Company at Elkhart, Indiana, and editor of the *Herald of Truth*, published in the interest of the Old Mennonite Church.

---

* See Germantown Records.

The Keysers.

THE Keyser family was notable in Europe on account of their strict adherence to the doctrine of the Old Evan gelical Church, in consequence of which one of its great ancestors, Leonard Keyser, was publicly burned to death at the stake, near Scharding, Bavaria, on the 16th day of August, 1527. On account of the then raging persecution, the family appears to have shifted about from place to place, until they settled at Amsterdam, the chief city of Holland; from whence Peter Dirk Keyser emigrated to America in 1688, and was one of the original settlers of Germantown.

His marriage certificate I have copied from an old Hol land or Dutch Bible, now in possession of Gideon Keyser, in Germantown, where it is recorded in the language of Holland; also in English in the following words:

"That Dirk Keyser and Joanna Snoeck, upon their desire after three Sundays having been published at Amsterdam in all the churches, on the undersigned date in the church at Buiksloot, lawfully and in presence of the Lord's congregation are married, declare I, the undersigned Secretary at Buiksloot, the 22d November, 1683, and was signed. B. VREDENHUIS, *Secretary.*

This must have been the same Dirk Keyser of whom S. W. Pennypacker, Esq., makes mention in his *Bio-*

graphical Sketches, p. 41, where he says: "And Dirk Keyser, a silk merchant of Amsterdam, and a Mennonite, connected by family ties with the leading Mennonites of that city, arrived in Germantown in 1688." He was chosen a minister in the Germantown Mennonite congregation and officiated at the marriage of Jacob Kolb and Sarah Van Sintern, May 2d, 1710, in the presence of the full congregation, in the old log meeting-house in Germantown. His son, Dirk Keyser, Jr., was born in Germantown, September 26th, 1701, who then had a son, born August 8th, 1732, named Peter Keyser, who was a tanner by occupation, and was the first Keyser who united himself with the Dunkards or Brethren. He had a son, Peter Keyser, Jr., born November 9th, 1766, who was the renowned Dunkard preacher. He was a very tall man, being six feet three inches high. He was married March 30th, 1790, to Catharine Clemens, of Horsham Township, Montgomery County. She was the daughter of Garret and Keturah Clemens. He died in Germantown, in the same house in which he was born, in May, 1849, in his eighty-third year.

Biography of the Kolbs in America.

PETER SCHUMACHER came to Germantown in 1685 and died in 1707, aged eighty-five years.

His fifth child, a daughter, married Dielman Kolb. She died in 1705, aged fifty-three years, and is buried at Wolfsheim, in the Palatinate. He died in 1712, aged sixty-four years, and is buried at Manheim. Their children were: Ann Kolb, Peter Kolb, Martin Kolb, Johannes Kolb, Jacob Kolb, Dielman Kolb and Henry Kolb. The two first named died and were buried in Europe; the other five came to America about the year 1707, with the exception of Dielman, who came later, between 1710 and 1720. Peter, Martin, Dielman and Henry were Mennonite ministers.

Ann Kolb, born 1676, married Balthasar Kolb. She died February 26th, 1738, at Wolfsheim.

Martin Kolb, born 1680, married May 19th, 1709, in the house of his bride's father, Magdalena, daughter of Isaac Van Sintern, born September 4th, 1662, and was a great-grandson of Jan de Voss, a burgomaster at Handschooten, in Flanders, about 1550. He married in Amsterdam, Cornelia Claassen, of Hamburg, and came to Pennsylvania with four daughters after 1687. He died August 23d, 1737, and is buried at Skippack. Martin Kolb had seven children, five daughters and two sons—Dielman and Isaac.

Dielman married Wilhelmina Rittenhouse, a first cousin

of David Rittenhouse, the astronomer, and daughter of Henry Rittenhouse and great-granddaughter of Willem Rittenhouse, the first Mennonite minister and Bishop in Germantown, also the first in America. Dielman had eight children, as follows: Esther, married to Samuel Funk; Magdalena, married to Isaac Cassel, minister; Wilhelmina, married to Dirk Keyser; Henry, married to Esther Metz; Daniel, married to Elizabeth Funk; Matthias, married to Anna Funk; Martin, died single; Isaac, moved to Maryland, and married —— Kiser. Their descendants are now numerous in Chester, Montgomery and Philadelphia Counties, also in Maryland.

Jacob Kolb, born May 21st, 1685, married to Sarah Van Sintern (a sister to Magdalena, Martin's wife), May 2d, 1710, in the presence of the full congregation, in the Mennonite church at Germantown, by Dirk Keyser. They had nine children, six daughters and three sons— Isaac, Henrich and Dielman.

Isaac was generally called " der grosse Isaac," or " der sehr starke Mann."

Henrich, the second son of Jacob, married Elizabeth Cassel, May 10th, 1744. Their first son, Jacob, born March 2d, 1745, was the grandfather of Henry Kolb, at the Branch Creek, in Upper Salford, Montgomery County, now deacon (Vorsteher) in the Salford Mennonite congregation. Their fourth son, Yelles, was the father of Joseph Kolb. Their sixth son, Isaac, lived at North Wales, and was the father-in-law of Hubert Cassel and grandfather of big Jesse Cassel, of Franconia, and Isaac Cassel, at Kulpsville.

It appears by examining records and dates, that Isaac had a son named Isaac, or Isaac the younger, who died in

1862, at the great age of eighty-two years, and was the father of several children, now landholders in that vicinity His wife was a Miss Hoxworth, sister of the wife of Benjamin Hancock, of Norristown, father of General Hancock. This is how the present Kulp family is related to that distinguished commander, General Winfield Scott Hancock, late Democratic candidate for President.

A number of the Kulps are yet living in Gwynedd. John B. Kulp, who died several years ago, and his sister, Mary B. Kulp, are both buried at Germantown, in the Mennonite graveyard. Their parents are also buried there. John B. Kulp provided in his will that "five hundred dollars" should be paid, clear of all taxes and other charges, to the Society of Mennonites at Germantown in trust, to be invested forever, and the interest to be used to keep in repair and in order the graves of his and his late father and brother. His estate was settled April 1st, 1885, by Algernon S. Jenkins, executor, and the money paid over to Daniel K. Cassel, Treasurer of the Board of Trustees of the Society of Mennonites at Germantown, and by him invested in real estate on mortgage, in trust for the Society.

Jacob Kolb the first, Martin's brother, lived in Skippack. An obituary notice of him says: "On the 4th instant (October, 1739) Jacob Kolb, of Skippack, as he was pressing cider, the beam of the press fell on one side of his head and shoulder, and wounded him so that he languished about half an hour, and then died, to the exceeding grief of his relatives and family, who are numerous, and concern of his friends and neighbors, among whom he lived many years in great esteem; aged fifty-five years."

Of Johannes Kolb, a brother of Martin, we have no reliable records.

Henry Kolb came to America with his brothers, Martin and Jacob. He died in 1730, leaving a family of seven children, three sons and four daughters, viz.: Peter Kulp, David Kulp, Tielman Kulp, Mary Karsdorp, Dorithy Gotshalk, Annie Swarts and Agnes Kulp. Peter died in 1748. Jacob was the eldest son of Peter, born March 7th, 1740; he died June 28th, 1818, aged 78 years. His bones lie away in the Mennonite churchyard, at Kulpsville, Montgomery County, Pa. His marriage certificate, dated November 6th, 1766, states that he was a resident of Whitepain Township, County of Philadelphia, in the Province of Pennsylvania, It is in the possession of George B. Kulp, member of the Bar of Wilkesbarre, Luzerne County, Pa., and is a remarkably well-preserved document, which is historically interesting, and commences as follows:

" WHEREAS, Jacob Kulp, of the Township of Whitepain, in the County of Philadelphia, in the Province of Pennsylvania, and Mary Cleamans, daughter of Abraham Cleamans, of Lower Salford, in the County and Province aforesaid, having published their intentions of marriage with each other, according to law in that case provided," etc., with thirteen names attached as witnesses, some written in German.

The above-named Jacob Kulp had three sons and five daughters, viz.: Abraham, Jacob, David, Elizabeth, intermarried with —— Lloyd; Catharine, married to Abraham Sellers; Mary, married to David Reiner (father of Jacob K. Reiner, minister of the Dunkards or Brethren); Susanna, married to Christian Stover, and Nancy, married to John Snare.

Abraham Kulp, the eldest son of Jacob, was born July 19th, 1770. His first wife, the grandmother of George B. Kulp, was Barbara Sellers. His second wife was Elizabeth, daughter of Daniel Wampole. Abraham died February 11th, 1847, near Linden, Lycoming County, Pa. His only son by his first wife is Elder Jacob S. Kulp, of Pleasant Hill, Mercer County, Ky.

David C. Kulp, a brother of Abraham, was one of the most prominent and distinguished men of his native County of Montgomery. He was a Justice of the Peace in the County named for over forty years, and also held the positions of Treasurer, Auditor, Commissioner and other County offices, all acceptably to the people he served.

Dielman Kolb, a brother of Martin, came from Manheim, where he attended as a preacher to the Mennonite congregation, "making himself most valuable by receiving and lodging his fellow-believers who had to flee from Switzerland," as appears from a letter dated August 27th, 1710. He settled himself in Salford, now Montgomery County, where he purchased at different times about 500 acres of land. He married widow Snavely, and had by her one daughter named Elizabeth, who was afterwards married to Andrew Ziegler, son of Michael Ziegler a Mennonite minister at Skippack.

Dielman Kolb appears to have been prominent in the affairs of the Mennonite Church. He was very intimate with Henry Funk, also a minister and Bishop of the Mennonite faith. It was through the perseverance and zeal of those two men that the Mennonite congregation in Salford was organized in 1738. Dielman Kolb and Heinrich Funk were appointed a committee by the Mennonites to arrange and supervise the translation of the *Martyrs' Mirror* from the Dutch to the German language.

It was through the influence of Dielman Kolb that Christopher Dock was induced to write his method of keeping school, which was afterwards printed by Christopher Saur

On the 8th of July, 1748, Dielman Kolb made his last will and testament, in writing, and he must have lived nine years after that, for his will was not proved before April 30th, 1757. His witnesses were Robert Jones, Martin Kolb and Jacob Kolb; his executors were his widow, Elizabeth Kolb, and his son-in-law, Andrew Ziegler.

The Kolbs, as already stated, were among the leaders of the Mennonite Church. All the Kolbs or Kulps of the older time lent their efforts to good works, and from the earliest settlement of the Germans in Pennsylvania to the present time there has been a large number of Mennonite preachers of the name of Kulp, particularly in the Counties of Bucks and Montgomery, in this State.

Jacob Kolb, Martin's brother, had a son Heinrich, born September 26th, 1721, who was married to Elizabeth Cassel, May 10th, 1744.

From Jacob Kolb's family Bible, which he bought February 28th, 1728, we have the following:

Mother died February 7th, 1705.

Father Dielman Kolb died October 13th, 1712.

Mother-in-law Neltgan Van Sintern died May 29th, 1735.

My father-in-law, Isaac Van Sintern, died August 23d, 1737.

Jacob Kolb born May 21st, 1685, died at the age of 54 years, 4 months, 13 days.

My wife was born January 6th, 1690, died at the age of 76 years 2 months 15 or 16 days.

Isaac Kolb, a son of Dielman and Wilhelmina Kolb, as stated above, moved to Maryland, in the vicinity of Frederick City, and married a Miss Kiser, by whom he had three sons, named David, Samuel and Matthias, and two daughters; their Christian names I could not obtain. One married Isaac Meach, the other Samuel Franer— both Pennsylvanians. Isaac died August 30th, 1828, and is buried in the burying-ground near Utica Mills, in Frederick County, Maryland. Both daughters moved West and died there, and we have no accounts or record.

David Kolb was born in 1793; died in 1862; was married to Elizabeth Caston, of Pennsylvania, June 13th, 1813; she died about 1826.

His children by the first wife were: David Rittenhouse Kolb, John Wesley Kolb, Samuel Kolb, Susan Kolb, Catharine Kolb.

By the second wife, Magdalena Staup: George W. Kolb, James T. Kolb, Martin L. Kolb, Charles Kolb, Isaac Kolb, Ann Kolb, Elenora Kolb.

John Wesley Kolb, a son of David, married Eliza Hitchew, March 14th, 1847. Their children were: John David Kolb, Oliver Grason Kolb, Calvin Wesley Kolb, Laura Virginia Kolb, Mars Alice Kolb, Susan Elizabeth Kolb, two of whom are married.`

Matthias Kolb's children were: Josiah Kolb, Reuben Kolb, William Kolb, Michael Kolb, Mary Ann Kolb.

Samuel Kolb, son of Isaac, died single, in the State of Ohio.

Cassel Family in America.

YILLIS KASSEL came to Pennsylvania in the year 1727, and was a preacher at Skippack and one of the representative men of the Church. His father, Yillis Kassel, was also a Mennonite preacher at Kriesheim in 1665, and wrote a confession of faith and a number of MS. poems, which are now in the possession of his descendant, Abraham H. Cassel, of Harleysville, the noted antiquary. They describe very vividly the horrible condition of the Rhine country at that time, and the sufferings of the people of his faith. The composition was frequently interrupted by such entries as these: "And now we must flee again to Worms." "In Kriesheim, to which we have again come home."

From one of them is extracted the following:

> "Denn es ist bekannt und offenbar,
> Was Jammer, Elend und Gefahr
> Gewesen ist umher im Land.
> Mit Rauben, Plündern, Mord und Brand,
> Manch Mensch gebracht in Angst und Noth,
> Geschändeliert auch bis zum Tod.
> Zerschlagen, verhauen manch schönes Haus,
> Vielen Leuten die Kleider gezogen aus;
> Getreid und Vieh hinweggeführt,
> Viel Jammer und Klag hat man gehört."

A copy of the first German edition of Menno Simons' Foundation (1575), which belonged to the younger Yillis,

(351)

and is, so far as known, the only copy in America, is now in the library of Abraham H. Cassel.

Yillis Kassel was born before 1618 and died after 1681.

Johannes Kassel, a weaver, with Mary, his wife, and five children, viz.: Arnold, Peter, Elizabeth, Mary and Sarah, Germans from Kriesheim, came over by way of London in the ship Jeffries, and landed at Philadelphia on the 20th of November, 1686, and died April 17th, 1691. His son, Arnold, married Susannah Delaplaine in 1693, 9th day of April. She was the daughter of Nicolaes Delaplaine * Arnold was Recorder in Germantown during 1692 and 1693. There is a number of old deeds in existence in Germantown with Arnold Kassel's name as Recorder, and his brother, Peter Kassel, was "Ausrufer" (town-crier) in 1695 and 1696. Arnold had eight children, five sons and three daughters: Johannes, Daniel (died young), Arnold, Jr., Nicholas, Daniel, Veronica, Susannah and Elizabeth.

Hupert Cassel, a weaver by trade, then a single young man, emigrated to this country about the year 1715 or 1720 from the Palatinate. On his arrival in America he stopped at Germantown, and during his stay there he hired his services to different individuals both as a husbandman and weaver, until he became acquainted with a Dutch girl (a native of Holland), whose Christian name was Psyche, with whom he afterwards joined in the holy bonds of matrimony. The above-named Hupert Cassel occupied afterwards about one hundred and fifty acres of land in what is now Skippack, Montgomery County, Pa., which he bought from Dirk Renberg on the 16th

---

* See Notes of Walter Cresson.

day of November, 1725, which was constantly occupied by his descendants until the year 1855, a period of about one hundred and thirty years. The last occupant of the Cassels was Samuel, son of Henry Cassel, who died without issue.

On October 16th, 1727, Illes or Yelles, and Johannes Cassel, brothers of the aforesaid Hupert, arrived. Yelles and Johannes then lived with Hupert, who received them with kindness. Johannes soon afterward moved to Lancaster. The above-named Yelles was a noted preacher among the Mennonites in Skippack. The father of this Yelles, John and Hupert was also named Yelles. He was a very pious and talented man and a pretty good poet, as numerous pieces, in the possesion of Abraham H. Cassel, the antiquarian at Harleysville, will testify. He appears to have been the brother of the above-named Johannes Cassel, which will make him our ancestor's (Hupert Cassel's) uncle, as above stated, and accounts for the perpetuation of the name, but he was very sickly, and died in Germany just about the time that Johannes emigrated.

The above-named Hupert Cassel had five children, viz.: Yelles; Abraham, married Catharine Oberholzer (?); Magdalena, married Nicholas Halteman, no issue; Henry, died single, 1807; Mary, no record.

Yelles Cassel[1] had six children, viz.: Hupert, grandfather of A. H. Cassel, of Harleysville, married Magdalena Jantz, daughter of Nicholas Jantz, or Claes Jansen; Barbara, married Isaac Wisler; Christian, married Susie Henrich; Henry; Elizabeth, married a Benner (not positive); Abraham,[2] married Feige Grimly.

Abraham[2] had five children, as follows; Jacob,[3] married

23

Susanna Clemens; Catharine, married Abraham Haas; Elizabeth, married John Reiff (no issue); Mary, married Jacob Kline; Magdalena, married Henry Musselman.

Jacob Cassel,[3] son of Abraham Cassel, married Susanna Clemens, daughter of Abraham Clemens and Catharine (Bachman) his wife, and granddaughter of Gerhard Clemens, who arrived in America and settled in the neighborhood of the present village of Lederachsville prior to 1712.

Jacob Cassel[3] and Susanna had seven children, viz.: Abraham, born March 15th, 1782, married Polly Bean; Catharine, born March 11th, 1784, married Jacob Bergey; Elizabeth, born February 22d, 1786, married Abraham Kratz; Mary, born October 17th, 1789, married Samuel Bergey; Jacob,[4] born July 5th, 1792, married Wilhelmina Kulp; John, born November 18th, 1794, married Sallie Bean; Susanna, born September 11th, 1799, married Daniel Pennypacker.

Jacob Cassel[4] had four children, viz.: Daniel,[5] born April 22d, 1820, married Elizabeth Kulp; Abraham, born March, 20th, 1822, married Mary Kulp; Samuel, born July 20th, 1826, married Elisabeth Hendricks; Jacob, M.D., born November 13th, 1834, married Kate Weeks; Daniel,[5] author of this work.

There was also a Heinrich Cassel, who was of considerable note in Germany, who with some of the other Cassels first worshiped with the Quakers, because they had no church or congregation, but in 1708 he identified himself with the Mennonites again. He was also of the same family as Johannes and Yelles, Sr.

Hupert Cassel (probably a son of Yelles Cassel and brother of Abraham Cassel, as the records appear), a joiner by trade, bought a tract of land containing about one hundred and six acres in Hilltown Township, Bucks County, Pa., in 1758. He was married to Susanna Schwartz, a sister of Abraham Schwartz, who was the first Mennonite minister at Deep Run, Bucks County, Pa. It appears that Hupert Cassel had two brothers living in Skippack, Montgomery County, viz.: Abraham and Isaac.

It further appears that Hupert Cassel had only four children, viz.: Barbara, married to Dillman Kolb, father of Bishop Jacob Kolb, of Hatfield Township, Montgomery County, Pa.; Molly Cassel was married to Gottschall Gottschall, of Lower Salford Township, Montgomery County, Pa.; Elizabeth Cassel to Joseph Mangle, and Isaac Cassel to Catherine Trumbore. Abraham Cassel, brother of Hupert, resided in Skippack, Montgomery County, Pa.

Isaac Cassel, also a brother of Hupert, was a Mennonite minister, and officiated in Skippack and Germantown. He was married to Magdalena Kolb, daughter of Dielman and Wilhelmina Kolb. Their children were Abraham, Jacob, Susanna and Catharine.

For further information of Johannes Cassel, who settled at Columbia, Lancaster County, Pa., mentioned in the beginning of this sketch, see *Biographical History of Lancaster County*.

Abraham H. Cassel, the self-taught scholar and noted antiquarian of Harleysville, Montgomery County, Pa., the son of Yelles Cassel and grandson of Hupert Cassel, of Towamencin Township, Montgomery County, Pa., has an extensive collection of very rare and valuable books, pamphlets and Colonial documents, etc., many of which could not be found elsewhere. Among many other rarities he has about fifty different editions of old Bibles in their various translations. A number of them are over three hundred years old, and among them is the very rare *Uralte Deutsche Bibel*, bearing date 1470–73, said to have been printed from wooden blocks, movable types not then being in use, leaving blank spaces for the capitals, which were afterwards inserted with a pen and red ink. This whole Bible was completed about ten years before Martin Luther was born, and about fifty years before he made any attempt at translating it, but Luther still has the honor of having given the first German Bible to the world. Mr. Cassel has also a very fine copy of the first edition of King James' English Bible, printed in the Gothic, or old English black letter, and an English translation of the ancient Jewish, or Massoretic Bible, also the Mormon Bible by Joe Smith, the seer, and the Pentapla or *five* translation Bible, besides al most innumerable other matters of interest that cannot here be mentioned.

According to records it appears that Johannes Cassel, a brother of Yillis, the preacher at Kriesheim, and uncle of Hupert Cassel, who came over in 1715, shortly after his arrival moved to Lancaster County and settled in the vicinity of Columbia. It also appears that his son, Abraham, moved to Sporting Hill, then a wilderness. Here Abraham Cassel the second was born on the 18th of April, 1775; his oldest son, Henry Cassel, was born March 12th, 1776. In after years he located at Marietta. He was one of the leading men of that place, and was President of the old Marietta Bank. He had three children; the youngest, A. N. Cassel, was a member of the Legislature in 1838 and 1839, and was afterwards one of the most honored citizens of Marietta.

Abraham Cassel, the youngest of these three children, owned a farm in Rapho Township, the old homestead. He was a sound and practical thinker, and served in several public positions. He had three sons and two daughters. The oldest son, Dr. John H. Cassel, studied medicine with Dr. Washington L. Atlee, and afterwards located at Pittsburgh.

An incident occurred shortly after the arrival of the Cassels at Germantown, which we find recorded in *Harris' Biographical History of Lancaster.* They were members of the Mennonite church at Germantown, and the incident will show, in a very striking manner, the simplicity of the Church at that time. A letter came from Europe to the Cassels that a large legacy was left them by the death of a relative, amounting to nearly a million dollars, and that they should send out and get the treasure. A Church council was called and the matter freely discussed, when it was decided by a unanimous vote not to receive the money, as it would have a tendency to make them proud. Simplicity of manner, plainness of dress, frugality, honesty and economy were some of the characteristics of this people.

Gerhard Roosen.

Mennonite Minister of the Hamburg Altona Con gregation. Born 1612, died 1711.

His first ancestor known to us was Kord Roosen who lived in Kassembrook, now Prussia, Rhine Province, before Menno Simons renounced the Catholic faith. There were many at that time who advocated the doc-trine of adult baptism, and Kord Roosen was one of them. It is said that his parents were Waldenses, which sect was numerous in that province, and in the vicinity of Köln, in the latter part of the fourteenth century, and that many families of the Hamburg and Altona Mennonite congregation were also of Waldens origin. Be that as it may, Kord Roosen had four children by his first wife, three sons and one daughter, but we have not the dates of their birth.

In the year 1531 he married his second wife ; her parents were Catholics. By her he had one son, who was named Geerlink Roosen, but before this son was born, Kord Roosen was compelled to choose either to join the Catholic Church or leave wife and home. He remained true to his faith, and chose the latter, and fled with his four children, the two youngest being so young that he had to carry them the greater part of the way, a distance of about sixty miles. The whole journey he made on foot, and settled in Holstein, in the year 1532, in the vicinity of Lübeck, and commenced to manufacture powder. His wife, who was not permitted by her Catholic parents to accompany him, stayed at home, against her and his will, but she never forgot him. His son Geerlink, who was born shortly after his flight, was nearly grown up when his mother and her parents died. Young Geerlink Roosen then made up his mind to go to his father; so he left his home in the year 1554, at the age of about twenty-two years, but when he arrived he found that his father had died about six months before his arrival. But he stayed with his half-brothers and half-sister, who were all living at a place called Steenrade. In 1563 Geerlink Roosen married a Mennonite widow, whose maiden name was Elizabeth Van Sintern, in the vicinity of Meierhofe Holzkamp. Geerlink Roosen then leased the above-named place and lived there, and died in the year 1611. He had five children. The oldest son remained on the premises, so the place was in the Roosen name over one hundred years.

Paul Roosen, the youngest son of Geerlink Roosen, was born in 1582. He was a tanner by trade, at Oldesloe. He was a Mennonite, and a member in the Friesenburg congregation, and in 1611 he moved to Altona and continued the tannery business and prospered. He had a place of his own, and also owned a warehouse in Hamburg. Altona was not a place of much note until 1601, when the Mennonites and German Reformed settled there, and started into business, when the place began to improve, so that in 1604 it was incorporated into a borough. Paul Roosen must have been a prominent man. He was the first deacon (Vorsteher) in the

new Mennonite congregation at Altona; he gave the
congregation the privilege of building a church on his
own ground, which is the same place on which the first
Altona Mennonite preacher, François Noé, built his
house. The Altona Mennonite church still stands on
the same ground.

Gerhard Roosen, son of Paul Roosen, was born on
the 8th day of March, 1612, between five and six
o'clock in the morning. His mother (Hanchen) Hannah was the daughter of Hans Quins, the first Mennonite
in Hamburg· who had to flee from Brabant in 1570.
Gerhard Roosen often spoke of his grandmother Elizabeth, Geerlink Roosen's widow, who was eighty-nine
years old when she died, and had been personally acquainted with Menno Simons, and frequently heard him
preach. Geerhard Roosen was personally acquainted
with an old minister who moved to Altona from the
Friesenburg congregation, who was ordained as a Bishop
by Menno Simons, and was the third minister in the
Altona congregation.

Paul Roosen, Gerhard's father, died February 27th,
1649, at the age of about sixty-seven years, and Gerhard
was selected a deacon (Vorsteher) in his father's place.
In his forty-ninth year he was called to the ministry, and
on the 15th of April, 1660, he preached his first sermon,
text, Micah 6: 8. On the 6th of July, 1663, Gerhard
Roosen was installed a Bishop by Bastiaan Van Weeni-
gen, a Bishop from Rotterdam, and on the 20th of March,
1664, he held his first baptismal service and baptized
eleven persons, when he selected for his text Matthew
28: 18–20. Eight days later he held his preparatory
sermon and chose for his text 1 Cor. 5: 7; eight days

after that he administered Holy Communion and preached from the text 1 Cor. 11 : 23. In his ninetieth year he signed a letter with three other ministers, namely, Pieter Van Helle, Jacob Van Kampen and Jean de Lanoi, instructing the brethren at Germantown, Pennsylvania, to ordain Willem Rittenhouse as Bishop of the Germantown congregation.

Gerhard Roosen died November 20th, 1711, aged 99 years 8½ months. He had the good of the congregation at heart, and therefore recommended Heinrich Teunis de Jäger, who was chosen as preacher in the Hamburg Altona congregation, July 12th, 1711, to the great satisfaction of Gerhard Roosen, as his successor. In the year 1702, when Gerhard Roosen was in his ninetieth year, we see, as, proof of his fidelity to the Church, how he had the welfare of the Altona congregation at heart, as he manifested great interest in getting an honest and God-fearing Christian man as one of his followers. Such a man he found in Jacob Denner, son of Balthaser Denner, a Mennonite minister, who died in Hamburg, December 15th, 1681, in his fifty-seventh year.

Jacob Denner wrote a large work called "Denner's (Predigten) Sermons," containing 1,502 pages, a copy of which is now in my possession, printed at "Frankenthal am Rhein" in 1792 ; his introduction to it is dated November, 1730. He was born September 20th, 1659, at Hamburg. He was chosen a minister of the Altona congregation, September 29th, 1684, and remained in Altona till 1714, when, after the great fire, he lived at Friedrichstadt; in 1715 he moved again to Altona, where he remained and preached his last sermon, in the latter part of 1745, not quite two months before he died, which was on the 17th of February, 1746, at the age of 86 years 4 months and 22 days. It is believed that he read the Bible through more than fifty times, besides reading many of the best theological works he could procure.—BEREND KARL ROOSEN.

A Biographical Sketch of the Rittenhouses.

In Holland they were called Ruddínghuysen, Rittenhusius and Rittenhausen, finally in this country Rittenhouse.

In 1688 Willem, Wilhelm or William Rittenhouse, his wife, two sons, Claus, Klaus or Nicholas and Gerhard, Gerrit, and a daughter named Elizabeth arrived in Germantown from New Amsterdam (New York), where they lived a short time only. Barton, in his *History of David Rittenhouse*, says he came from Arnheim prior to 1674 and settled in New Amsterdam, which must be an error, because the following records show that he was yet in Amsterdam in 1678. He built the first paper-mill in America in 1690, on a branch of the Wissahickon, in Roxborough Township, Philadelphia, near Germantown. He was elected the first Mennonite minister in the Germantown congregation; afterwards, in 1701, he was ordained Bishop in the same congregation. It appears from a letter in the Mennonite archives in Amsterdam, that he endeavored to have the Confession of Faith translated into English and printed by Bradford. He was born in 1644, and died in 1708, aged sixty-four years.

His daughter Elizabeth married Heivert Papen, who came from Kriesheim in 1685. He declined to be Burgess of the Borough of Germantown in 1701 on account of conscientious scruples.

On the opposite page is a fac-simile copy of the " Oath of Citizenship " of Willem Ruddinghuysen subscribed at Amsterdam June 23d, 1678, taken from the original copy printed on parchment now in the possession of Hon. Horatio Gates' Jones, of Roxborough, Philadelphia, to whom I am greatly indebted for the use of it. It is printed in the Holland or Dutch language.

Translated into English it reads as follows ·

OATH OF CITIZENSHIP.

You do swear that you will be a good and true citizen of this city, and be subject to the Burgomasters and rulers, and take part in watches, beats and other protections and burdens of this city; and that you will apprize them of any threatening danger of which you may be informed; and that you will, by advice and act, further its welfare to the utmost of your power ; and that you will perform and omit all that a good citizen should perform and omit.

So truly may God Almighty help you.

WILLEM RUDDINGHUYSEN Van Mülheim, papermaker, took the above-mentioned oath and paid the citizen fee to the gentleman of the Treasury.

Done in Amsterdam the 23d day of June, 1678.

J. GEELRINCK.

The above document conclusively proves that he was not a Mennonite at the time, for had such been the case he most decidedly would not have affirmed such an oath as the above, but have limited himself to a vow or a promise. It may be that he joined one of the congrega-

Eedt van Poorters.

DAt sweert ghy, dat ghy een goe ende
getrouw Poorter deser Stede, den
Burgemeesteren ende Regeerders in
der tijt onderdanigh wesen sult in Wa-
ken, Bijten ende andere beschermen s-
fen ende lasten deser Stede u goetwillig
hebben sult, dese goede Stede voor t
quaet, dat ghy sult vernemen, waerschou-
wen, ende tot alle welvaert, met raed ende daet, naer allen uwen vermogen, vor-
deren ende helpen sult; Ende voors alles
sult doen ende laten, dat een goe Poorter sc u d gh s te doen ende laten.
Soo waerl ck moet u Godt almachtigh helpen.

tions in Amsterdam later on, or perhaps after he came to America.

Nicholas Rittenhouse, a son of William, was born June 15th, 1666; married Wilhelmina Dewees, and died in 1734, aged sixty-eight years. He was also a Mennonite minister at Germantown, ordained as such shortly after the death of his father. He had seven children, viz.: William, Henry and Matthias, Psyche, Mary, Catharine and Susanna.

William, the first son of Nicholas, had a son named Nicholas, born in 1719, who had a son, Martin, born February 12th, 1747, old style, who had a son, Nicholas, born July 2d, 1774, who had a son, Nicholas, Jr., born October 20th, 1806, who is yet living (1887) in Roxborough, Philadelphia, and in his eighty-first year, a near neighbor of his esteemed friend, Hon. Horatio Gates Jones, a Vice-President of the Historical Society of Pennsylvania, to whom I am indebted for valuable information.

Gerrit, or Gerhard, had the paper-mill after the death of his father. Afterward Jacob, a son of Gerhard, owned the mill.

Henry, the second son of Nicholas, had one daughter only, and several sons, of whom I have no record. The daughter, Wilhelmina, born August 5th, 1721, died May 5th, 1791, aged 69 years 9 months, was married to Dielman Kolb, who was born March 2d, 1719, and died October 19th, 1799, aged 80 years 5 months and 6 days. Both are buried at Skippack Mennonite Church, Montgomery County, Pennsylvania. For their children see *Biography of the Kolbs in America.*

Matthias, the third son of Nicholas, was born in 1703;

and in 1727 married Elizabeth Williams, the daughter of a native of Wales. Matthias was the father of David Rittenhouse, the philosopher, who was born April 8th, 1732, and on February 20th, 1766, married Eleanor Colston. She died December, 1770, and in December, 1772, he married Hannah Jacobs, his second wife. He died June 26th, 1796, aged 64 years 2 months and 18 days. Among Matthias' three elder children, David was the eldest who survived the age of infancy. The house in which David Rittenhouse was born is still standing (1887), right back of the Rittenhouse Baptist Chapel. It was built in 1707, as appears from the date-stone in the gable end.

A monument of granite, about twelve feet high, was erected to his memory a few years ago in the court-house yard at Norristown, Montgomery County, Pennsylvania.

In 1751, Thomas Barton, of Lancaster County, Pennsylvania, an alumnus of Trinity College, Dublin, who afterwards married the sister of David Rittenhouse, and became a Professor in the University of Pennsylvania, supplied him with books, and taught him Latin and Greek.

Emigration of the Stauffers to America.

THE original "Vaterland" of the Stauffers was Switzerland. According to tradition they owe their origin to a generation of Knights called Stauffacher, at Hoenstauffen, who, at the time of the freeing of Switzerland by William Tell, were wealthy farmers and rendered great assistance. Definite information only is given as far back as Hans Stauffer, son of Daniel Stauffer. Hans was married in Switzerland in the year 1685, to a widow named Kinget Heistand (who was first married to Michael Risser). He was a Mennonite, and was driven out of Switzerland shortly after his marriage by the followers of Zwingli, on account of his religious faith. He fled to the Palatinate and had to leave his father behind.

On November 5th, 1709, he started with his family on his great journey, by way of London, to America. After many hindrances on his journey he landed in London on the 20th of January, 1710. Further we have no record, except that they had a stormy passage. They landed in America in the Spring of the same year, and settled in the vicinity of Valley Forge, in Chester County, Pennsylvania. His family consisted of eight persons: himself and wife, three sons, Jacob thirteen, Daniel twelve and Henry nine years old; and one daughter, Elizabeth, who was married to Paul Friedt, and one child, Maria. The sons afterwards bought large tracts of land

(367)

in the vicinity of Colebrookdale, Berks County, Pennsylvania, which was at that time almost a wilderness.

The Stauffer descendants multiplied fast, so that they are at present numerous in the counties of Bucks, Montgomery, Berks, Lehigh, Chester, York and Lancaster, also in the West and Canada. It is remarkable that the majority of them remained true to the Mennonite Church, to which their fathers belonged, and as far as this world is concerned, the majority of them are in moderate circumstances. The writer of this article wishes that he might be furnished with all possible information in regard to their immigration.

Milford Square, Pa.   J. G. STAUFFER.

Custom of Baptism in the Early Centuries.

BENJAMIN EBY, a prominent Mennonite minister and Bishop at Berlin, Waterloo County, Canada, in his *History of the Mennonites*, published by Henry Eby, in 1841, writes about the Second Commandment as follows·

Christ said, "Thou shalt love thy neighbor as thyself," and also commanded His disciples, Matt. 28 : 19, as follows: "Go ye therefore, and teach all nations, baptizing them in the name of the Father, and of the Son, and of the Holy Ghost." The above commandment was closely observed by the Apostles and their followers; they held strictly to the teachings and doctrines of Christ. They taught that taking up the sword against their fellow men in times of war, and swearing an oath, were not in accordance with the doctrine of the New Testament or the teachings of our Saviour; neither would they baptize any person before they had been instructed in the doctrine of Christ, and then baptized them upon their own confession of faith.

Many Jews and heathens were converted and adopted Christ through the preaching of the Gospel by the Apostles, and were organized as a congregation at Antioch, where they were first called Christians, Acts 11 : 26. The evangelical doctrine of Christ was extensively spread throughout Asia, Africa and Europe, notwithstanding the severe persecutions they had to endure on account of their teachings, and though many were put to death.

Still they prospered and increased in numbers, as the blooming roses among the thorns.

Through the first two hundred years we do not find, through any reliable history or any records, that any of the Christians deviated from the true doctrine of Christ. But in the third century men appeared who commenced to advocate infant baptism, but it was accepted only by a few. The ingenious and renowned Tertulianus, about the year 204, remonstrated in strong terms against baptizing too young, and strongly advocated the order of baptism according to the doctrine of Christ. But it was impossible for the pious and zealous teacher at that time to keep the Christians as St. Paul says, 1 Cor. 1 : 10, all of one mind.

In the time of Cypriani, about the year 250, in a Council held at Carthage, it was resolved that young children *should* be baptized, but it was not generally observed, and many Christians held that faith should precede baptism, and therefore baptized only adults upon their own confession of faith. They also denied the swearing of an oath, also the taking up the sword against the enemy; but the hatred of their opponents steadily increased, so that at a Council held at Rome, in the year 470, it was resolved and an edict issued to anathematize and put in the ban and treat as heretics those who would not baptize infants.

This was a terrible edict, but the old Christians could not be persuaded to deny Jesus, and to abandon His doctrine and seek the friendship and favors of this world, but preferred to follow the will of God and His intentions as harmless sheep, to subject themselves rather to suffer as martyrs, and in consequence many have sealed their confession with their blood. For more than sixteen hundred years were the harmless defenders of adult baptism kept in fear by persecution, through imprisonment, and many other kinds of cruel punishment, by fire, sword, hunger and drowning; nevertheless, there have been, through many centuries, even from the time of the Apostles, many Christians who advocated adult baptism and preached the true doctrine of Christ, notwithstanding the severe persecutions they had to endure.

The year 1160 is remembered at all times and mentioned with joy by many devout and well-meaning Christians at that time, and principally a short time afterwards, when the true doctrine of God's Word lifted its head with joy and flourished in glory. The doctrine against infant baptism, and against swearing an oath, and against carrying on war, was preached and defended openly and without fear. The beginning of this liberty or freedom of speech was made through Peter Waldus, at Lyons, which was afterwards carried out by his successors, as the following will show.

T. J. Van Braght, in his *Martyrs' Mirror*, Part I, p. 217, etc., writes as follows:

About the year 1160 several prominent citizens were assembled together at Lyons, in France, conversing together about matters and things occurring at that time, and it happened that one of them fell down suddenly and died. Over this terrible occurrence and example of the mortality of man, Peter Waldus, a very rich merchant, who happened to be among them, was so terrified at this occurrence that he took it to heart and resolved (and through the motive of the Holy Ghost) to repent and live in the fear of the Lord. He commenced with his

own household and his friends, as they assembled at convenient times, to exhort and admonish them in piety and
godliness. As he had done much good to the poor for
some time, the people began to assemble more frequently.
From time to time he began to preach the Holy Scripture
to them in the French language. He remained strictly
in the doctrine and teachings of Christ and the Apostles,
and endeavored to imitate the customs and teachings of
the first Christians.

His confession of faith corresponded with that of the
(Taufgesinnten) adult-baptism Christians. He advocated
the baptism of adults only, and against swearing an oath,
and against taking up the sword to carry on war. His
followers were called Waldenses, Albigenses, Poor of
Lyons, etc., and afterwards were called by various other
names according to the names of places where they lived,
or the names of the preachers they had.

Peter Waldus' doctrine met with great approval in
France and Italy, but then persecution commenced again
and they met with much opposition ; many were banished
from the country, others suffered martyrdom in various
ways, many others fled in large numbers into various
other countries. Their departure from Lyons, their
flight to strange countries and towns, their innocent and
patient sufferings, their firmness until death, and all this
without any resistance, revenge or self-defence, is ample
proof of their faith and the spirit which guided them.

Sebastian Frank divides the Waldenses in three parties
First, those who accepted Peter Waldus as their teacher
and followed his teachings, says he, hold in all things
with the Taufgesinnten (adult-baptism Christians), because
they do not baptize infants, they do not swear an oath,

in any form, they believe that it is not proper for a Christian to do so; they suffer no beggars among them, but assist each other in a brotherly way; they lead a Christian and unspotted life, etc. These are true Waldenses, whose ñame at the same time agrees with their deeds, as well in their faith as in their conduct, showing that they are Christians indeed, which is the topic of our sketch.

The second party are those who deviated from the teachings and doctrines of their leader, and accepted and followed other doctrines, but still call themselves Waldenses.

The third party was improperly called Waldenses, or Albigenses, because they suffered or allowed a few of the Waldenses to live among them and protected them.

T. J. Van Braght, Vol. I, p. 220, says that Jacob Mehrning in his book remarked by what name the harmless Christians were first designated. With us as Germans, he says, they are, with contempt, called Anabaptists, but in the Netherlands they are called Mennonites, after Menno Simons, one of their most influential teachers, but their proper and true name is and properly should be, Christians, or Christian-baptists, because, according to the order and command of our Saviour, they baptized none but those who, according to Christ's command, confess Christ and His Holy Gospel and believe on Him, and upon such confession they are baptized in the name of the Father, and of the Son, and of the Holy Ghost.

Among the Waldenses, or Taufgesinnten Christians, arose Hans Koch and Leonhard Meister, two excellent and educated men, who have done much towards spreading the doctrine of their people, but on that account they were imprisoned at Augsburg, in the year 1524, and suffered martyrdom. Besides them, there were several others who gave evidence of the truth of the teachings of the above, who acted as instruments in getting ready for the great work of the Reformation, namely, Felix Mantz, who at the same time was instrumental in bringing about a better condition in religious matters of faith in Germany, but was eventually drowned at Zurich, in the year 1526, by the enemies of their doctrine ; also the highly learned and firm Michael Sattler, who was imprisoned at Horb, in Germany, in the year 1527, and tortured, and torn to pieces, and afterwards burnt.

Leonhard Kaiser (S. W. Pennypacker, in his *Biograph ical Sketches*, p. 41, mentions him as the ancestor of Dirk Keyser, who came to Germantown in 1688, 3d day, 3d month, a silk merchant and a Mennonite), an eloquent and zealous preacher at Scharding, in Bavaria, who was sentenced to be burnt in 1527, was tied on a ladder and with it was pushed into a great fire to burn him to ashes ; after the wood was all burnt, he was taken out unharmed. Wood was gathered a second time, and a great fire was built, and he was pushed in again; after the wood was all burned the second time, he was found among the ashes smooth and clear, unharmed. Then they cut him into pieces, threw them into the fire, but they could not burn them. Then at last they threw them into the River Inn. This was a miracle of God, and should have served those bloodthirsty people as a warning.

Thomas Herrman, a zealous and devout preacher of the Gospel, was taken a prisoner in the year 1527, at Kitzpil, and was tortured and sentenced to be burned, but his heart they could not burn; at last they threw it into the lake which was close by.

Leonard Schoener, a defender of the doctrine of Christ, was burned to ashes at Rotenburg, in the year 1528.

George Blaurock, who spread the Gospel truth in Switzerland, also traveled to Tyrol, to carry out the duties of his calling and to preach the Gospel there, was taken a prisoner there in the vicinity of Clausen, in the year 1529, and was burned at the stake.

All these and many others taught that, first, the swearing an oath was not in accordance with the New Testament and doctrine of Christ, and therefore not allowed. Second, they believe that taking up the sword to carry on war is contrary to the doctrine of Christ, therefore it cannot be sanctioned. Third, that infant baptism has no foundation in the New Testament.

The above is evidence that the doctrine of the (Taufgesinnten) adult-baptism Christians has been preached at all times among nations, and was believed and carried out, whose authors, since their existence, had many names, whose confession and the devout conduct they followed could be recognized as the true Church of Christ.

According to the following evidence it is clear that the (Taufgesinnten) adult-baptism Christians, Waldenses and Mennonites were in close similarity with that of the first Christians. T. Jan Van Braght, Part I, page 95, states that from the time of Sylvester, about the year 315, the doctrine which has been preached and defended by the (Taufgesinnten) adult-baptism Christians and Waldenses has been preached and sanctioned by an innumerable multitude of people, and was at that time preached and sanctioned—yea, the same churches that existed in the eleventh, twelfth, thirteenth and following centuries were called Waldenses, Albigenses, and lastly Mennonites, or (Taufgesinnten) adult-baptism Christians, who had also existed a long time before.

A certain celebrated author in the Romish Church made the following complaint in his book : " That the above-mentioned Christians at all times had many sects among them, but among all that ever existed, none were more dangerous to the Romish Church than the Waldenses, or (Taufgesinnten) adult-baptism Christians, because they had been in existence at so early a period, even at the time of Sylvester, yea, others will date them back in the time of the Apostles."

Jacob Mehrning writes about the above-mentioned people, in his book, the following· " This is by no means a new sect, that became popular through the revivals of Peter Waldus ; it is a well-known fact that Papist writers themselves acknowledge that they already existed at the time of Pope Sylvester—yea, long before him, even at the time of the Apostles."

He also writes again that Flaccius made mention of the same, which he took out of an old book written by a Papist, stating " that the above-mentioned sects existed at the time of Sylvester, yea, at the time of the Apostles, and that Thuanus does mention of those people and says they existed through many centuries back."

T. Jan Van Braght, Part I, p. 120, makes mention of a controversy between the Inquisitor of Leuwarden and Jaques d'Auchy, a martyr. The Inquisitor based his remarks on the Edict of Cæsar, and said: " It is already twelve or thirteen hundred years since Cæsar Theodosius issued an edict that all heretics should be killed, namely, those who at that time had been re-baptized, even as your sect, being, the Inquisitor said, that they were re-baptized." " Even as your sect," he gives to understand, or acknowledges that such people as Jaques d'Auchy was, and those (Taufgesinnten) adult-baptism Christians, who, at the same time, namely, in the year 1558, left their lives for the same doctrine as those against whom the Edict had been issued twelve or thirteen hundred years ago.

T. Jan Van Braght, Part I, p. 293, gives a remarkable history of the Oriental Christians previous to the year 1540, and says : " Likewise have we information that there are yet at this time Christians at Thessalonica, who, in all religious points, agree with the Mennonites, two of them lived yet at the time of our forefathers (written in 1540), with the brethren at Moravia, afterwards in the Netherlands among the Mennonites and communed with them.   They explicitly stated that those at Thessalonica had in their possession, in their archives, two epistles written by St. Paul's own hand, in perfect preservation. There are even yet many of their brethren in Greece and other Oriental countries, scattered here and there, who, from the beginning of the Apostles, have held on to the ancient custom of adult baptism, to the present time ; so it seems God has preserved His own through all times to the present."

About the year 1536, the highly educated and enlightened Menno Simons, that great Reformer, left the Catholic priesthood and adopted the principles of the Waldenses, and commenced to preach for them.   From that time they were called Mennonites.

The following is from Arthur Penrhyn Stanley, D.D.,

Dean of Westminster, Episcopal, entitled, "Christian Institutions; or, Essays on Ecclesiastical Subjects," pp. 23
and 24: "In the Apostolic age, and in the three centuries which followed, it is evident that, as a general rule,
those who came to baptism, came in full age, of their
own deliberate choice.   We find a *few cases* of the baptism of children; in the third century we find one case of
the baptism of infants.   Even amongst Christian house-
holds the instances of Chrysostom, Gregory, Nazianzen,
Basil, Ephrem of Edessa, Augustine, Ambrose are de-
cisive proofs that it was not only not obligatory, but not
usual.   All these distinguished personages had Christian
parents, and yet were not baptized till they reached maturity.   The old liturgical service of baptism was framed
for full-grown converts, and is only by considerable
adaptation applied to the case of infants.   Gradually the
practice of baptizing infants spread, and after the fifth
century the whole Christian world, East and West,
Catholic and Protestant, Episcopal and Presbyterian
(with the single exception of the sect of the Baptists
before mentioned) * have adopted it.   Whereas, in the
early ages, adult baptism was the rule, and infant baptism
the exception; in later times infant baptism is the rule,
and adult baptism the exception."

Also, on page 27, he says further: "It declares that
in every child of Adam, whilst there is much evil, there
is more good; whilst there is much which needs to be
purified and elevated, there is much also which in itself

---

* All denominations who rejected infant baptism and only baptized adults,
were called Baptists, or Anabaptists. By the Catholics they were called
heretics, and those who refused to recognize the state church were called
sects.

shows a capacity for purity and virtue. In those little children of Galilee, all unbaptized as they were, not yet even within the reach of a Christian family, Jesus Christ saw the likeness of the kingdom of heaven; merely because they were little children, merely because they were innocent human beings. He saw in them the objects, not of Divine malediction, but of Divine benediction. Lord Palmerston was once severely attacked for having said, 'Children are born good.' But he, in fact, only said what Chrysostom had said before him, and Chrysostom said only what in the Gospel had been already said of the natural state of the unbaptized Galilean children, 'Of such is the kingdom of Heaven.'"

As authority for the above article, I will give the following

"The well-known Arthur Penrhyn Stanley, D.D., LL.D., Dean of Westminster, and member of the English New Testament Company of Revisers, born December 13th, 1815, was a favorite student of Dr. Arnold, at Rugby; distinguished himself as a student in the preparatory school and in the University College, where he graduated in 1838, and where he subsequently taught and held many honorable offices. He became Chaplain to Prince Albert in 1854; to Queen Victoria and the Prince of Wales in 1862; became Dean of Westminster, January, 1864. He made a tour of the East, accompanying the Prince of Wales, in 1862. He has been one of the most prominent men of the English Church for many years. He married Lady Augusta Bruce, the Queen's most intimate friend, in 1862. His works are of immense value, and altogether he was one of England's most scholarly men. He died July 18th, 1881."

The question whether the proper mode of baptism is by sprinkling or immersion was, with Menno Simons, like all other Baptists of the sixteenth century, entirely strange. Morgan Edwards, D. Benedict, J. N. Brown and other American writers refer to two claims in Menno's writings, where immersion is said to be given as the proper mode of baptism, but the citations are errors, as the passages do not appear in Menno's explanation of Christian baptism, where they are said to appear, nor in any other of Menno's writings.

The best biography of Menno is, " Het leven en de verrichtingen van Menno Symons." " The life and doings of Menno Simons, by A. M. Cramer, Amsterdam, 1837," afterwards translated into English, and from the English into German, by J. N. Brown, and published by the American Baptist Publication Society of Philadelphia, 1854.—*American Conversations Lexicon*, July 16th, 1872, p. 203.

Munsterites not Connected with Mennonites.

In a book printed by Henry Eby, in Berlin, Canada, in the year 1846, entitled " Christian Duty," and " Con fession of Faith of the Mennonites," with an Appendix on non-resistant Christians, we read the following, p. 187 : " Herewith this report might be closed, if our experience had not taught us how many people, through ignorance and not being properly acquainted with us, or for want of (to our sorrow and without cause) love continued to trouble and molest us with scandalous remarks about the riots and riotous enthusiasm of Thomas Münzer and his associates, who, about the time of the Reformation, or shortly afterwards, came into existence. After so many prosperous congregations of defenceless Christians already existed in many localities who held meetings, public as well as private (on account of the severe persecutions), and after so many excellent and enlightened men had been persecuted, tormented and put to death on account of their non-resistant doctrine and belief, then finally the Münster riots started, in the year 1533,. not by the Mennonites, as their enemies would charge them; neither were they supported, assisted or even recognized by the Mennonites.* The Münster riots

---

* When the Münster riots occurred and the battles at Münster were fought, in 1533 and 1535, Menno Simons was yet a Catholic priest in Witmarsum, his birthplace. He left Popery January 12th, 1536, one year after the battle at Münster was fought.—B. Karl Roosen, p. 24, at Hamburg, Altona.

were supported and carried on by men who left the darkness of Popery, and saw a glimmer of light, yet inex-
perienced. They, with Johann Von Leiden,* through
several Lutheran ministers, were persuaded to take up
the sword, and to establish the kingdom of Christ by
force and compulsion, by the sword. They also adopted
adult baptism and rejected infant baptism, therefore the
enemies of the non-resistant Christians have tried to
classify them with the Mennonites."

We also read, p. 188, the following: " See the 'Onnoosel-
heyts Peyl,' that is, fundamental searches of the innocence
on the part of the Mennonites in the Münster riots, in
print, whereby Schleidanus, Guido de Vres, Heinrich
Bullinger and Heinrich Dorzio, definitely, and on various
occasions, mention has been made of the Münster Process
and can be seen in their writings, that the following
named persons were the principal authors of the Münster
riots, viz.: Bernhard Rottman, Heinrich Rollius, Gott-
fried Stralen, Herman Staprede, all Lutheran ministers,
who caused and started the Münster riot."

N. B.—Whereas, we do not baptize infants, but only
such persons who can be baptized upon their own confession of faith, according to the Word of God; they call
us Anabaptists, when the followers of Zwingli retained
infant baptism and other customs of the Romish Church
and are called Reformers. We will let the reader judge
impartially who is nearest the truth, or nearest the Word
of God, or who has reformed best and who is most de-
serving the name of Reformer.

---

* Generally called Johann Von Leyden by historians. His proper name
was Johann Bockhold, a tailor of Leyden.—*Encyclopædia Britannica.*

Origin of the Munsterites.

For more than a century, up to the present day, people have been made to believe that the Anabaptists, contemptuously so-called, have but recently sprung from some erring spirits—some say from the Münsterites, etc., whose fabulous faith, life and conduct the true Anabaptists have never recognized; for no one will ever be able to show with truth, so far as we have been able to ascertain, that the articles of religion of those Münsterites, whereby they have drawn the attention of the world upon themselves, and which consist in commotion, rebellion and such like, have ever been adopted or acknowledged as good, much less professed and lived by any formal church of the Anabaptists, or by any well-known member of the same. But, on the contrary, they have from that time on and ever since declared that they would have neither lot nor part with them or their transactions, and admonished one another not to follow such ways, because these could not stand the test before God and His Word, nor before the mind of a true and meek Christian, as being contrary to the Gospel of Christ and the most holy faith. Were we disposed to pay them in their own coin, we might say the Münsterites were fellow-members of those who sanction war and claim that one must propagate and defend his religion with the

(383)

sword, for this is what they did; but *we* speak against it with heart, soul and mind.

Aside from the fact that the Anabaptists did not spring from the Münsterites, but have existed through all the times of the Gospel, as has been sufficiently shown, we would, moreover, state that the pernicious and evil proceedings which took place at Münster about the year 1534 cannot, according to the truth, be laid to the charge of the Anabaptists, who, at that time, like innocent doves fleeing before the talons of the hawk into clefts of the rock, or into hollow trees, had to hide themselves; but must be placed to the account of some Lutheran preachers, to whom a certain Jan van Leyden had recommended and taught Anabaptism. According to old and authentic authors, these proceedings happened as follows:

In the year 1532, Bernaert Rotman, a Lutheran (at that time called Evangelical) preacher, began to preach at Münster, in St. Maurice Church, against the doctrine of the Papists; when, however, the Papists of Münster came to know this, they bribed him with money to go away. But repenting of it a few months afterwards, he came back and drew such crowds that he, being sustained by some of the chief men of the city of Münster, erected his pulpit in the entry of the church. He also sought to have other churches opened in order that his doctrine might be propagated the more widely—if this were not done, they should be opened by force, etc. In the mean time, on the 14th of February, 1533, there arrived at Münster Jan van Leyden,* a strange, odd and opinionated man, who, though he maintained baptism upon faith, yet

* Whose proper name was Johann Bockhold, a tailor of Leyden.

in most other points never agreed with the Anabaptists. To be brief, after much controversy, he brought the matter so far that not only Bernaert Rotman, who had at first opposed him, but also his colleague, H. Staprede, and various others began to preach against the practice of infant baptism. On the other hand Jan van Leyden learned from them, especially from B. Rotman, the doctrine that one might defend and propagate his religion with external weapons.

In the meanwhile, the magistrates, apprehending serious mischief which might be expected to spring from this, forbade those whom they thought were giving the most occasion to it in the city; they indeed left the city, yet on the instigation of B. Rotman, entered it again by another way. Finally matters came to such a pass that the aforementioned, and supporters of the Lutheran (or miscalled Evangelical) doctrine, who had become agreed with Jan van Leyden in the article of baptism, collected together and resolved to bring about a total restoration of religion; deciding also, that to this end, as it could not be effected quietly, it should be done by force of arms; further, that in Münster the beginning should be made. Jan van Leyden was constituted the leader; and through B. Rotman's proclamation (many) ignorant and simple people from the surrounding places were summoned to help carry out said restoration, which, however, was not made known to them at first. These were promised that in Münster they should receive tenfold for their goods which they had to abandon on this account. Without loss of time they opposed the power of the Bishop.*

---

* Count Waldeck.

25

They erected fortifications, seeking not only to defend themselves, but also to exterminate their opponents—that is, the true adherents of Rome and the Pope. But matters took quite a different turn from what they had intended; they were defeated and the Bishop and those of the city triumphed. Rotman himself (notwithstanding that his associates were in equal distress), despairing of his life, ran to the enemies to be killed by them; so that he might not, like Jan van Leyden, be taken alive and come to a shameful end.

This, then, was the tragedy enacted at Münster; the instigation, progress and execution can and may not be attributed to the so-called Anabaptists, but to the first risen Lutherans, especially to B. Rotman and his followers. Had this restoration been successful, the Lutherans would not have been ashamed of it; on the contrary, they would have boasted of it, and never would have left the honor of it remain in the hands of the Anabaptists. To this alludes the following old ditty ·

> Had successful been the glorious restoration,
> Never would the much-despised Anabaptists
> Have obtained the honor; Luther or some other,
> By the sword of Rotman, lord would have been crowned.

[Compare tract Onnooselheyds Peyl, etc., edit. Harl. Anno. 1631. Annex Hist. Mart. a little before the introduction: with the various attestations of Bernhard Rotman, Godfrey Stralensis, Rollins, and other Lutheran leaders at Münster; whose writings concerning this matter were published shortly after the transaction, and have also come down to us. Also the notes of Melanchton, Guido, Sleydan; and also in the great atlas, old edition.]—*The Bloody Theatre, or Martyrs' Mirror*, by Thielman J. Van Braght, p. 16.

German Translations of the Bible by the Waldenses.

By Dr. Ludwig Keller.

In the fourteenth century, under the administration of Kaiser Ludwig, of Bavaria, the great opposition of the Roman Catholic Church to Protestantism was broken. This was an important period in the history of the Germans, when public opinion began to awaken and the enthusiasm began to develop itself in natural affairs as well as in religion, which was of much importance to coming centuries, when the opposition to the Roman Catholic Church began to grow stronger than ever before, and the " heretics " (so called by Roman Catholics) commenced to establish their churches everywhere. The history of the translation of the German Bible was a remarkable period in the fourteenth century, which has been brought about through the introduction of the German music, which was followed by a number of German translations of the Bible (more particularly the New Testament), many of which have become extinct. There are nine hymns in the Catholic hymn books composed by Bohemian brethren. The States Library at München contains twenty-one different copies of Gospels and Epistles translated into German by Waldenses. Only one of the German Bibles of the fourteenth century became particularly popular; it was called the Tepler Bible, and was issued in parts; also a German version of the New Testament, including an Epistle of Paul to the Laodiceans, a copy of which is now in the Gymnasial Library at Freiburg, in Saxony, and another in possession of J. M. Goeze. After printing was invented in the year 1466, the first German Bible was given to the press. In the same year a second edition was issued by John Mentel, in Strasburg, and another edition in 1473, at Augsburg. The names of the translators, also that of the printers, were carefully withheld on account of the severe persecution at that time.

It is an important question to consider that the German translations of the New Testament by the different translators, almost word for word agreed with the first or Tepler Bible; not only those three above-mentioned editions, but all editions from 1470 to 1522, both High German and Dutch, have the Tepler version as their basis. These are the editions printed without the printers' names (except one printed at Nürnberg or Augsburg), two by Günther Zeiner, between 1473 and 1477, at Augsburg; further, the two editions by Anton Sorg, also at Augsburg, 1477 and 1480; the Anton Koburg edition, 1483; the Grüninger, of Strasburg, 1485; the fifth and sixth of Augsburg (Hans Schoensperger), 1485 and 1490; the seventh and eighth of Augsburg, by Hans and Silvan Otmar, 1507 and 1518. The Dutch translations appeared at Cöln in two editions; at Lübeck (1494) and at Halberstadt, 1522. Further information may be obtained by referring to *Kehrcins' History of the German Translation of the Bible before Martin Luther*, Stuttgart, 1851, p. 33, also p. 49. According to the statements of

Kehrems, it appears that the "Tepler" Bible was extensively circulated and became very prominent.

Thus far we have an account of the German editions of the Bible prior to 1522. Translations of parts of the Bible appeared in large numbers prior to 1518. The Gospels of the New Testament appeared not less than twenty-five times prior to 1518, and the Psalter thirteen times prior to 1513, and other Epistles in large numbers.*

The following is taken from the "History of the Revision" of the New Testament, and corresponds with the above. It reads as follows ·

"Portions of the Bible were translated into German as early as the latter part of the ninth century. These translations increased in number until the invention of printing. Five undated editions were issued before 1477, all of them from the Vulgate. The first of these is thought to have been printed as early as 1466 in Strasburg. Between 1477 and 1522 nine other editions followed, besides translations of detached portions.

"Luther's New Testament appeared in 1522. It was published at Wittemberg in two folio volumes. In 1524 the whole Bible, with the exception of the prophetical books, was published in three folio volumes at Nuremberg. Luther's Bible was translated from the original languages.

"The Zürich Bible† was published shortly after Luther's, and was a combination of his translation with the translations of Leo Judä and other German scholars."

---

* See Dr. Keller, Leipzig, p. 43.   *Waldenser und die Deutschen Bibel uebersetzungen.*

† In 1530, by Christopher Froschauer. My ancestor, Martin Kolb, brought one of them from Holland in 1707. It is now in the possession of Jonathan Kulp, of North Coventry, Chester County, Pennsylvania, and is (1888) 358 years old.—AUTHOR.

The Community and the Church.

Dr. Keller writes in the "Badisches Gemeindeblatt" about the names "Mennoniten," "Taufgesinnten," "Alt-evangelische Taufgesinnte." He maintained that when the several confessions of the "Taufgesinnten," from 1591 to 1665, be thoroughly examined, it will show that the above-mentioned people invariably only designated themselves as the congregations (Gemeinden), the con-gregations of Christ ("die Gemeinden Christi"), or con-gregations of God ("oder Gemeinden Gottes"), also "Taufgesinnten Gemeinden Gottes."

On the other hand, the name Mennonite does not ap-pear in a single instance in all their official acts previous to the year 1664, even in their conferences, where the Flanders, the Frieslanders and the German congrega-tions were partakers. In the year 1665, for the first time, we find the name Mennonite in a single instance only. It is certain that the above-mentioned conferences pre-ferred the name "Gemeinde Christi" to the name Men-nonite, but it should be observed that the name Menno-nite only became general in later years.

Menno Simons' Memorial.

THE following sketch I found among a lot of waste paper, and as it is so full of interest I placed it on these pages. It seems there was an illustration attached to it, which I was not able to obtain.

ONE OF THE PLACES WHERE MENNO SIMONS AFTER HIS RENUNCIATION OF THE CHURCH OF ROME FIRST PREACHED THE GOSPEL.

There are many localities in the world that will be long remembered, and around which cluster many precious memories. The places in themselves may not be more than a thousand other places, and indeed may possess less of beauty and less of the romantic than a hundred other places of which no notice is taken; but the events that transpired there, and men who have lived and labored and suffered in them, make these places of intense interest to all who possess a knowledge of them.

With what solemnity of feeling do men, to-day, walk the streets of ancient Jerusalem, the pathway across the Brook Kedron, the Garden of Gethsemane, the Mount of Olives and many other places in Palestine, the soil of which, more than eighteen hundred years ago, was pressed by the sacred feet of the Son of God; and because here

(391)

He labored and suffered and died to save us from our
sins; and here, too, the Gospel was first preached, and
here transpired the tragic scenes of sorrow and suffering
connected with the lives and death of many who loved
the poor, despised Nazarene.   All these things give a
deep and lasting interest to localities of this character,
which is precious to every Christian.

With similar feelings we must ever regard the localities
where God's children in the ages past have lived and
suffered and died, and especially so is it with those who
have held like faith and maintained like principles with
ourselves.   When we follow the fortunes of God's people through the Eastern countries, when we think of the
Donatists, the Paulicians, the Waldenses or Poor Men of
Lyons, the Albigenses, the Mennonites and others, every
spot, where the precious blood of these faithful martyrs
flowed, must be to the Mennonites to-day, as it were,
hallowed ground.

So the place represented by the illustration on the opposite page has a historic record, which will forever en-
dear it to all the followers of that noble champion of
Gospel truth, who here so boldly, against all opposition,
declared the whole counsel of God unto the people. The
place is a parcel of ground containing only a few acres
near the village of Witmarsum, in the province of Friesland, in Holland.

Witmarsum was the birthplace of Menno, as he himself relates in his Renunciation of the Church of Rome,
and to this place he again returned and preached, after he
had served as priest for a time in his father's village,
called Pingjum, and gained some notoriety as an ex-
pounder of the Scriptures.

On the parcel of ground above referred to there was still standing, in 1828, a small, dilapidated, old building, which throughout that vicinity was known as *Menno Simons' Oud Preekhuis* (Menno Simons' Old Meeting house), and was then still used by the Mennonites of that day as a house of worship.

In this place, according to old traditions, Menno Simons, for some time after his renunciation of the Church of Rome, preached the Gospel, and it is even claimed that he preached in this very house, but it is hardly probable that on this rough coast, so much exposed to the storms and tempests of that locality, the house could have withstood the ravages of time for a period of three hundred years.

In 1828 the old house, which so long bore the name of Menno, was taken down and a new one erected in the same place and in the same style as the old one, with the exception that a small cupola was added in the middle of the roof. The illustration on the opposite page is a representation of this house, built in 1828. In later years, during the winter, when the weather was more rough and the roads muddy, it seemed too severe and unpleasant a task for the people to go from the village, through storm and rain against the bleak winds and through marshy roads, to the meeting-house, and for this reason it was determined, in 1876, to build a new meeting-house in the village of Witmarsum, which was done in 1877, and in December of the same year the congregation took leave of the old meeting-house, and later on the place erected a memorial stone or monument, on the sides of which are the following inscriptions:

IN MEMORY OF
MENNO SIMONS,
Born in Witmarsum 1492.
Heb. XIII, Vs. 7.

According to tradition
Menno here preached to his
first followers.

For a period of three hundred years'
the Anabaptists of Witmarsum
met in this place for worship.

1 Corinthians III, Vs. 11.
1536.

Origin of the Old Evangelical Church.

THE first Christians from the time of the Apostles did not bind themselves down to any system of teaching, or any symbol, only the plain doctrine and example of Christ and the Apostles. Of theology or theological education they knew very little, and just so little did they consider ceremonial forms essential to salvation. Baptism only followed the teaching of religious belief, and in that whole epoch, to the year A.D. 150, not the least trace of infant baptism can be proven; only adults were baptized upon their own confession of faith, and such baptism was called the seal of faith. For the performance of all these religious exercises no temples nor altars were needed, consequently no churches were needed down to the year A.D. 175. (Dr. Keller.)

Since the year A.D. 300 we find the Church was called the Church of the *Novatians*, or sometimes in the Oriental countries were called the Congregations of the Katarer, who from the third to the fifth century spread themselves from Syria to Spain.

Novatian, a prominent leader, but not the originator of these churches, was already by their opponents or enemies charged as a schismatic and heretic. Cæsar Constantine, who for a while tolerated them, at last treated them as heretics, forbade their religious meetings, took away their churches and ordered their books to be destroyed. Cæsar

Honorius, also, in the year A.D. 412 included them in
his edict against the heretics, and Theodosius the Second
followed the same example, but notwithstanding all these
persecutions these churches maintained themselves and
prospered throughout the Orient until the sixth and
seventh century, when they still claimed to be the "True
Evangelical Church."*   And it is an established fact that
they possessed some very valuable literary works.

The question is, were these Katarers (Albigenses), who
were also called Bogomilen (friends of God) since the
seventh and eighth century in the Orient and Occident,
as also later the so-called Paulicians, who simply called
themselves Christians, in close connection with the older
Katarers in any respect?   Certain it is that all those
churches claim to be in immediate historical connection with the Apostolic times.

These Katarer or Albigenser churches continued down
to the twelfth century, when Peter Waldus, so prominent
in the Church, became their principal leader, and from
that time were called Waldenses, or Evangelische Chris-
ten, until the Lutherans and others also called themselves
Evangelische, then, to distinguish, they called themselves
the Altevangelische Gemeinden until the sixteenth century, when Menno Simons, the highly educated and enlightened Dutch Reformer, connected himself with the
Church and became a leader among them, in the year
1537.   After that time they were called Mennonites by
their enemies only, but they invariably designated themselves as the Congregations, or Congregations of Christ.
Even Heinrich Funk, of Franconia, Pa., in his will dated
June 13th, 1759, says, "ye Elders in the Congregation

* See *Herzog & Plitt Realencyclopædia*, Bd. X, p. 666.

of Christ," "named ye Mennonists." The name Mennonite does not appear in a single instance in all their offi
cial acts previous to the year 1664.

The same principle claimed by those Middle Age
Katarern corresponds also with many of the later so-
called sects, above all, the so-called " Waldenses " or
" Tisserands" (weavers), " Friends of God," " Pickarden,"
" Anabaptists," etc. (as these sects may be called by their
enemies), was taught through all ages from the time of
the Apostles down to the present, no matter by what name
they were called. They were at the same time known
as the " True Congregations of Christ," or Evangelical
Christians. And that they existed from the Apostles
down to the present is plainly shown by the following:

An old writer in the Romish Church said, among all
sects none were so injurious to the Romish Church as
the Waldenses or Taufgesinnten, because they existed at
so early a time, even the time of Sylvester or the time of
the Apostles. Jacob Mehrning also writes about the
above-named sects thus: This is by no means a new sect
that took its start with Peter Waldus; Papist writers
themselves acknowledge that they existed at the time of
Pope Sylvester—yea, even at the time of the Apostles.

These so-called sects claim continual connection from
time to time with the old Christian, Apostolic, or Old
Evangelical churches through all times. But their
enemies continually claim that they were nothing else
than new and self-constituted sects, except some few who
are better informed, as above-mentioned, and who do
acknowledge that they already existed at the time of
Sylvester—yea, long before him, even from the time of
the Apostles.* The time of Sylvester was A.D. 315.

* See T. J. V. Braght, 1st part, p. 95.

If any of the churches or denominations of the present day will go back and claim those old sects, as they call them, as their starting point, or foundation, or their principles, are they also willing to accept and adopt those principles or confessions of faith that they preached and practiced, and lived up to and testified to, and sealed with the blood of thousands of them who were persecuted and murdered by the Roman Catholics in Spain and the Netherlands, and by the Calvinists in Switzerland, viz.:

1st. Against swearing an oath.

2d. Against taking up the sword and waging war.

3d. Against infant baptism as not in accordance with the Scripture.

Closing Chapter.

WE must say, it is indeed a very remarkable history which greets us in the records of the idea and experience of these old evangelical churches. They have been persecuted through centuries; they have been stigmatized as heretics; they have been slaughtered as outcasts; yet their opponents have never succeeded in exterminating them and rooting out their principles and ideas. On the contrary, in spite of all opposition, they have gained ground more and more as the centuries marched on. Out of the graves of the martyrs of these churches there sprouted up new blossoms of life, exhaling the fragrance of a true, living, Christian faith among the nations, thus verifying the words of Christ: "If a grain falleth into the ground and die, it beareth much fruit."

Penetrating into the details of their history, the reader is struck with astonishment to find these annals replete with records of most heroic suffering without equal; they show the fulfilment of Christ's words: "Behold, I send you forth as sheep in the midst of wolves," and "If they have persecuted me, they will also persecute you;" but at the same time these records prove the truth of the statement, "They have hated me without a cause."

Let me close with pointing to the words of a circular which has lately been sent to the Protestant denominations, in which attention is solicited to the old Waldensian

churches.   It is there set forth that a Church which has
become remarkable and venerable through a long history
of suffering and persecution, naturally claims the sympathy of all those that take a true interest in the pure
doctrines of the Gospel.   What is said here in respect to
the venerable Waldensian churches of Italy might, as I
believe, be fitly applied also to the descendants of the
old evangelical churches of all centuries and those who
have adopted their principles.   These churches may well
claim to have gained through long and intense suffering
a citizenship among other Protestant denominations ; this
citizenship carries with it, it is true, duties and obligations,
but it also carries with it a most just claim, the only one
which the evangelical churches make in accordance with
their principles—*the claim of liberty of conscience ; the
claim of being tolerated and permitted to live according to
their principles of faith, as they see them laid down in the
Word of God.*

FINIS.

APPENDIX.

First Impulse or Motive of the Cassels Emigrating to America.

WILLIAM PENN made his first visit through Germany in 1671 as a missionary, and only followed the example of his brothers in faith, and stopped at Emden, Crefeld and Westphalia.

His second visit he made in the year 1677, in the thirty third year of his age, and not yet known as the founder of Pennsylvania. Four years later, it appears, he made a third trip; and from Cassel he gave notice of a meeting he proposed to hold at Frankfort. From Frankfort he went to Kriesheim, where he arrived August 23d, 1681, and intended to preach. A meeting had been previously announced for that purpose; but upon the urgent request of a Calvinist minister, all preaching was forbidden by the bailiff's deputy. However, a silent meeting was held, in which all took part; also those from Worms, who followed them in a wagon. Penn, however, got permission from Count Karl Ludwig to preach again, consequently, on Sunday, August 26th, Penn traveled on foot from Worms to Kriesheim, a distance of six miles, and preached to the people of Kriesheim in a barn. Count Ludwig quietly entered the barn, and stood behind a door listening; but Penn did not know it. Ludwig afterwards reported to the Calvinist minister, that nothing of a heretical nature occurred, but, on the contrary, all that he heard was actually very good.   Penn preached in the German language, which he had learned from his mother, she being a Dutch woman from Rotterdam.   During his discourse he pictured the then raging persecutions of the non-resistant Christians; how they were denied the right to worship God according to the dictates of their conscience, and how they were driven from one place to another, and their property confiscated.

He further explained their principles of faith regarding swearing an oath and waging war, and of revenge, which corresponded very nearly with that of the Mennonites, and gave great satisfaction to those present.   Among them were Heinrich Cassel and Yilles Cassel, who were so well pleased with his remarks that as soon as the meeting closed they took him by the hand and embraced him, and invited him to go with them, which he did. Then they had a long consultation about matters of religion.   He told them that he had a large tract of land in America, which had been granted to him by King Charles II, March 4th, 1681, and made it free by purchase to enable the conscientiously scrupulous to settle and enjoy their religious opinions without restraint.   Thus by promising them perfect freedom and liberty of conscience to worship God according to the dictates of their conscience, was given the first impulse or motive of the Cassels emigrating to America.*

---

* From MSS. in the library of A. H. Cassel at Harleysville.

The Mennonite Shipbuilder.

AT the time of the truce between the Spaniards and the Dutch, in 1609, there lived at Hoorn, in North Holland, a Mennonist, Peter Jansen, who took the notion that he would build a ship of the same proportions as Noah's ark, only smaller, that is, 120 feet long, 20 feet broad and 12 feet high. While it was building every one laughed at him; but, Dutchman-like, he kept sturdily on, and found in the end that it justified his expectations, for, when launched, it proved to be able to bear a third more freight than other ships of the same measurement, required no more hands to manage it than they, and sailed much faster. The result was that the Dutch built many others like it, calling them Noah's arks, and they only ceased to be used after the close of the truce in 1621, because they could not carry cannon, and thus were not safe against privateers.—J. D. MICHAELIS.

Extract from an Address delivered by Dr. W. J. Mann.

Dr. WILLIAM J. MANN delivered a most interesting historical sermon in the Zion Church, on Franklin Street, Philadelphia (*German Lutheran*), which we find in the *Philadelphia Press*, Monday, October 8th, 1883, basing his remarks on Genesis 21 : 33, 34, viz.: Abraham, whose name the confessors of the three most important forms of religion on the earth keep in reverence, is by Israelites called the father of their nation ; by the Mahomedans, a prophet; and by us Christians in a higher sense, the father of the faithful and the friend of God. Two hundred years ago the first German emigrants came to our beautiful Pennsylvania. They were small in numbers,* but they were an energetic, industrious and persevering people. They came as Christians,† and not being provided with churches they united with the Quakers and

---

* Thirteen families, consisting of thirty-three souls.

† Dr. W. J. Mann failed to mention here that those Christians, as he says, were the thirteen families of Mennonites, viz. : Lenart Arets, Abraham Op den Graeff, Dirk Op den Graeff, Herman Op den Graeff, Willem Streypers, Thonis Kunders, Reynier Tyson, Jan Seimens, Jan Lensen, Peter Keurlis, Johannes Bleikers, Jan Lukens and Abraham Tunes, who arrived October 6th, 1683.

worshiped with them,* and indeed, in 1688, undertook to lay the first protest against Slavery before the monthly meeting of the Quakers.† It took almost 180 years and a mighty war which shook our whole Union to the foundation to bring about what these Germans in their simple-heartedness had considered as the right and Christian thing at too early a period. ‡ Within the course of a few decades other Germans arrived in Pennsylvania, and some of them of very peculiar notions, deeply interested in the Kingdom of God, and thinking that leading a hermit § life they could best serve their Lord, settled around our romantic Wissahickon. || Lutherans and Reformed churchmen also followed the invitation given by William Penn, that great and good man, who through-

---

* The first religious meeting held by these people was held in the house of Thonis Kunders, in 1683. From that time they held their meetings in private houses. Sometimes in Summer, in the shade under the trees; sometimes they worshiped with the Quakers, and the Quakers with them, but were not connected with them. In 1708 these Mennonites built their first meeting-house at Germantown Road and Herman Street, Germantown.

† This protest was drawn up in Germantown in the year 1688 and signed by Garret Hendricks (it is held that he was a Mennonite, see *Germantown Independent* of July 28th, 1883), Derick Op den Graeff and Abraham Op den Graeff, both Mennonites (see *Biographical Sketches* by S. W. Pennypacker, p. 28), and Francis Daniel Pastorius, who was a Pietist (see notes on his Pamphlets, pp. 17 and 49, by S. W. Pennypacker).

‡ The Mennonites never held slaves, even those who lived in Slave States did not; they believed it to be contrary to the doctrine of Christ.

§ There was only one person at that time near Germantown who lived a hermit life, named Herman Dorst. He died October 14th, 1739, at the age of eighty years.

|| In 1694 Johannes Kelpius, the Hermit of the Wissahickon, and others of his followers, all Pietists, who were expelled from the College at Helmstedt, arrived and settled on the Wissahickon near Roxborough, where they founded the Society of the "Woman in the Wilderness." The Mennonites had no connection with them.

out his province at once established perfect religious tolerance. In 1703 we discover the first German Lutheran congregation on this continent at New Hanover, thirty-six miles from Philadelphia.

An Interesting Address.

By MATTEO BROCHET, OF ROME.

An interesting address was delivered some time ago in Berlin by Dr. Matteo Brochet, of Rome, President of the Evangelization Committee of Italy. He touched briefly upon the early history of the Waldenses, not only those of the twelfth century, but those of the tenth century. He mentions thirty-three persecutions, where their towns had been burned, their members and brethren tormented and killed, and yet they have been wonderfully preserved in their Church and their principles through all the persecutions they had to endure. It seems to have been the object of the All-wise Preserver of the universe that through *these* people the Gospel should be preached to all the Italian inhabitants. Although it would have been much more convenient for them to have remained at home on their farms in the valleys, yet since religious liberty was guaranteed in Italy (1848), the twelve or fourteen thousand members of the Waldenses commenced their mission work.

In 1855 they founded a theological seminary at Florence and sent preachers and Bible colporteurs through all Italy. In 1860 they had fifteen stations and the same number of messengers in Italy. At present (1887) their field of labor extends from Mont Blanc to the south point of Sicily. They have 44 organized congregations, 38 stations and 120 missionaries, and among them 36

(409)

ordained ministers and 57 teachers; they visit many cities and towns. During the last year they counted (independent of the old valley congregations) 4,000 communicant members, 1,961 scholars in their elementary schools and over 3,000 scholars in their Sunday and evening, schools. They raised about 70,000 francs to defray expenses.

The conduct toward these Waldenses on the part of the Italians is very favorable, but the Romish clergy try to put every obstacle in their way, viz.: that the Bible only originated from Luther, and they were buying souls, and other reports. They also hinder and injure the Waldenses in their business. In the year 1560 a minister of the Waldenses was publicly burned to death in the presence of the Pope and his cardinals; in 1860 an attempt was made to burn a house occupied by Waldenses.

At present there is in Rome an Evangelical church, at the Piazza di Venezia, open with the following superscription "Light shineth out of darkness," and the Evangelical preacher there has many attentive listeners in his audience. At present many of the Catholic population take part in religious affairs with the Waldenses. In an Evangelical school, among 200 children there are 180 children of Catholic parents; that is a great blessing for the Waldenses, for which they are thankful to God, but at the same time they in return are very thankful for the privileges they received on the part of the government of Italy. May Italy and Germany, not only in matters of science and politics, but in matters of religion, go hand in hand. God bless them.

July 4th, 1887.

The Mennonites and Temperance.

ALREADY in the founding of the Mennonite Church in this country, two hundred years ago, at Germantown, Pa., we find them taking a decided stand on the temperance question, and they have ever since been noted for their temperance principles, and as the liquor question is becoming the most prominent that the public and the religious world has to deal with, it is only fitting that they should declare their principles now.

At the last session of the Semi-annual Conference of Eastern Pennsylvania, held in Churchville, Berks County, May 3d and 4th, 1887, and to which a number of the churches of said denomination in Bucks County belong, the following resolution was passed without a dissenting word or vote:

" Acknowledging the pernicious influence on the body and soul which the manufacture, sale and use of intoxicating drinks exert on mankind, we rejoice at the steps which our State government has taken for the suppression and final prohibition of this evil. We acknowledge it to be the duty of every Christian to take a decided stand in suppressing this evil, and in no way, either by word or action, to promote the sale or use of intoxicating drinks."—*Bucks County Intelligencer.*

(411)

Early Churches of Germantown.

THE Mennonites held their first religious service in the house of Tonis Kunders (afterwards called Conrad, later Cunard), in 1683; from that time the Mennonites date their organization. Some historians call them the German Friends. As soon as the Friends settled in German town they frequently worshiped together, until in 1705 the Friends or Quakers built a meeting-house of their own, but the Mennonites continued worshiping in private houses until the year 1708, when they built their first meeting-house, which was a log house, on the same lot where their present stone house now stands (built in 1770).

The Dunkards came to Germantown in 1719. The log house was built in 1731 by John Pettikoffer, for his dwelling, who procured his funds by asking gifts therefor from the inhabitants. Because it was the first house in the place and procured by begging, it was called "Beggarstown." The stone church on the same premises was built in 1770.

The German Reformed built their first meeting-house opposite to the market-house about the year 1733. The front was first built; the back part was added in 1762.

The Methodists began to preach in Germantown about the year 1798, and in 1800 they built their stone meeting-house in the lane opposite to Mr. Samuel Harvey's house.

The Lutheran church.—It is not accurately known when this was built, but it is certain there was a Lutheran church in Germantown before the first one in Philadelphia which was erected in 1743. The first ordained minister, Dr. H. M. Muhlenberg, came to Philadelphia in 1742.

The Protestant Episcopal church of St. Luke was built in the year 1819.

The lower burying-ground of half an acre was the gift of John Streeper, of Germany, per Leonard Aret, one of the first Mennonites at Germantown; it is now called Hood's cemetery. The upper one was given by Paul Wolff, afterwards called Ax's graveyard, now Concord burying-ground. Paul Wolff was a Mennonite, and a number of the old Mennonites are buried there.

Old Germantown.

Its Division into Lots.—The Curious Names of the
Original Settlers and Something of their
Holdings.

THE German Township, first called "The German
Town," and when incorporated by William Penn as a
borough was named Germantown, was laid out by virtue
of three warrants—one for six thousand acres to Francis
Daniel Pastorius for the German and Dutch purchasers,
dated October 12th, 1683, another to Francis Daniel
Pastorius for two hundred acres, dated February 12th,
1684, and the third to Jurian Hartsfelder, who was at
one time the owner of the district of the Northern Liberties, for one hundred and fifty acres, dated April 25th,
1684. The land was laid out on April 3d, 1684, and the
patent was issued in 1689.

Germantown began fourteen perches below Shoe
maker's Lane (now Penn Street) and extended to Abing-
ton Road (now Washington Lane). The town lots num
bered fifty-five and were divided into twenty-seven and a
half on each side of the main road (now Germantown
Avenue). The original settlers cast lots for the ground,
in the cave of Francis Daniel Pastorius, in Philadelphia,
and the following curious document was in existence
fifty years ago, and is probably still in preservation:

"We, whose names are to these presents subscribed, do hereby certify, unto all whom it may concern, that soon after our arrival in this province of Pennsylvania, in October, 1683, to our certain knowledge, Herman Op der Graff, Dirk Op der Graff, and Abraham Op der Graff, as well as we ourselves, in the cave of Francis Daniel Pastorius, at Philadelphia, did cast lots for the respective lots which they and we then began to settle in German- town ; and the said Graffs (three brothers) have sold their several lots, each by himself, no less than if a division in writing had been made by them.

Witness our hands this 29th November, A.D. 1709.

> LENART ARETS,
> JAN LENSEN,
> THONES KUNDERS,
> WILLIAM STREYPERS,
> REYNIER TYSEN,
> ABRAHAM TUNES,
> JAN LUCKEN."

The lots were numbered from the north southward, and the names of the original holders, as well as the owners twenty-five years later, were as follows ·

EAST SIDE OF MAIN ROAD.

1689.	1714.
1. Peter Keurlis.	Peter Keurlis.
2. Tunis Kunders.	Tunis Conrad.
3. John Lensen.	John Lensen.
4. Lenart Arets.	Leonard Arets.
5. Rynier Tyson.	Isaac Van Sintern.
6. John Lucken.	Herman Carstorp.

1689.	1714.
7. Abraham Tunis.	Jacob Gottschalk.
8. Gerhard Hendricks.	Isaac Schumacher.
David Sherges.	
9. Walter Simon.	Walter Simon.
10. Dirk Kolk.	James Delaplaine.
Wiggert Levering.	
11. Herman Van Bon.	Herman Van Bon.
12. Gerhard Levering.	John Doeden.
Henry Sellen.	
13. Isaac Scheffer.	John Henry Sprogell.
Henry Buchholtz.	
Frankfort Co.	
14. Cornelius Bom.	Paul Kestner.
15. Isaac Dilbeck.	Daniel Geissler.
16. Enneke Klosterman.	Francis Daniel Pastorius.
17. John Doeden.	John Doeden.
18. Andreas Souplies.	Christian Warner.
19. William Rittenhouse.	Arnold Van Fossen.
20. Claus Rittenhouse.	Paul Engle.
21. Claus Rittenhouse.	Hans Henry Lane.
22. Dirk Keyser, Sr.	Dirk Keyser.
23. William Streypers.	Paul Engle.

WEST SIDE OF MAIN ROAD.

1. John Streypers.	Joseph Shippen, Jr.
2. Dirk Op de Graeff.	Widow Op de Graeff.
3. Herman Op de Graeff	Joseph Shippen, Sr.
Abraham Op de Graeff.	
4. John Simons.	John Neiss.
5. Paul Wolf.	Conrad Jansen.
6. John Bleikers.	Herman Tunes.

	1689.	1714.

7. Frankford Co. John Henry Sprogel.
8. Jacob Schumacher. Quaker Meeting-house.
9. J. Isaac Van Bebber. John Jarrit.
Jacob Tellner.
10. Heivert Papen. Heivert Papen.
11. J. Jansen Klinges. Tunis Conrad.
12. Cornelius Siverts. Cornelius Siverts.
13. Hans Peter Umstad. Geo. Adam Hogermeed.
14. Peter Schumacher. Peter Schumacher
15. Jacob Tellner. John Williams.
Jurian Hartsfelder.
16. Claus Thompson. Claus Thompson.
17. Hans Millan. Dirk Johnson.
18. Henry Fry. Philip C. Zimmerman.
19. Johannes Kassel. John Henry Sprogel.
20. Abraham Op de Graeff. Anthony Klinken.
Anthony Klinken.
21. John Silans. Paul Engle.

Fifty years later these lots were owned principally by Edward, Joseph and William Shippen, Theobold Endt, Jacob Ritter, Christopher Saur (printer of the first Bible in America), Justus Fox, John Bockius, Abraham Griffith, John Wynne, William Ashmead, O. Bensell, Christopher Meng, Mathias and John Knorr, John, Frederick and Peter Ax, John Weiss, Jr., George Dannenhower, Godfrey Bockius, Christian Eckstein, John Bringhurst, John Wister, Benjamin Shoemaker, Thomas Rose, Casper Wister, Paul Kripner, Jacob Bowman, John Lehman, Daniel Lucken, Christian Lehman, Wendell Heft, Conrad Reiff, Christian Warner. The descendants of many of

27

these early property-holders are still residents of and take a prominent part in the affairs of Germantown.

The roads leading from Germantown, as appeared on a map made by Christian Lehman, in 1746, were, as are now known, on the east, Fisher's Lane or Logan Street; Duy's Lane or Wister Street; Shoemaker Lane or Penn Street; Church Lane or Mill Street; Methodist Meeting Lane or Haines Street, and Keyser's Lane or Washington Lane; Oueen Lane, now Queen Street; Bensell's Lane, also known as Ashmead's Road, and Schoolhouse Lane, now School Street; Rittenhouse's Mill Road, afterwards Poor House Lane, and now Rittenhouse Street; Johnson's Lane, near where Walnut Lane is now, and Keyser's Lane, from Roxborough, now known as West Washington Lane. The above account is given, as part of Mennonite history or their doings, because all the signers of the "curious document" above mentioned were Mennonites, and the greater portion of the lot-holders were also Mennonites. Jacob Godshalk, owner of lot No. 7, in the year 1714 was a preacher, and came over in the year 1702.

Enneke Klosterman (lot No. 16) afterwards became the wife of Francis Daniel Pastorius; they were married November 26th, 1688, and had two sons, John Samuel and Henry. Pastorius wrote many books and poems in various languages, and many have been lost. The following letter is characteristic ·

Dear children, John Samuel and Henry Pastorius: Though you are (*Germano Sanguine nati*) of High Dutch parents, yet remember that your father was naturalized, and ye born in an English Colony, consequently each of you *Anglus natus* an Englishman by birth. Therefore, it would be a shame for you if you should be ignorant of the English tongue, the tongue of your countrymen, but that you may learn the better I have left a book for you both, and commend the same to your reiterated perusal. If you should not get much of ye Latin, nevertheless read ye the English part oftentimes OVER AND OVER AND OVER. And I assure you that *Semper aliquia hærebit.* For the dripping of the house-eaves in time maketh a hole in an hard stone. *Non vi sed sæpe cadendo,* and it is very bad cloath that by often dipping will take no colour.—F. D. P.

The book he left, as stated above, is a large volume written in Greek, Latin, German, French, Dutch, English and Italian. The book is in a good state of preservation and is in possession of the Pastorius family in Germantown, corner of Main and Pastorius Streets.

Ephrata.

AT Ephrata, Lancaster County, was located an institution of learning which was for many years the seat of learning and the fine arts, and many families of Philadelphia and Baltimore resorted thither to have their children educated. There the Declaration of Independence was translated by Peter Miller into seven different languages, to be sent to the Courts of Europe.

The first Sabbath school, too, on record was established there; for as early as 1740, full forty years earlier than Robert Raikes' much applauded system was known in England, this one at Ephrata was begun by *Ludwig Strecker*.

"GOD WILLING."—This was once of universal declaration, in announcing forthcoming sermons to be preached at given places. Now it is almost as universally discontinued, and ministers come and go without any such rest on contingencies. No cause has been published for the change.—*Watson's Annals*, Vol. II.

Old Clock.

In the house of Mrs. Thomas Givens, in Rittenhouse-town, is an old-fashioned tall clock, which has struck the hours for more than three centuries since it was first wound up by the manufacturer in Holland. It has but one hand; this, however, works around the silver dial plate, and indicates the exact time.

The clock was the property of the late Jacob C. Rittenhouse, son of John Rittenhouse. It then became the property of Mrs. Spencer, daughter of Jacob C. Rittenhouse, and is now in possession of Mrs. Thomas Givens, daughter of Mrs. Spencer, and a member of the Mennonite Church at Germantown. The clock was evidently brought over from Holland by Willem Rittenhouse, the first papermaker in America, also the first Mennonite minister and first Bishop of the Mennonite Church in Germantown, and the first in America.

Indian Contract and Deed with William Penn.

THE following contract of peace brought about with the wild Indians or savages, without the use of musket or sword, is recorded in a survey book, No. 14, in the Land Office, and extracts from the warrant of survey by Holme:

"Philadelphia.

"To my very loving ffriends Shakhoppah, Secaming, Malebore, Tangoras—Indian Kings; and to Maskecasho, Wawarrin, Tenoughan, Tarrecka, Nesonhaikin—Indian Sakamackers, and the rest concerned:

"WHEREAS, I have purchased and bought of you, the Indian Kings and Sakamackers, for the use of Governor William Penn, all your land from Pemapecka Creek to Upland Creek, and so backward to Chesapeake Bay and Susquehanna, two days' journey; that is to say, as far as a man can go in two days, as under the hands and seals of you the said kings may appear; and to the end I may have a certain knowledge of the land backward, and that I may be enabled and be provided against the time for running the said two days' journey, I do hereby appoint and authorize my loving ffriend, Benjamin Chambers, of Philadelphia, with a convenient number of men to assist him, to mark out a westerly line from Philadelphia to Susquehanna, that so the said line may be prepared and

(422)

made ready for going the said two days' journey backward hereafter, when notice is given to you the said kings, or some of you, at the time of going the said line; and I do hereby desire and require, in the name of our said Governor Penn, that none of you, the said Kings, Sakamackers, or any others, Indians whatsoever, that have formerly been concerned in the said tracts of land, do presume to offer any interruption or hindrance in making out the said line, but rather I expect your ffurtherance and assistance, if occasion be herein; and that you will be kind and loving to my said friend, Benjamin Chambers, and his company, for which I shall, on the Governor's behalf, be kind and loving to you hereafter, as occasion may require.

" Witness my hand and a seal, this seventh day of the fifth month called July, being the fourth year of the reign of our great King of England, and eighth of our Proprietary, William Penn's government.

" THOMAS HOLME."

A true copy from the original, by Jacob Taylor. With the foregoing paper is a diagram of the ground plot of the survey. It goes direct from Philadelphia City to a spot on the Susquehanna about three miles above the mouth of the Conestoga, near to a spot marked, " fort demolished."

In the book of " Charters and Indian Deeds," page 62, is given the deed of the foregoing granted lands, to wit:

" WE, Shakhoppah, Secane, Malebore, Tangoras, Indian Sakamackers, and right owners of ye lands lying between Macopanackan, *alias* Upland, now called Chester River

or Creek, and the River or Creek of Pemapecka, now
called Dublin Creek, beginning at a hill called Conshohockin, on the River Manaiunck, or Schoolkill, from
thence extending a parallel line to the said Macopanackan
(*alias* Chester Creek), by a southwesterly course, and
from the said Conshohockin hill to the aforesaid Pemapecka (*alias* Dublin Creek), by the said parallel line northwesterly, and so up along the said Pemapecka as far as
the creek extends, and so from thence northwesternly
back unto the woods, to make up two full days' journey,
as far as a man can go in two days from the said station
of the said parallel line at Pemapecka, as also beginning
at the said parallel at Mecopanackan (Chester Creek), and
so from thence up the said creek as far as it extends, and
from thence northwesternly back into the woods, to make
up two full days' journey, as far as a man can go in two
days from the said station of the said parallel line at the
said Macopanackan, *alias* Chester Creek, *For and in
consideration* of 200 fathoms of wampum, 30 fathoms of
duffells, 30 guns, 60 fathoms of strawed waters, 30 kettles,
30 shirts, 20 gun belts, 12 pairs shoes, 30 pairs stockings, 30 pairs scissors, 30 combs, 30 axes, 30 knives, 21
tobacco tongs, 30 bars of lead, 30 pounds powder, 30
awls, 30 glasses, 30 tobacco boxes, 30 papers of beads,
44 pounds red lead, 30 pairs of hawks' bells, 6 drawing
knives, 6 caps, 12 hoes—to us in hand well and truly
paid by William Penn, Proprietary and Governor of
Pennsylvania and territories,

"DO BY THESE PRESENTS *grant, bargain, sell, etc.*, all right,
title and interest *that we or any others shall or may* claim
in the same, hereby renouncing and disclaiming forever
any claim or pretence to the premises, *for us, our heirs
and successors, and all other Indians whatsoever.*

" In Witness whereof, we set our hands and seals, etc., this thirtieth day of the fifth month called July, and in the year 1685.

Signed,

SHAKAHAPPOH,   SECANE,

MALEBORE,   TANGORAS.

" Sealed and delivered to Thomas Holme, President of the Provincial Council, in the presence of us:

Tareckhoua,	Lasse Cock,
Penoughant,	Mouns Cock,
Wesakant,	Swan Swanson,
Kacocahahous,	Ism Frampton,
Nehallas,	Sam'l Carpenter,
Toutamen,	Will Asley,
Tepasekenin.	Arthur Cook,
	Tryall Holme."

Mennonites.

A SECT of Baptists in Holland, so called from Mennon Simonis of Frizeland, who lived in the sixteenth century. This sect believes that the New Testament is the only rule of Faith; that the terms Person and Trinity are not to be used in speaking of the Father, Son and Holy Ghost; that the first man was not created perfect; that it is unlawful to swear or to wage war upon any occasion; that infants are not the proper subjects of baptism, and that ministers of the Gospel ought to receive no salary. They all unite in pleading for toleration in religion, and debar none from their assemblies who lead pious lives and own the Scripture for the Word of God. The Mennonites meet privately, and every one in the assembly has the liberty to speak, to expound the Scripture, to pray and sing. They assemble twice every year, from all parts of Holland, at Rynsbourg, a village about two leagues from Leyden, at which time they re ceive the Communion, sitting at a table where the first distributes to the rest; and all sects are admitted, even the Roman Catholics, if they please to come.—*Dictionary of Arts and Science.* London. Printed for W. Owen at Homer's Head, in Fleet-Street, 1764.

Origin of New Year's Day, or First of January.

ANCIENTLY the year began with March. This was in the day of Romulus, the founder of the once famed city of Rome. That legislator, for the use of his people, divided time into several periods; but, being more of a military man than an astronomer, he made his years to consist of ten months, fancying the sun to pass through all the seasons in three hundred and four days. This distribution occasioned great inconvenience. It, however, continued to exist until Numa Pompelius ascended the throne, when a remedy was suggested which, it was thought, would obviate the difficulty. The introduction of two additional months was recommended, and, finally, under the names of January and February, were interpolated between December and March. The year was than made to begin with January. Respecting the origin of this name, we are taught that it came to us from the Latin *Januarius,* a word given to it by the Romans. The latter derived it from Janus, one of their divinities, who was said to preside over all new undertakings. In all sacrifices the first libations of wine were offered to him and all prayers prefaced by a brief address to the same distinguished personage. When in the flesh, he is said to have ruled as the first king over Italy, and to have endeared himself to his subjects by his generous and merciful conduct towards strangers and by the kindness and consideration which he showed to them selves. His reign was marked by wisdom, judgment and prudence and by the reforms which he brought about. It was he who taught them that civility raised the standard of their morals, and instructed them how to improve the vine, raise the corn and make bread.

So great and powerful a king could not fail to impress by his actions a simple-minded and superstitious-loving people. What more natural than for them to love and serve him while living, and, when dead, to deify and place him on the pinnacle of heaven as an object of admiration and worship? No longer blessed with his presence, and unable to see him with the bodily eye as he sat enthroned on high, they must needs have something tangible.

Undertakers for Funerals.

THIS is wholly a modern affair. It was formerly the case that long trains of friends, male and female, walked in procession. It seemed more solemn than now ; and when the coffin was accompanied by pall and pall-bearers for respectable funerals, it was more dignified and imposing. It was a kind of willing homage of friends, who thereby signified a willing respect and regard for the deceased.

First Mennonites Represented as Quakers.

THE Germans who originally arrived came for conscience sake to this land, and were a very religious community. They were usually called *Palatines*, because they came from a Palatinate, called Cresheim and Crefeld. Many of the German Friends had been convinced by William Penn in Germany. Soon after their settlement, in 1683, some of them, who were yet in Philadelphia, suffered considerably by fire, and were then publicly assisted by the Friends.—*Watson's Annals*, Vol. II, p. 19.

The above is a specimen by which the reader will see how the Mennonites are represented as Quakers. Those who originally arrived were thirteen families, all Mennonites, who came from Cresheim and Crefeld in 1683. The Friends mentioned above were a different party.

No Union of Church and State.

In Bullinger's Widertöufferen Vrsprung, page 165, printed by Froschower, at Zurich, 1560, we find the following:

Dan sy haltend styff das widerspyl, vnd leerend, die Oberkeit möge und solle sich der Religion vnd Gloubens sachen nüt annehmen. * * Es bedunckt die Töuffer vngebürlich syn, dass in der kirchen ein ander schwärdt dan nun dess Göttlichen worts solle gebrucht werden; vnd noch vil vngebürlicher, dass man menschen, das ist, denen die in der Oberkeit sind, solle die sachen der Religion oder Gloubens hendel vnderwerffen.

Habits of First Settlers.

In their early days all the better kind of houses had balconies in the front, in which, at the close of the day, it was common to see the women, at most of the houses, sitting and sewing or knitting. At that time the women went to their churches generally in short gowns and petticoats, and with check or white flaxen aprons. The young men shaved smooth and wore white caps; in summer they went without coats, wearing striped homespun trowsers, and barefooted; the old men wore wigs. —*Watson's Annals.*

Watson says, when speaking of the first settlers of Germantown:—"They used no wagons in going to market, but the woman went and rode on a horse with two panniers slung on each side of her. The women, too, carried baskets on their heads, and the men wheeled wheelbarrows—being six miles to market. Then the people, especially man and wife, rode to church, funerals and visits both on one horse ; the woman sat on a pillion behind the man."

Another writer states:—Pastor John Minnich, one of the old Mennonite preachers, used to come each Sunday from Dolly Lolly Corner, near Shoemakertown, on horseback, his wife, Nanny, riding on behind. Preachers in his day did not require a coach and six.

It was also no uncommon occurrence to see Pastor

Heinrich Hunsicker, of Perkiomen, go out on a Sunday morning at two o'clock, and fetch his horse from pasture, and put a saddle, which he had made of straw, on the horse, and then he and his wife would ride to Germantown, both on one horse, a distance of twenty miles, where he was to preach.

How does the above compare with many of our six thousand dollar preachers of to-day?

In going to be married the bride rode to meeting behind her father, or next friend, seated on a pillion; but after the marriage the pillion was placed, with her, behind the saddle of her husband.—*Watson's Annals.*

Obituary.

WILLIAM F. WILLIAMS died Friday, April 9th, 1885, in the seventy-sixth year of his age. The deceased was a member of the Mennonite Church at Germantown, and was elected one of the Trustees for the last eight years, and succeeded Peter Schriver, as sexton of the church, until about two years ago, when he moved to his son-in-law, in Cheltenham Township, Montgomery County, where he died. He was a devoted Christian gentleman, and was universally respected. The funeral services were conducted by N. B. Grubb.

Samuel Rittenhouse died September 5th, 1885, in the eighty-fourth year of his age. Deceased was a deacon in the Germantown Mennonite Church for many years, and was the Secretary of the congregation, and had in his possession and care all books and papers belonging to the congregation. He is buried in the Mennonite graveyard at Germantown. He was highly respected, and served in his official capacity to the satisfaction of all. The burial services were conducted by N. B. Grubb.—*Church Records.*

Index.

29

Made in the USA
San Bernardino, CA
21 July 2018